P9-CDN-710

# THE SATIRES

OF

# A. PERSIUS FLACCUS

EDITED BY

BASIL L. GILDERSLEEVE, Ph.D. (Göttingen), LL.D.,

PROFESSOR OF GREEK IN THE UNIVERSITY OF VIRGINIA.

NEW YORK:

HARPER & BROTHERS, PUBLISHERS,

FRANKLIN SQUARE.

1875.

# PREFACE.

THE text of this edition of Persius is in the main that of Jahn's last recension (1868). The few changes are discussed in the Notes and recorded in the Critical Appendix.

In the preparation of the Notes I have made large use of Jahn's standard edition, without neglecting the commentaries of Casaubon, König, and Heinrich, or the later editions by Macleane, Pretor, and Conington, or such recent monographs on Persius as I have been able to procure. Special obligations have received special acknowledgment.

My personal contributions to the elucidation of Persius are too slight to warrant me in following the prevalent fashion and cataloguing the merits of my work under the modest guise of aims and endeavors. I shall be content, if I have succeeded in making Persius less distasteful to the general student; more than content, if those who have devoted long and patient study to this difficult author shall accord me the credit of an honest effort to make myself acquainted with the poet himself as well as with his chief commentators.

In compliance with the wish of the distinguished scholar at whose instance I undertook this work, Professor Charles Short, of Columbia College, New York, I have inserted references to my Latin Grammar and to the Grammar of Allen and Greenough, here and there to Madvig.

B. L. GILDERSLEEVE.

UNIVERSITY OF VIRGINIA, *February*, 1875.

# CONTENTS.

*Quando cerco uome di gusto, vado ad Orazio, il più amabile; quando ho bisogno di bile contra le umane ribalderie, visito Giovenale, il più splendido; quando mi studio d'esser onesto, vivo con* PERSIO, *il più saggio, e con infinito piacere mescolato di vergogna bevo li dettati della ragione su le labbra di questo verecondo e santissimo giovanetto.*　　　　　　　　　VINCENZO MONTI.

———

Συνίσταντο οἱ μὲν ὡς τοῦτον, οἱ δ' ὡς ἐκεῖνον πλὴν μόνου τοῦ Ἴωνος· ἐκεῖνος δὲ μέσον ἑαυτὸν ἐφύλαττεν.　　　　ΛΟΥΚΙΑΝΟΥ.

———

PERSIUS *das rechte Ideal eines hoffärtigen und mattherzigen der Poesie beflissenen Jungen.*　　　　　　　MOMMSEN.

# INTRODUCTION.

An ancient *Vita Persii*, of uncertain authorship, of evident authenticity, gives all that it is needful for us to know about our poet—much more than is vouchsafed to us for the rich individuality of Lucilius, much more than we can divine for the unsubstantial character of Juvenal.

Aulus Persius Flaccus was born on the day before the nones of December, A.U.C. 787, A.D. 34, at Volaterrae, in Etruria. That Luna in Liguria was his birthplace is a false inference of some scholars from the words *meum mare* in a passage of the sixth satire, where he describes his favorite resort on the Riviera.

The family of Persius belonged to the old Etruscan nobility, and more than one Persius appears in inscriptions found at Volaterrae. Other circumstances make for his Etruscan origin : the Etruscan form of his name, *Aules*, so written in most MSS. of his Life ; the Etruscan name of his mother, Sisennia ; the familiar spitefulness of his mention of Arretium, the allusions to the Tuscan haruspex, to the Tuscan pedigree ; the sneering mention of the Umbrians—fat-witted folk, who lived across the Tuscan border. Most of these, it is true, are minute points, and would be of little weight in the case of an author of wider vision, but well-nigh conclusive in a writer like Persius, who tried to make up for the narrowness of his personal experience by a microscopic attention to details.

Persius belonged to the same sphere of society as Maecenas. Like Maecenas an Etruscan, he was, like Maecenas, an *eques Romanus.* The social class of which he was a member did much for Roman literature; Etruria's contributions were far less valuable, and Mommsen is right when he recognizes in both these men, so unlike in life and in principle—the one a callous wordling, the other a callow philosopher—the stamp of their strange race, a race which is a puzzle rather than a mystery. Indeed, the would-be mysterious is one of the most salient points in the style of Persius as in the religion of the Etruscans, and Persius's elaborate involution of the commonplace is parallel with the secret wisdom of his countrymen. The minute detail of the Etruscan ritual has its counterpart in the minute detail of Persius's style, and the want of a due sense of proportion and a certain coarseness of language in our author remind us of the defects of Etruscan art and the harshness of the Etruscan tongue.

Persius was born, if not to great wealth, at least to an ample competence. His father died when the poet was but six years old, and his education was conducted at Volaterrae under the superintendence of his mother and her second husband, Fusius. For the proper appreciation of the career of Persius, it is a fact of great significance that he seems to have been very much under the influence of the women of his household. To this influence he owed the purity of his habits; but feminine training is not without its disadvantages for the conduct of life. For social refinement there is no better school; but the pet of the home circle is apt to make the grossest blunders when he ventures into the larger world of no manners, and attempts to use the language of outside sinners. And so, when Persius undertakes to rebuke the effeminacy of his time, he outbids the worst passages of Horace and rivals the most lurid indecencies of Juvenal.

When Persius was twelve years old he went to Rome,

as Horace and Ovid had done before him, for the purpose
of a wider and higher education, and was put to school
with Verginius Flaccus, the rhetorician, and Remmius
Palaemon, the grammarian. Verginius Flaccus was ex-
iled from Rome by Nero, with Musonius Rufus, on account of the prominence which he had achieved as a
teacher, and Quintilian quotes him as an authority in his
profession. Remmius Palaemon, the other teacher of Persius, a man of high attainments and low principles, was
one of the most illustrious grammarians of a time when
grammarians could be illustrious. A freedman, with a
freedman's character, he was arrogant and vain, grasping
and prodigal—in short, a Sir Epicure Mammon of a professor. But his prodigious memory, his ready flow of
words, his power of improvising poetry, attracted many
pupils during his prolonged life, and after his death he
was cited with respect by other grammarians—a rare
apotheosis among that captious tribe. The first satirical
efforts of ingenuous youth are usually aimed at their pre-
ceptors, and the verses which Persius quotes in the First
Satire are quite as likely to be from the school of Palaemon as from the poems of Nero.

But the true teacher of Persius, the man to whom he
himself attributed whatever progress he made in that
'divine philosophy' which deals at once with the constitution of the universe and the conduct of life—his 'spiritual director,' to use the language of Christian ascetics
—was Cornutus. Persius is one of those literary celeb-
rities whose title to fame is not beyond dispute; and
while some maintain his right to high distinction on the
ground of intrinsic merit, others seek with perhaps too
much avidity for the accidents to which he is supposed
to owe his renown. If it is necessary to excuse, as it
were, his reputation, the relation of Persius to Cornutus

A 2

might go far to explain the care which schoolmasters have taken of the memory of the poet. No matter how crabbed the teacher may be, how austere the critic, the opening of the Fifth Satire, with its warm tribute to the guide of his life and the friend of his heart, calls up the image of the ideal pupil, and touches into kindred the brazen bowels of Didymus.

Lucius Annaeus Cornutus, of Leptis in Africa, was a philosopher, grammarian, and rhetorician. It has been conjectured that he was a freedman of the literary family of the Annaei; and this is rendered probable by the fact that Annaeus Lucanus, the nephew of Annaeus Seneca, was his pupil. The year of his life and the year of his death are alike unknown. He was banished from Rome by Nero because he had ventured to suggest that Nero's projected epic on Roman history would be too long if drawn out to four hundred books, and that the imperial poem would find no readers. When one of Nero's flatterers rejoined that Chrysippus was a still more voluminous author, Cornutus had the bad taste to point out the practical importance of the writings of Chrysippus in contrast with Nero's unpractical project; and Nero, who had a poet's temper, if not a poet's gifts, sent him to an island, there to revise his literary judgment. Cornutus was not only a man of various learning in philosophy, rhetoric, and grammar, but a tragic poet of some note, and perhaps a satirist. Whether the jumble that bears the name of Cornutus or Phurnutus, *De Natura Deorum*, is in any measure traceable to our Cornutus, is not pertinent to our subject. Of more importance to us than his varied attainments is his pure and lofty character, which made him worthy of the ardent affection with which Persius clung to his 'Socratic bosom.' It is recorded to his honor that Persius having bequeathed to him his library and a considerable sum of money, he accepted the books only, and relinquished the money to the family of Persius. Nor did he cease his loving care for his friend after his ashes, but revised his satires, and suppressed the less mature performances of the young poet.

The social circle in which Persius moved was not wide. The mark of the beast called Coterie, which is upon the foreheads of the most plentifully belaurelled Roman poets, is on his brow also. But it must be said that the men whom he associated with belonged to the chosen few of a corrupt time, albeit they would have been of more service to their country if they had not recognized themselves so conspicuously as the elect. The Stoic *salon* in which Persius lived and moved and had his being reminds M. Martha of a Puritan household; it reminds us of the sequestered Legitimist opposition to the France of yesterday. We are so apt to see parallels when we are well acquainted with but one of the lines—or with neither.

Let us pass in review some of the associates and acquaintances of Persius.

Among his early friends was Caesius Bassus, to whom the Sixth Satire is addressed: an older contemporary, who had studied with the same master, next to Horace, by a long remove, among the Roman lyrists. To his fellow-pupils belong Calpurnius, who is more than doubtfully identified with the author of the Bucolics; and Lucan (Annaeus Lucanus), the poet of the Pharsalia, who shared with him the instructions of Cornutus, and is said to have shown the most fervent admiration of the genius of his school-fellow. We are told that when the First Satire was recited, Lucan exclaimed that these were true poems. Whether he accompanied this encomium with a disparagement of his own performances, or simply had reference to the modest disclaimer of Persius's Prologue, as Jahn is inclined to think, does not appear. The anecdote is in perfect keeping with the perfervid Spanish temper of Lucan and Lucan's family. But this momentary burst of admiration is no indication of any genuine sympathy between the effusive and rhetorical Cordovan and the shy, philosophical Etruscan. Nominally they belonged to the same school—the Stoic; but Persius was ready to resist unto blood, Lucan's Stoicism was a mere parade.

While this anecdote leaves us in suspense as to the relations between Lucan and Persius, we have express evidence that there was no sympathy between Persius and Seneca. They met, we are informed, but the poet took little pleasure in the society of the essayist. This is not the place to attempt a characteristic of this famous writer, who, like Persius, leaves few readers indifferent. Once the idol of the moralists—who of all old birds are the most easily caught with chaff—Seneca has fallen into comparative disfavor within the last few decades; yet sometimes a vigorous champion starts up to do battle for him, such as Farrar in England, and, with more moderation, Constant Martha in France; and his cause is by no means hopeless if the advocate can keep his hearers from reading Seneca for themselves. It is impossible not to admire Seneca in passages; it seems very difficult to retain the admiration after reading him continuously. The glittering phrase masks a poverty of thought; 'the belt with its broad gold covers a hidden wound.' To Persius, the youthful Stoic, with his high purpose and his transcendental views of life, Seneca the courtier, the time-server, the adroit flatterer, must have appeared little better than a hypocrite, or, which is worse to an ardent mind, a practical negation of his own aspirations. The young convert—and Persius's philosophy was Persius's religion—in the first glow of his enthusiasm, must have been repelled by the callousness of the older professor of the same faith. And yet so strong was the impress of the age that Persius and Seneca are not so far asunder after all. To understand Persius we must read Seneca; and the lightning stroke of Caligula's tempestuous brain, *harena sine calce*, illuminates and shivers the one as well as the other.

If the family of the Annaei did not prove congenial, there were others to whom Persius might look for sympathy and instruction. Such was M. Servilius Nonianus, a man of high position, of rare eloquence, of unsullied fame. Such was Plotius Macrinus, to whom the Second Satire is addressed, itself a eulogy. Even in his own family circle there were persons whose lofty characters have made them celebrated in history. His kinswoman Arria, herself destined to become famous for her devotion to her husband, was the wife of Thrasea Paetus, and the daughter of that other Arria, whose supreme cry, NON DOLET, when she taught her husband how to meet his doom, is one of the most familiar speeches of a period when speech was bought with death. Thrasea, the husband of the younger Arria, was one of the foremost men of his time, and bore himself with a moderation which contrasts strongly with the ostentatious virtue of some of the Stoic chiefs. He rebuked the vices of his time unsparingly, but steadily observed the respect due to the head of the state; and even when the decree was passed which congratulated Nero on the murder of his mother, he contented himself with retiring from the senate-house. But Thrasea's silent disapproval of one crime fired Nero to another, and his refusal to deprecate the wrath of the emperor was the cause of his ruin—if that could be called ruin which he welcomed as he poured out his blood in libation to Jupiter the Liberator.

That the familiar intercourse with such a man should

have inspired a youth of the education and the disposition of Persius with still higher resolves and still higher endeavors is not strange. That it sufficed, as some say, to penetrate Persius with the sober wisdom of maturer years, and made up to him for the lack of personal experience and artistic balance, is attributing more to association than association can accomplish.

To Thrasea's influence Jahn ascribes Persius's juvenile essays in the preparation of *praetextae*, or tragedies with Roman themes, and it is not unlikely that a poetical description of his travels (ὁδοιπορικῶν) referred to some little trip that he took with Thrasea. Thanks to Cornutus, this youthful production—which doubtless was nothing more than a weak imitation of Horace, or haply of Lucilius—was suppressed after the death of the author, and with it his *praetexta*, and a short poem in honor of the elder Arria also.

The purity of Persius's morals, and the love which he bore his mother, his sister, his aunt, stand to each other reciprocally as cause and effect; and the occasional crudity of his language is, as we have already seen, the crudity of a bookish man, who thinks that the sure way to do a thing is to overdo it. Persius was a man of handsome person, gentle bearing, attractive manners, and added to the charm of his society the interest which always gathers about those whom the gods love.

He died on his estate at the eighth milestone on the Appian Road, *vitio stomachi*, eight days before the kalends of December, A.U.C. 815—A.D. 62—in the twenty-eighth year of his age.

Cornutus first revised the satires of his friend, and then gave them to Caesius Bassus to edit. The only important change that Cornutus made was the substitution of *quis non* for *Mida rex* (1, 121), a subject which is discussed in the Commentary. Other traces of wavering expression and *duplex recensio* are due to the imagination of commentators, who attribute to the young poet a logical method and an exactness of development for which the style of Persius gives them no warrant. *Raro et tarde scripsit,* the statement of the Life of Persius, explains much.

The poems of Persius were received with applause as soon as they appeared, and the old *Vita Persii* would have us believe that people scrambled for the copies as if the pages were so many Sabine women. Quintilian, in his famous inventory of Greek and Roman literature, says that Persius earned a great deal of glory, and true glory, by a single book, and here and there the great scholar does Persius homage by imitating him; and Martial holds up Persius with his one book of price, as a contrast to the empty bulk of a half-forgotten epic. But it would not be worth the while to repeat the list of the admirers of Persius in the ages of later Latinity. It suffices to say that he was the special favorite of the Latin Fathers. Augustin quotes or imitates him often, and Jerome is saturated with the phraseology of our poet. Commended to Christian teachers by the elevation of his moral tone, by the pithiness of his maxims and reflections, and the energy of his figures, he was set up on a high chair, a big school-boy, to teach other school-boys, and scarcely a voice was raised in rebellion for centuries. But since the time of the Scaligers, who were not to be kept back by any consideration for the feelings of the Fathers, there has been much unfriendly criticism of Persius; and the world owes him a debt of gratitude for provoking an animosity that has opened the way to a freer discussion of the literary merits of the authors of antiquity. To be subject all one's life through fear of literary death to the bondage of antique dullness, as well as to the thraldom

of contemporary stupidity, would have been a sad result
of the revival of letters.

The first and last charge brought against Persius is his
obscurity.    Admitted by all, it is variously interpreted,
variously excused, variously attacked.    Now it is accounted for by the political necessities of the time.    Now
it is attributed to the perverse ingenuity of the poet,
which was fostered by the perverse tendencies of an age
when, as Quintilian says, *Pervasit iam multos ista persua-
sio ut id iam demum eleganter dictum putent quod inter-
pretandum sit.*    Some simply resolve the lack of clearness
into the lack of artistic power; others intimate that the
fault lies more in the reader than in the author, whose
dramatic liveliness, which puzzles us, presented no difficulties to the critics of his own century.    But the con-
troversy is not confined to the obscurity of the satires.
Persius is all debatable ground.    Some admire the pithy
sententiousness of the poet; others sneer at his priggish
affectation of superiority.    Some point to the bookish
reminiscences, which bewray the mere student; others recall the example of Ben Jonson, of Molière, to show that
in literature, as in life, the greatest borrowers are often
the richest men, and bid us observe with what rare and
vivid power he has painted every scene that he has witnessed with his own eyes.    To some he is a copyist of
copyists; to others his real originality asserts itself most
conspicuously where the imitation seems to be the closest.
Julius Scaliger calls him *miserrimus auctor;* Mr. Conington notes his kindred to Carlyle.

No critic has put the problem with more brutal frank-
ness than M. Nisard, who, at the close of his flippant but
suggestive chapter on Persius, asks the question, *Y a-t-il
profit à lire Perse?*    Though he makes a faint show of
balancing the Ayes and Noes, it is very plain how he

himself would vote. The impatient Frenchman is evidently not of a mind 'to read prefaces, biographies, memoirs, and commentaries on these prefaces, these biographies, these memoirs, and notes on these commentaries, in order to form an idea that will haply be very false and assuredly very debatable, of a work about which no one will ever talk to you, and of a poet about whom you will never find any one to talk to.' But the question, which may be an open one to a critic, is not an open one to an editor; and editors of Persius are especially prone to value their author by the labor which he has cost them, by the material which they have gathered about the text. The thoughts are, after all, so common that parallels are to be found on every hand; the compass is so small that it is an easy matter to carry in the memory every word, every phrase; and so-called illustrations suggest themselves even to an ordinary scholar in bewildering numbers, while the looseness of the connection gives ample scope to speculation. Hence the sarcasm of Joseph Scaliger: *Non pulchra habet sed in eum pulcherrima possumus scribere ;* and the well-known criticism of the same scholar: *Au Perse de Casaubon la saulce vaut mieux que le poisson.* But this artificial love on the part of the editors has not contributed to the popularity of the author, and the youthful poet has been overlaid by his erudite commentators. Besides this disadvantage, Persius, when he is read at all, comes immediately after Juvenal, and, as if to enhance the contrast, is generally bound up with him; and the homeliness of his tropes, the crabbedness of his dialogue, the roughness of his transitions repel the young student, who finds the riddance of the historical and archæological work which Juvenal involves a poor compensation for the lack of the large manner and the dazzling rhetoric of the great declaimer. On the other hand, maturer scholars have been found to reverse the popular verdict, and to say, with Mr. Simcox, that 'the shy, youthful fervor of the dutiful boy, combined with the literary honesty which kept Persius from writing any thing which was not a part of his permanent consciousness, makes him improve upon every reading, which is more than can be said of Juvenal, who writes as if he thought and felt little in the intervals of writing.' But, while it is easy to get tired of Juvenal, it is not so easy to become enamored of Persius; and it must be admitted that the pleasure is questionable. Yet, in spite of M. Nisard, there is no real question about the utility of the study of the poet, who illustrates by what he does not say even more than by what he says the character of an age which is of supreme importance to the historian. Even if we put the study on lower ground, we must admit that Persius's title to a prominent position in the annals of Roman literature is indefeasible. However desirable it may be to get rid of him, an author who has left his impress on Rabelais and Ben Jonson, as well as on Montaigne and Boileau—an author whose poems have furnished so many quotations to modern letters, can not be dismissed from the necessities of a 'polite education' with a convenient sneer. Persius deserves our attention, if it were only as a problem of literary taste.

To the end of the study of Persius, it is best to look away from the conflicting views of the critics, and to abandon the attempt to distinguish between the weight of facts and the momentum of rhetoric in the balanced antitheses of praise and blame. The position of the poet will be most accurately determined by the calculation of the statics of his department and his age.

The Satire is the only extant form of Latin poetry that can lay claim to a truly national origin; and the error into which the early historians of classical literature were led by the resemblance between the name of the Roman satire and the name of the Greek satyr-drama has long been corrected. But the truth which this error involves, the connection between the comic drama and the satire, remains. The satire goes back to the popular source of comedy, and holds in solution all the elements which the Greeks combined into various forms of dramatic merriment. As the rhythmical movements, which culminate in such perfections as the dactylic hexameter and the iambic trimeter, are common to our whole race, and the rude Saturnian verse is one with the heroic, so the rustic songs of harvest and vintage are common to Greece and Italy; and it is no marvel that, as the satire was working itself out to classic proportions, it should have felt its kindred to Greek comedy, and should have drawn its materials and its methods from that literature on which Roman literature in its other departments was more directly dependent. And so the satire, though a genuine growth of Italian soil, was none the less subject to Greek influences. It was trained into Greek forms, it was permeated by Greek thought; and here as elsewhere the retranslation into Greek, of which the older commentators were so fond, is often the key to the meaning; here as elsewhere our appreciation of the author, as a whole, is conditioned by our knowledge of Greek literature.

Horace, the master of Roman satire, has more than once drawn the parallel between satire and comedy; and Persius, who follows the literary, though not the philosophical creed of his predecessor, aims even more distinctly than Horace does at reproducing the mimicry of comedy on the narrow stage of the satire. At the close of the First Satire he goes so far as to demand of his readers the intense study of the Old Attic Comedy as the preparation for the enjoyment of his poems—an extraordinary demand, if we do not make due allowance for the rhetorical expression of high aims and earnest endeavors. A comparison of the triumvirate of the *comoedia prisca* of Attica reveals little trace of direct influence, abundant evidence of extreme diversity in expression and conception. I say 'expression,' not 'language.' It is true that the language of Persius has a virile tone, but the masculine energy of his words is often out of keeping with the scholastic tameness of his thoughts. The breezy Pnyx of the Athenian and the stuffy *lecticula lucubratoria* of the Roman are not further apart than Aristophanes and Persius.

The New Attic Comedy, the comedy of situation and manners, furnished themes that lay nearer to the genius of Persius, although the grace of a Menander was much further from his grasp than from Terence, the half-Menander of Caesar's epigram. One passage is all but translated from Menander's Eunuch; and if Persius did not borrow traits for his picture of the miser and the spendthrift from the master of the New Comedy, it was not for lack of models. Indeed, so unreal is Persius, with all the realism of his language, that one of the most striking features of his poems—the opposition to the military— loses somewhat of its significance when we remember that the Macedonian period, to which the New Comedy belongs, is crowded with typical soldiers of fortune, with their coarse love of sensual pleasure—their coarse contempt of every thing that can not be eaten, drunk, or handled. Every line of Persius's centurion can be reproduced from the Greek; and although it would be going too far to say that there was no counterpart to his sketch in his own experience, although, on the contrary, Persius seems to have verified by actual observation whatever he learned from books, the historical value of his portrait is very much reduced by the existence of the Greek type. As a specimen of a kind of clerico-political opposition to an empire which its enemies might call an empire of brute force and military mechanism, the hostility of Persius to a class whose predominance was making itself felt more and more is not without its point and interest, and it is unfortunate that we have to leave its reality in suspense.

Yet another form of the comic drama was the Mime, and we have the explicit statement of Joannes Lydus that Persius imitated the famous mimographer, Sophron; and although the fragments of Sophron are so scanty that this statement can not be verified, it is not without its intrinsic probability. The mimetic power of Sophron is notorious, and Persius might well have taken lessons from the man whom Plato acknowledged as his master. The dialogue, thus borrowed from the mime, became the artistic form of philosophic composition, and, as Persius's Satires are essentially moral treatises, it is not surprising that he should have made large use of the same machinery. Plato himself furnished the movement for two of his essays, and we can detect a community of models between Persius and some of the later Greek writers. Lucian, the mercurial, and Persius, the saturnine, often work on the same theme, each in his way; and when the dialogue is dropped, and the bustle of the drama is succeeded by the effects of the scene-painter's craft, we are reminded of another group of copyists, and find all the picturesque detail for which Persius is so famous in the letters of Alkiphron and Aristainetos, themselves far-off echoes of the New Comedy.

Surely these are originals enough, the Attic Comedy, the Mime, Sophron and Plato, Menander and Philemon. But we find other models nearer home, and, passing by the reflections of Greek comedy in Plautus and Terence, its refractions in Afranius and Pomponius, we come to the satiric exemplars of Persius—Lucilius and Horace. *Mox ut a scholis et magistris divertit, lecto libro Lucilii decimo, vehementer saturas conponere instituit.* This statement of the old *Vita Persii* is much more consonant with the character of Persius than his own affected mirthfulness. His 'saucy spleen' had as little to do with his verse-writing as righteous indignation with the rhetorical out-pouring of Juvenal. His laughter was as much a part of the conventionalities of the satire as the *Camena* was of his confidences to Cornutus. School-boys all imitate circus-riders; here and there one mimics the clown; and Persius, who had not outgrown the tendencies of boy-hood, straightway began to make copies of verses in the manner of Lucilius. At the same time he was too much under the influence of Horace to follow Lucilius in his negligences, and too little master of the form to strike the mean between slovenly dictation and painful composition. As an imitator of Lucilius he boldly lashes men of straw where Lucilius flogged Lupus and Mucius, and breaks his milk-teeth on Alkibiades and Dama where Lucilius broke his jaw-teeth on living and moving enemies. As an imi-tator of Horace he appropriates the garb of Horatian diction; but the easy movement of roguish Flaccus is lost, and the stiff stride of the young Stoic betrays him at every turn.

As in the case of the Old Attic Comedy, Persius's intel-lectual affinity with Lucilius was purely imaginary; and for the purposes of this study it is unnecessary to repro-duce the lines of Horace's portrait of the 'great nursling of Aurunca,' or to attempt to form a mosaic out of the chipped chips of Lucian Müller's recent collection. The wide range of theme, the manly carelessness of style, the bold criticism, the bright humor, the biting wit—in short,

almost every characteristic of Lucilius that we can distinguish, shows how little kindred there must have been between the two men. The dozen scattered verses of the
Tenth Book of Lucilius, which is said to have suggested
the theme of the First Satire of Persius, and the fragments
of the Fourth Book, which is imitated by Persius in his
Third Satire, though more significant, give us no clew to
the manner or the extent of his indebtedness. Here and
there a verse, a hemistich, a jingle may have been taken
from Lucilius, and he may have enriched his vocabulary
here and there from Lucilius's store of drastic words; but
his obligations to Lucilius, real and imaginary, are all as
nothing in comparison with the large drafts which he
drew on the treasury of Horace.

The obligations of Persius to Horace have been the
theme of all the editors. The scholiasts themselves have
quoted parallels, and Casaubon has written a special treatise on the subject, and commentators, with almost childish rivalry, have vied with each other in noting verbal co-
incidences and similar trains of thought. The fact of the
imitation is too evident to need proof, and it would have
been much more profitable to examine the causes and
significance of this dependence, and to study the modifi-
cations of the language and the thought as they passed
through the alembic of Persius's brain, than to multiply
examples of words and phrases that are common, not only
to Horace and Persius, but to the language of every-day
life. Indeed, some go so far as to make Persius quibble
on Horace; and 'How green you are,' of the modern
street, and 'What means that trump?' of the modern
card-table, are as much Shakespearian as some of Persius's 'borrowings' are Horatian.

Horace had long been a classic when Persius dodged
his school-tasks and was a dab at marbles. Indeed, noth-

ing is more remarkable about Roman literature than the rapidity with which the images of its Augustan heroes took on the *patina* of age. The half-century that lay between Horace and Persius drew itself out to a distant perspective, and Virgil and Horace had all the authority of *veteres*. They not only dictated the forms of poetry, but permeated and dominated prose. True, the hostility to Virgil and Horace had not ceased; the *antiquarii* were not dead; but the ground had been shifted. The admirers of republican poetry in the time of Horace were republicans—in the time of Persius they were imperialists; and the maintenance of the authors of the Augustan age as the true classics was a part of the programme of the opposition. The court literature of the Neronian period found its models in the earlier epic essays of Catullus rather than in the poems of Virgil. Virgil had modified the Greek norms to suit the Latin tongue; but these men went back of malice aforethought to the Greek standard, and emulated the proportions of the Greek versification of the Alexandrian period. They were impatient of the classic vocabulary, and found the classic rhythms tame; and so they betook themselves to the earlier language, and set it to more exact harmonies. It was no heresy with this set to consider Virgil at once light and rough. The mouth-filling words of the older and bolder period, marshaled in serried ranks, no gap, no break, as they kept time to a rhythmical cadence that was marked by all the music of consonance and assonance—this was the ideal of the school which Persius assailed, just as an admirer of Pope or Goldsmith might assail the dominant poetry of our day, with its sensuous melody and its revived archaisms. Surely the worshippers of recent poets might pause before accepting the narrow literary creed of Persius. But, not to imitate the example of Ni-

sard, and indulge in dangerous parallelisms, it is sufficient
for our purpose to note that Persius's close study of the
language of Horace was not only a part of a liberal education, but a necessity of the school to which he belonged.
If he was to write satire at all, he must needs take Horace for his model. If he had written an epic, he would
have taken Virgil.

Besides this, we may boldly say that reminiscence is
no robbery. The verses, the phrases, the arguments that
we know by heart often become so wholly ours that they
weave themselves unconsciously into the texture of our
speech. We use them as convenient forms of expression,
without the least thought of plagiarism. We quote them,
thinking that they are as familiar to others as they are
to ourselves. They constitute, as it were, a sympathetic
medium between men of culture. And so Persius repeated group after group of the words of Horace as innocent-
ly as the Augustan poets translated their Greek models,
and thought no more harm than did the Emperor Julian
when he Platonized, or Thackeray when he transfused the
classics that he learned at the Charter House into his own
matchless English. That he did it to excess is not to be
denied. He never learned the lesson of Apelles—what is
enough.

Having thus briefly disposed of those turns which are
common to the Latin tongue, and those which ran freely
into the pen of the writer, we have now to deal with a considerable number of passages in which the memory of Persius must have lingered over the words of Horace, in which
his painstaking genius has hammered the thoughts of
Horace into a more compact or a more angular utterance.
To the majority of readers his condensations and his am-
plifications will alike appear to be so many distortions of
the original. So, notably, where he characterizes Horace

B

himself, and substitutes for the simple *naso adunco* the
puzzling *excusso naso*, where 'the dreams of a sick man'
become the 'dreams of a sick dotard,' where 'telling
straight from crooked' is twisted into 'discerning the
straight line where it makes its way up between crooked
lines,' and where he wrings from the natural phrase 'drink
in with the ear' the odd combination 'bibulous ears.'
In the longer passages the wresting is still more pronounced; and those who refuse to take into consideration the moral attitude of Persius may well wonder
at the perversity with which he distorts the lines and
overcharges the colors of the original. But it is tolera-
bly evident that, with all Persius's admiration of Horace
as an artist, he felt himself immeasurably superior to
him morally, and looked upon these adaptations and
alterations as so much gained for the effect of his discourse. The slyness of Horace might have answered
well enough for his day and for the kind of vices that
he reproved, but the depth over which Persius stood
gave him a more than Stoic stature. Horace might have
been content with a flute; nothing less resonant than a
trumpet would have suited the moral elevation of Persius.
Horace is a consummate artist, and not less an artist in
the conduct of his life than in the composition of his
poems. Persius is the prototype of the sensational preacher, and preachers of all centuries, from Augustin and Jerome to Macleane and Merivale, have had a weakness for
him.

Aside from the moral tone, which is enough to give a
different ring to the most similar expressions in the two
poets, there is an artistic difference of great significance
in the handling of the dramatic element, which they both
recognized as fundamental in the satire. The dramatic
satires of Horace will not bear dislocation without de-

struction. In Persius the characters are always shifting, always fading away into an impersonal *Tu*. This may be partly due to the interval which he allowed to elapse between the periods of composition; but it is possible that he recognized the limitation of his own powers, that his satires were intended to be a knotted thong, and not a smooth horsewhip. This piecemeal composition, be it the result of poverty or of economy, makes Persius the very author for 'Elegant Extracts.' Hence it is not hard to defend him, as it is not hard to defend Seneca, and on similar grounds. Single verses ring in the ear for months and years. What line, for instance, more quoted than

*Tecum habita : noris quam sit tibi curta supellex ?*

What line sinks deeper than the sombre verse,

*Virtutem videant intabescantque relicta ?*

Single scenes, whether of dialogue or of description, possess every requirement of dramatic vividness. On every page of the commentary we call him bookish, and yet his pictures stand out from the canvas with a boldness which makes us concede that his books did not keep him from seeing, if they did not teach him to see, what was going on around him. What is not a little remarkable in so young a man is the honesty of his painting. A home-keeping youth, Persius gives us living pictures of what he saw at home, whether at Rome, at Volaterrae, or at Luna; in the school-room, in the lecture-room, in the court of justice, on the wharf, at the country cross-roads. He has watched the carpenter stretching his line, the potter whirling his wheel, the physician adjusting his scales. He has heard the horse-laugh of the burly centurion, and shivered; has heard, with a young Stoic sneer, a cooing and mincing declaimer. He knows all about ink and paper and parchment and reeds; he has not outlived his knowledge of marbles, and one might fancy that the lustral spittle of his aunty was still fresh on his brow. The fact that there is no breeziness about his poems, nothing that tells us of the liberal air beyond, is another sign of his truthfulness. His life is like his own 'ever retreating bay' of the Sixth Satire, with the cliffs of Stoic philosophy between him and the wintry sea without. Arretium he knows—it was not so far from Volaterrae—and Bovillae, in the neighborhood of which he had a farm, and Luna, and the world of Rome; but the rest of his geography is in the inane. Horace, on the other hand, ambles all over Italy, and treats us every now and then to a foreign tour with the air of a man who had run across the sea in his time; and even if he who takes us in his sweeping flight from Cadiz to Ganges be not the real Juvenal, the undisputed Juvenal has a far wider geographical outlook than Persius. This very limitation is one of the best signs of the artistic worth of Persius, and justifies the regret that he had not made himself the Crabbe of Roman poetry.

We have seen that Persius was not slavishly dependent on Horace, assimilated the material that he derived from him, raised the worldly wisdom of Horace to the ideal standard of the Stoic, and followed a different canon of dramatic art. To this we may add that Persius, with a certain aristocratic disdain of conventionalities, goes deeper into the current of vulgar diction than the freedman's son dared. Persius felt that he could afford to talk slang, and he talked it; and the commentators have found it necessary to hold Petronius in the left hand, as well as Horace in the right.

We now proceed to yet another formal element, which is no less significant to the close student of antique literature. The Roman handling of the hexameter was arti-

ficial in the extreme. Reasoning backward from the
Latin hexameter, scholars have been prone to transfer
the conscious symbolism of the Roman poets to the Greek
originals; and if they had stopped, say, at Apollonius
Rhodius, they might have been justified, for in the later
Greek poets something of the sort is not to be denied.
But the healthier period of Greek poetic art was lifted
far above such toying adaptations of sound to sense as
commentators still discover in Homer when they enlarge
on the symbolism of this or that spondaic verse, the beauty of this or that combination of diaeresis and caesura. A
recent comparison of Homer with his successors has shown
that, of all the spondaic verses in Homer, scarcely one in
a hundred can be traced to any 'picturesque' motive,
and the rapid movement of so many five-dactyl hexameters is simply the normal pace of the verse. When we
come to Latin metres, however, we must take a different
standard, and recognize a conscious modification of the
Greek rule. The Ovidian pentameter of the best period
—to cite a familiar instance—is subject to minute laws,
which are transgressed at every turn in Greek elegiac
poetry, and the different ideals of Persius and Horace are
distinctly traceable in their treatment of the hexameter.
Horace, as is well known, broke the lofty movement of
the hexameter to suit the easy gait of the satire. Persius is more rhetorical than Horace, and, although he admits elision with as great freedom as his master, his verse
has a more mechanical structure than the verse of Horace, and many of the conversational peculiarities of the
Horatian hexameter are much less conspicuous in Persius.
Horace weakens the caesura, employs a great number of
spondaic words, and neglects the variety at which the
epic aims; and perhaps the trained ear of a determined
scholar might hear in the jog-trot of his satiric rhythms

the hoofs of his bob-tailed mule and the lazy flapping of his portmanteau. Persius, on the other hand, hammers out his thoughts in a far more orthodox cadence. Comparing the first six hundred and fifty verses of the first book of the satires of Horace with the six hundred and fifty verses of Persius, we find that more than eight per cent. have five spondees against less than five per cent. in Persius. The so-called third trochee or feminine caesura of the third foot is found in one of ten of Horace's hexameters, and only in one of twenty-six in Persius—a low proportion even for a Latin poet. Still more striking is the rare use which Persius makes of the masculine caesura of the sixth foot, with its consequent monosyllabic close. Aside from all idle symbolism, this arrangement, which is comparatively common in Horace, gives the verse a certain familiar roughness, especially where the final word forces a union with the following line. These diversities can not be accidents, and serve to show that, although Persius might weave himself a garment from the dyed threads of Horatian diction, he was not bold enough to wear the *discincta tunica* of Horace's Muse. But we must not forget to be just, and it is only fair to add that such a garb would have been as inappropriate to his severe and lofty, though narrow spirit, as the Coan vestments of Ovid's 'kept goddess'—if we may borrow the *déesse entretenue* of Heinrich Heine.

A comparison of Persius with Juvenal — a favorite theme with editors—does not enter into the plan of this study. It suffices for our present purpose to note that the practiced rhetorician of the time of Trajan could not have shared Quintilian's admiration of his youthful predecessor. The parallel passages which have been cited belong to the common stock of satirical strokes or to the thesaurus of proverbial phrases. Who can believe that

Juvenal took *usque adeo* from Persius, or borrowed from him the familiar *rara avis?* There are three or four touches in the Tenth Satire which recall some of the more striking expressions of Persius; but Ribbeck's objections to the genuineness of this sophistic declamation, if not convincing, are at least sufficiently well founded to make us pause in citing them. In moral earnestness, Persius is as far superior to Juvenal as he is inferior to him in the rhetorical treatment of his themes; and so long as men will take into consideration this moral element, which modern critics are prone to eliminate from works of art, so long as they will say *pectus est quod satiricum facit* as well as *quod theologum*, Persius will command a personal esteem which does not attach to the satires of Juvenal. The ingenious theory of Boissier, that the great satirist of the Caesars was a snubbed snob, brings out in still more striking contrast the figure of Persius as the reserved provincial aristocrat, and may be worthy of a more ample development than it has yet received. But Juvenal is a dangerous theme. As M. Martha has admirably observed, Juvenal is an author whose declamatory tone has infected his eulogists; and those who are not carried away by an 'admiration which disfigures while it exalts,' may readily be tempted into the opposite extreme. Let us turn, then, to other matters which illustrate more directly the character of our author's compositions. And first a word or two of Stoicism.

With the strong practical tendencies of the Romans, the only systems of Greek philosophy that ever found large acceptance at Rome were the Epicurean and the Stoic; and in the Stoic school the only doctrines that commanded much attention were the ethic. The subtle dialectic of the Stoics, of which we have some unjoyous specimens in Cicero's philosophical compilations, was not congenial to the Roman mind; but the Stoic creed was the creed of the nobler spirits of the imperial time. Excluded from public life, or, at all events, from the satisfactory exercise of public functions, the elect few took refuge in Stoic philosophy.*

The object of Stoicism is by means of virtue and knowledge to make men independent of all without them, and happy in that independence. It is a pantheism: God revealed in every thing; God's law recognized in every thing; God the substance from which every thing proceeds, to which every thing returns; the Original Fire, from which every thing is born again. God is the all-pervasive Spirit, Fate, Providence. Obedience to his eternal laws constitutes virtue and happiness. Good and evil are to be measured by this standard. All that brings us toward this is Good; all that carries us away from it is Evil. Every thing else is indifferent.

In Grace or out of Grace, says the Christian; or, as Calvin expresses it in his nervous language, *Qui Christum dimidium habere vult, totum perdit.* In Virtue or out of Virtue, says the Stoic. There is nothing between. The wise are perfectly wise; the foolish are totally foolish. 'There is not a half-ounce of rectitude in the fool.' The vicious man is as mad as Orestes—nay, madder.

The difference between human beings is slight. Alkibiades, the high-born and the handsome, is no better than shriveled old Baukis, who makes her livelihood by selling greens. All external distinctions sink into utter insignificance by the side of this great contrast of knowledge and ignorance into which virtue and vice are resolved.

All humanity is one people; all the world one state;

---

* In this section of the Introduction I follow Zeller's Essay on Marcus Aurelius (*Vorträge u. Abhandlungen*) so closely that some special acknowledgment seems to be necessary.

its ruler the Deity; its constitution the eternal law of the universe. The more unconditionally a man submits to the guidance of this law, the more exclusively he seeks his happiness in virtue, the more independent he will be of all without him, the more contented in himself, and yet the readier to enter into communion with others, and to do his duty to the whole of which he is a part.

But it is to be observed that the Stoicism of Persius, like the Stoicism of Marcus Antoninus, was of a softer, milder, more religious character than that of Zeno and Chrysippus; and when the Stoic discourses on the nothingness of all earthly things, the ills of life, man's moral weakness, and his need of help, we hear language that reminds us now of the epistles of the New Testament, now of the doctrines of Buddha. 'The philosopher,' says Zeller, 'is a physician for the soul, a priest and servant of the Deity among men, and this he shows by the most unlimited, devoted, unreserved philanthropy.' And not only so, but the Stoic does not disdain to make life brighter in the social circle; and the Sixth Satire of our author, which Nisard considers to be a youthful escapade of the poet—*qui s'évertue comme un écolier qui sort de classe*—is no less truly Stoic than the high-strung Third.

In speaking of this subject it is difficult to keep from using the word religion, for the emotional element, which is so characteristic of religion, is not wanting in a system which is the popular synonym for suppression of emotion. This is the thesis which M. Martha has brought out into clear relief, and illumined by many apposite examples—a thesis which will not be strange to those who have studied with any care the social aspects of the later life of antiquity. Under the empire morality was more than morality—it was a religion; and all the formulae of certain phases of Christian ascetics may be applied to the ethical side of Stoic philosophy. It is difficult to approach the subject without seeming irreverence; but the faith of the Christian must be far from robust who can shrink from a parallel that goes no farther than the machinery—that does not involve the motive power. It is not the aim of this study to determine whether this parallelism is to be recognized as a *praeparatio Evangelica*, or as the like result of similar forces at work in different systems of thought and belief. It is enough to present the parallelism, to excuse the phraseology.

Our ancestors, at all events, were not afraid to recognize 'natural Christians' in such men as Socrates, in such youths as Persius. Why, even Seneca figured for a long time as St. Seneca; and Jeremy Taylor was following old example when he cited the Stoic as well as the Christian code. It is only one step from the recognition of this spiritual kindred to the recognition of the practical methods of spiritual work as anticipated in the life of antiquity—practical methods which for our purposes are even better described by an unbeliever like Lucian than by a believer like Marcus Antoninus. In that age of transition we find father confessors, private chaplains, mendicant friars, missions, revivals, conversions, ecstasies—all showing the deep needs of the human heart, which refused to be satisfied with the outworn gods of the Pantheon, and, in ignorance of the divine Person, who alone can answer a personal love, sought solace in the mechanism of morality. In characterizing Cornutus, I have already borrowed a phrase from M. Martha, and called him, as M. Martha calls Seneca, a spiritual director; and I have already ventured to call Persius a sensational preacher. His stock of philosophy or theology is not as large as some commentators suppose; and all the elaborate attempts to show by the satires that Persius was a thoroughly trained and consistent Stoic have failed. The most elementary knowledge of Stoic ethics is sufficient for the comprehension of Persius. Whatever else he knew he kept back for practical considerations. He sticks to the marrow of morality, and reiterates the cardinal doctrines of Stoicism with the vehemence of a Poundtext. This vehemence, this enthusiasm, may be explained by his youth, his Etruscan blood, his profession as a moral reformer. A critic with M. Taine's resources might account for it by the climate of Volaterrae; but, however it may be accounted for, certain it is that he himself is much impressed with the profundity of the doctrines which he professes; that he warms and glows as he imparts to his auditors the great secret that they are not free because they are slaves to vice; that a man who does not understand his relations to his Maker can not move a finger without sinning; that in the flesh there is no good thing; and that the anguish of a tortured conscience is the worst of hells. But the difficulties of Persius are not due to recondite Stoic thought, and can not be cleared up by reference to Stoic philosophy. The trouble lies in the slangy expressions, the lack of organic development, the restless zeal to force his message home to the heart of every hearer, and the consequent shifting of the personages of his dialogue to suit the cases as they rose before his mind.

Persius, then, was a preacher of Stoicism—Stoicism, at once the philosophy and the religion of a time when serious and noble natures had no city of refuge except in their inmost selves, when the only possible activity seemed to be submission to the inevitable. The hydrostatic pressure of the imperial time forced all the better elements into this mould; and in so far Persius bears the stamp of his period, and the very absence of political and personal allu-

sions shows how imperfect life must have been. But one
school of commentators, headed by Casaubon, and represented to-day in Germany by Lehmann, in England by
Pretor, see in Persius much more than a disciple of the
Stoa; and the satires of our author—especially the First
and Fourth—are supposed to be full of more or less oblique references to Nero's person, his habits, his literary
pretensions, his aristocratic birth. At one time it seemed
as if this thesis, which was suggested by the scholiast, had
been abandoned, but the field for historical ingenuity is
too tempting; and one of the vaguest of all the satires,
the Fifth, has been discovered by Lehmann to be full of
the most stinging allusions to Nero. It is not enough
to grant to this school that Nero, as the type of his age,
may have been present to the mind of the author. They
scornfully reject this concession, and resort to all manner
of legerdemain in order to explain away the impossibili-
ties of such an attack and the improbabilities of its execution. With such scope as these scholars allow themselves we may find parallels every where, and covert
assaults may be detected in the most innocent literary
performances. But it would not answer the purpose of
this Introduction to enter into an elaborate discussion of
this question, which seems to be destined to an uncom-
fortable resurrection as often as it is laid. Every plausi-
ble coincidence has been mentioned in the Notes, and it
will be sufficient for ingenuous youth to know the opinions of distinguished scholars on the subject.

If this essay had not been prolonged beyond the limit
proposed, it might be well to give some account of the
grammatical and rhetorical peculiarities of the style of
Persius; but the grammar of Persius will present few
difficulties to those who are at all familiar with the poetic syntax of the Latin language; and enough has been

said to prepare the student, in a measure, for coping with the labored terseness of our author.

The manuscripts of Persius are remarkable for their age, their number, and the stupid bewilderment of the transcribers.   The best is the *Codex Montepessulanus*, or Montpellier manuscript, with which the *Codex Vaticanus* closely coincides; but, in the words of Jahn, *Nullus Persii codex tantae auctoritatis est ut in rebus dubiis eius vestigia tuto sequaris sed semper inter complures optio eaque non raro incerta datur.*

# A. PERSII FLACCI

# SATURARUM

### LIBER.

# A. PERSII FLACCI

# SATURARUM

## LIBER.

---

## PROLOGUS.

Nec fonte labra prolui caballino,
nec in bicipiti somniasse Parnaso
memini, ut repente sic poeta prodirem.
Heliconidasque pallidamque Pirenen
illis remitto, quorum imagines lambunt
hederae sequaces: ipse semipaganus
ad sacra vatum carmen adfero nostrum.
quis expedivit psittaco suum chaere
picamque docuit nostra verba conari?
magister artis ingenique largitor
venter, negatas artifex sequi voces;
quod si dolosi spes refulserit nummi,
corvos poetas et poetridas picas
cantare credas Pegaseium nectar.

5

10

## SATURA I.

O curas hominum! o quantum est in rebus inane!
'Quis leget haec?' Min tu istud ais? nemo hercule!
   'Nemo?'
Vel duo, vel nemo. 'Turpe et miserabile!' Quare?
ne mihi Polydamas et Troiades Labeonem
5 praetulerint? nugae. non, si quid turbida Roma
elevet, accedas examenque inprobum in illa
castiges trutina, nec te quaesiveris extra.
nam Romae quis non —? a, si fas dicere—sed fas
tum, cum ad canitiem et nostrum istud vivere triste
10 aspexi ac nucibus facimus quaecumque relictis,
cum sapimus patruos; tunc, tunc, ignoscite—'Nolo.'
Quid faciam? sed sum petulanti splene cachinno.
   Scribimus inclusi, numeros ille, hic pede liber,
grande aliquid, quod pulmo animae praelargus anhelet.
15 scilicet haec populo pexusque togaque recenti
et natalicia tandem cum sardonyche albus
sede leges celsa, liquido cum plasmate guttur
mobile collueris, patranti fractus ocello.
hic neque more probo videas nec voce serena
20 ingentis trepidare Titos, cum carmina lumbum
intrant, et tremulo scalpuntur ubi intima versu.
tun, vetule, auriculis alienis colligis escas?
auriculis, quibus et dicas cute perditus *ohe*.
'Quo didicisse, nisi hoc fermentum et quae semel intus

25 innata est rupto iecore exierit caprificus?'
En pallor seniumque! o mores! usque adeone
scire tuum nihil est, nisi te scire hoc sciat alter?
'At pulchrum est digito monstrari et dicier *hic est!*
ten cirratorum centum dictata fuisse
30 pro nihilo pendas?' Ecce inter pocula quaerunt
Romulidae saturi, quid dia poemata narrent.
hic aliquis, cui circa umeros hyacinthia laena est,
rancidulum quiddam balba de nare locutus,
Phyllidas Hypsipylas, vatum et plorabile si quid,
35 eliquat ac tenero supplantat verba palato.
adsensere viri: nunc non cinis ille poetae
felix? non levior cippus nunc inprimit ossa?
laudant convivae: nunc non e manibus illis,
nunc non e tumulo fortunataque favilla
40 nascentur violae? 'Rides' ait 'et nimis uncis
naribus indulges. an erit qui velle recuset
os populi meruisse et cedro digna locutus
linquere nec scombros metuentia carmina nec tus?'
Quisquis es, o, modo quem ex adverso dicere feci,
45 non ego cum scribo, si forte quid aptius exit,
quando haec rara avis est, si quid tamen aptius exit,
laudari metuam, neque enim mihi cornea fibra est;
sed recti finemque extremumque esse recuso
euge tuum et belle. nam belle hoc excute totum:
50 quid non intus habet? non hic est Ilias Atti
ebria veratro? non si qua elegidia crudi
dictarunt proceres? non quidquid denique lectis
scribitur in citreis? calidum scis ponere sumen,

scis comitem horridulum trita donare lacerna,
55 et ' verum' inquis ' amo : verum mihi dicite de me.'
qui pote? vis dicam? nugaris, cum tibi, calve,
pinguis aqualiculus protenso sesquipede exstet.
o Iane, a tergo quem nulla ciconia pinsit,
nec manus auriculas imitari mobilis albas,
60 nec linguae, quantum sitiat canis Apula, tantae!
vos, o patricius sanguis, quos vivere fas est
occipiti caeco, posticae occurrite sannae!

Quis populi sermo est? quis enim, nisi carmina molli
nunc demum numero fluere, ut per leve severos
65 effundat iunctura unguis? scit tendere versum
non secus ac si oculo rubricam derigat uno.
sive opus in mores, in luxum, in prandia regum
dicere, res grandis nostro dat Musa poetae.
ecce modo heroas sensus adferre videmus
70 nugari solitos graece, nec ponere lucum
artifices nec rus saturum laudare, ubi corbes
et focus et porci et fumosa Palilia faeno,
unde Remus, sulcoque terens dentalia, Quinti,
cum trepida ante boves dictatorem induit uxor
75 et tua aratra domum lictor tulit—euge poeta!
est nunc Brisaei quem venosus liber Acci,
sunt quos Pacuviusque et verrucosa moretur
Antiopa, aerumnis cor luctificabile fulta.
hos pueris monitus patres infundere lippos
80 cum videas, quaerisne, unde haec sartago loquendi
venerit in linguas, unde istuc dedecus, in quo
trossulus exsultat tibi per subsellia levis?

nilne pudet capiti non posse pericula cano
pellere, quin tepidum hoc optes audire *decenter?*
85 'Fur es' ait Pedio.   Pedius quid? crimina rasis
librat in antithetis: doctas posuisse figuras
laudatur 'bellum hoc!' hoc bellum? an, Romule,
    ceves?
men moveat? quippe et, cantet si naufragus, assem
protulerim.   cantas, cum fracta te in trabe pictum
90 ex umero portes? verum, nec nocte paratum
plorabit, qui me volet incurvasse querela.
   'Sed numeris decor est et iunctura addita crudis.
cludere sic versum didicit *Berecyntius Attis*
et *qui caeruleum dirimebat Nerea delphin*
95 sic *costam longo subduximus Appennino.*
*Arma virum,* nonne hoc spumosum et cortice pingui,
ut ramale vetus vegrandi subere coctum?'
'Quidnam igitur tenerum et laxa cervice legendum?
*Torva minalloneis inplerunt cornua bombis,*
100 *et raptum vitulo caput ablatura superbo*
*Bassaris et lyncem Maenas flexura corymbis*
*euhion ingeminat, reparabilis adsonat echo?'*
haec fierent, si testiculi vena ulla paterni
viveret in nobis? summa delumbe saliva
105 hoc natat in labris, et in udo est Maenas et Attis,
nec pluteum caedit, nec demorsos sapit unguis.
   'Sed quid opus teneras mordaci radere vero
auriculas? vide sis, ne maiorum tibi forte
limina frigescant: sonat hic de nare canina
110 littera.'   Per me equidem sint omnia protinus alba;

nil moror.  euge! omnes, omnes bene mirae eritis res.
hoc iuvat? 'hic' inquis 'veto quisquam faxit oletum.'
pinge duos anguis: pueri, sacer est locus, extra
meite! discedo.  secuit Lucilius urbem,
115 te Lupe, te Muci, et genuinum fregit in illis;
omne vafer vitium ridenti Flaccus amico
tangit et admissus circum praecordia ludit,
callidus excusso populum suspendere naso:
men muttire nefas? nec clam, nec cum scrobe? nus-
        quam?
120 hic tamen infodiam.  vidi, vidi ipse, libelle:
auriculas asini quis non habet? hoc ego opertum,
hoc ridere meum, tam nil, nulla tibi vendo
Iliade.  audaci quicumque adflate Cratino
iratum Eupolidem praegrandi cum sene palles,
125 aspice et haec, si forte aliquid decoctius audis.
inde vaporata lector mihi ferveat aure:
non hic, qui in crepidas Graiorum ludere gestit
• sordidus, et lusco qui possit dicere 'lusce,'
sese aliquem credens, Italo quod honore supinus
130 fregerit heminas Arreti aedilis iniquas;
nec qui abaco numeros et secto in pulvere metas
scit risisse vafer, multum gaudere paratus,
si cynico barbam petulans nonaria vellat.
his mane edictum, post prandia Calliroen do.

## SATURA II.

Hunc, Macrine, diem numera meliore lapillo
qui tibi labentis apponit candidus annos.
funde merum genio. non tu prece poscis emaci,
quae nisi seductis nequeas committere divis;
5 at bona pars procerum tacita libabit acerra.
haud cuivis promptum est murmurque humilisque su-
    surros
tollere de templis et aperto vivere voto.
'Mens bona, fama, fides' haec clare et ut audiat ho-
    spes;
illa sibi introrsum et sub lingua murmurat 'o si
10 ebulliat patruus, praeclarum funus?' et 'o si
sub rastro crepet argenti mihi seria dextro
Hercule! pupillumve utinam, quem proximus heres
inpello, expungam! namque est scabiosus et acri
bile tumet. Nerio iam tertia conditur uxor.'
15 haec sancte ut poscas, Tiberino in gurgite mergis
mane caput bis terque et noctem flumine purgas?
heus age, responde — minimum est quod scire laboro —
de Iove quid sentis? estne ut praeponere cures
hunc — 'cuinam?' cuinam? vis Staio? an scilicet
    haeres?
20 quis potior index, puerisve quis aptior orbis?
hoc igitur, quo tu Iovis aurem inpellere temptas,
dic agedum Staio, 'pro Iuppiter! o bone' clamet

'Iuppiter!' at sese non clamet Iuppiter ipse?
ignovisse putas, quia, cum tonat, ocius ilex
25 sulpure discutitur sacro quam tuque domusque?
an quia non fibris ovium Ergennaque iubente
triste iaces lucis evitandumque bidental,
idcirco stolidam praebet tibi vellere barbam
Iuppiter? aut quidnam est, qua tu mercede deorum
30 emeris auriculas? pulmone et lactibus unctis?

Ecce avia aut metuens divum matertera cunis
exemit puerum frontemque atque uda labella
infami digito et lustralibus ante salivis
expiat, urentis oculos inhibere perita;
35 tunc manibus quatit et spem macram supplice voto
nunc Licini in campos, nunc Crassi mittit in aedis
'hunc optet generum rex et regina! puellae
hunc rapiant! quidquid calcaverit hic, rosa fiat!'
ast ego nutrici non mando vota: negato,
40 Iuppiter, haec illi, quamvis te albata rogarit.

Poscis opem nervis corpusque fidele senectae.
esto age; sed grandes patinae tuccetaque crassa
adnuere his superos vetuere Iovemque morantur.

Rem struere exoptas caeso bove Mercuriumque
45 arcessis fibra 'da fortunare Penatis,
da pecus et gregibus fetum!' quo, pessime, pacto,
tot tibi cum in flammas iunicum omenta liquescant?
et tamen hic extis et opimo vincere ferto
intendit 'iam crescit ager, iam crescit ovile,
50 iam dabitur, iam iam!' donec deceptus et exspes
nequiquam fundo suspiret nummus in imo.

Si tibi creterras argenti incusaque pingui
auro dona feram, sudes et pectore laevo
excutiat guttas laetari praetrepidum cor.
55 hinc illud subiit, auro sacras quod ovato
perducis facies; nam fratres inter aenos
somnia pituita qui purgatissima mittunt,
praecipui sunto sitque illis aurea barba.
aurum vasa Numae Saturniaque inpulit aera
60 Vestalisque urnas et Tuscum fictile mutat.
o curvae in terris animae et caelestium inanes!
quid iuvat hoc, templis nostros inmittere mores
et bona dis ex hac scelerata ducere pulpa?
haec sibi corrupto casiam dissolvit olivo,
65 haec Calabrum coxit vitiato murice vellus,
haec bacam conchae rasisse et stringere venas
ferventis massae crudo de pulvere iussit.
peccat et haec, peccat: vitio tamen utitur.  at vos
dicite, pontifices, in sancto quid facit aurum?
70 nempe hoc quod Veneri donatae a virgine pupae.
quin damus id superis, de magna quod dare lance
non possit magni Messallae lippa propago:
conpositum ius fasque animo sanctosque recessus
mentis et incoctum generoso pectus honesto.
75 haec cedo ut admoveam templis et farre litabo.

C

## SATURA III.

'Nempe haec adsidue: iam clarum mane fenestras
intrat et angustas extendit lumine rimas:
stertimus indomitum quod despumare Falernum
sufficiat, quinta dum linea tangitur umbra.
5 en quid agis? siccas insana canicula messis
  iam dudum coquit et patula pecus omne sub ulmo
        est.'
unus ait comitum. "Verumne? itane? ocius adsit
huc aliquis! nemon?" turgescit vitrea bilis:
"findor" — ut Arcadiae pecuaria rudere dicas.
10 iam liber et positis bicolor membrana capillis
inque manus chartae nodosaque venit harundo.
tunc querimur, crassus calamo quod pendeat umor,
nigra quod infusa vanescat sepia lympha;
dilutas querimur geminet quod fistula guttas.
15 o miser inque dies ultra miser, hucine rerum
venimus? at cur non potius teneroque columbo
et similis regum pueris pappare minutum
poscis et iratus mammae lallare recusas?
"An tali studeam calamo?" Cui verba? quid istas
20 succinis ambages? tibi luditur. effluis amens,
contemnere: sonat vitium percussa, maligne
respondet viridi non cocta fidelia limo.
udum et molle lutum es, nunc nunc properandus et
        acri

fingendus sine fine rota.   sed rure paterno
25 est tibi far modicum, purum et sine labe salinum —
quid metuas? — cultrixque foci secura patella.
hoc satis? an deceat pulmonem rumpere ventis,
stemmate quod Tusco ramum millesime ducis,
censoremne tuum vel quod trabeate salutas?
30 ad populum phaleras! ego te intus et in cute novi.
non pudet ad morem discincti vivere Nattae?
sed stupet hic vitio et fibris increvit opimum
pingue, caret culpa, nescit quid perdat, et alto
demersus summa rursum non bullit in unda.
35 magne pater divum, saevos punire tyrannos
haud alia ratione velis, cum dira libido
moverit ingenium ferventi tincta veneno:
virtutem videant intabescantque relicta.
anne magis Siculi gemuerunt aera iuvenci,
40 et magis auratis pendens laquearibus ensis
purpureas subter cervices terruit, 'imus,
imus praecipites' quam si sibi dicat et intus
palleat infelix, quod proxima nesciat uxor?
    Saepe oculos, memini, tangebam parvus olivo,
45 grandia si nollem morituri verba Catonis
discere, non sano multum laudanda magistro,
quae pater adductis sudans audiret amicis.
iure; etenim id summum, quid dexter senio ferret,
scire erat in voto; damnosa canicula quantum
50 raderet; angustae collo non fallier orcae;
neu quis callidior buxum torquere flagello.
haud tibi inexpertum curvos deprendere mores,

quaeque docet sapiens bracatis inlita Medis
porticus, insomnis quibus et detonsa iuventus
55 invigilat, siliquis et grandi pasta polenta;
et tibi quae Samios diduxit littera ramos
surgentem dextro monstravit limite callem.
stertis adhuc, laxumque caput conpage soluta
oscitat hesternum, dissutis undique malis!
60 est aliquid quo tendis, et in quod dirigis arcum?
an passim sequeris corvos testaque lutoque,
securus quo pes ferat, atque ex tempore vivis?
helleborum frustra, cum iam cutis aegra tumebit,
poscentis videas: venienti occurrite morbo!
65 et quid opus Cratero magnos promittere montis?
discite, o miseri, et causas cognoscite rerum:
quid sumus, et quidnam victuri gignimur; ordo
quis datus, aut metae qua mollis flexus et unde;
quis modus argento, quid fas optare, quid asper
70 utile nummus habet; patriae carisque propinquis
quantum elargiri deceat; quem te deus esse
iussit, et humana qua parte locatus es in re.
disce, nec invideas, quod multa fidelia putet
in loculete penu, defensis pinguibus Umbris,
75 et piper et pernae, Marsi monumenta clientis,
menaque quod prima nondum defecerit orca.
    Hic aliquis de gente hircosa centurionum
dicat 'Quod sapio satis est mihi. non ego curo
esse quod Arcesilas aerumnosique Solones,
80 obstipo capite et figentes lumine terram,
murmura cum secum et rabiosa silentia rodunt

atque exporrecto trutinantur verba labello,
aegroti veteris meditantes somnia, *gigni*
*de nihilo nihilum, in nihilum nil posse reverti.*
85 hoc est, quod palles? cur quis non prandeat, hoc est?'
His populus ridet, multumque torosa iuventus
ingeminat tremulos naso crispante cachinnos.

'Inspice; nescio quid trepidat mihi pectus et aegris
faucibus exsuperat gravis alitus; inspice, sodes!'
90 qui dicit medico, iussus requiescere, postquam
tertia conpositas vidit nox currere venas,
de maiore domo modice sitiente lagoena
lenia loturo sibi Surrentina rogabit.
'Heus, bone, tu palles!'  "Nihil est."  'Videas tamen
    istuc,
95 quidquid id est: surgit tacite tibi lutea pellis.'
"At tu deterius palles; ne sis mihi tutor;
iam pridem hunc sepeli: tu restas." 'Perge, tacebo.'
turgidus hic epulis atque albo ventre lavatur,
gutture sulpureas lente exalante mofites;
100 sed tremor inter vina subit calidumque triental
excutit e manibus, dentes crepuere retecti,
uncta cadunt laxis tunc pulmentaria labris.
hinc tuba, candelae, tandemque beatulus alto
conpositus lecto crassisque lutatus amomis
105 in portam rigidas calces extendit: at illum
hesterni capite induto subiere Quirites.

'Tange, miser, venas et pone in pectore dextram.
nil calet hic.  summosque pedes attinge manusque.
non frigent.'  Visa est si forte pecunia, sive

110 candida vicini subrisit molle puella,
   cor tibi rite salit? positum est algente catino
   durum holus et populi cribro decussa farina:
   temptemus fauces.  tenero latet ulcus in ore
   putre, quod haud deceat plebeia radere beta.
115 alges, cum excussit membris timor albus aristas;
   nunc face supposita fervescit sanguis et ira
   scintillant oculi, dicisque facisque, quod ipse
   non sani esse hominis non sanus iuret Orestes.

## SATURA IV.

'Rem populi tractas?' barbatum haec crede magistrum
dicere, sorbitio tollit quem dira cicutae
'quo fretus? dic hoc, magni pupille Pericli.
scilicet ingenium et rerum prudentia velox
5 ante pilos venit, dicenda tacendaque calles.
ergo ubi commota fervet plebecula bile,
fert animus calidae fecisse silentia turbae
maiestate manus. quid deinde loquere? "Quirites,
hoc puta non iustum est, illud male, rectius illud."
10 scis etenim iustum gemina suspendere lance
ancipitis librae, rectum discernis, ubi inter
curva subit, vel cum fallit pede regula varo,
et potis es nigrum vitio praefigere theta.
quin tu igitur, summa nequiquam pelle decorus,
15 ante diem blando caudam iactare popello
desinis, Anticyras melior sorbere meracas!
quae tibi summa boni est? uncta vixisse patella
semper et adsiduo curata cuticula sole?
exspecta, haud aliud respondeat haec anus. i nunc
20 "Dinomaches ego sum," suffla "sum candidus." esto;
dum ne deterius sapiat pannucia Baucis,
cum bene discincto cantaverit ocima vernae.'

Ut nemo in sese temptat descendere, nemo,
sed praecedenti spectatur mantica tergo!
25 quaesieris 'Nostin Vettidi praedia?' "Cuius?"

'Dives arat Curibus quantum non miluus errat.'
"Hunc ais, hunc dis iratis genioque sinistro,
qui, quandoque iugum pertusa ad compita figit,
seriolae veterem metuens deradere limum
30 ingemit: *hoc bene sit!* tunicatum cum sale mordens
caepe et farrata pueris plaudentibus olla
pannosam faecem morientis sorbet aceti?"
at si unctus cesses et figas in cute solem,
est prope te ignotus, cubito qui tangat et acre
35 despuat 'hi mores! penemque arcanaque lumbi
runcantem populo marcentis pandere vulvas!
tu cum maxillis balanatum gausape pectas,
inguinibus quare detonsus gurgulio exstat?
quinque palaestritae licet haec plantaria vellant
40 elixasque nates labefactent forcipe adunca,
non tamen ista filix ullo mansuescit aratro.'
caedimus inque vicem praebemus crura sagittis.
vivitur hoc pacto; sic novimus. ilia subter
caecum vulnus habes; sed lato balteus auro
45 praetegit. ut mavis, da verba et decipe nervos,
si potes. 'Egregium cum me vicinia dicat,
non credam?' Viso si palles, inprobe, nummo,
si facis in penem quidquid tibi venit amarum,
si puteal multa cautus vibice flagellas:
50 nequiquam populo bibulas donaveris aures.
respue, quod non es; tollat sua munera cerdo;
tecum habita: noris, quam sit tibi curta supellex.

## SATURA V.

Vatibus hic mos est, centum sibi poscere voces,
centum ora et linguas optare in carmina centum,
fabula seu maesto ponatur hianda tragoedo,
vulnera seu Parthi ducentis ab inguine ferrum.
5 ' Quorsum haec ? aut quantas robusti carminis offas
ingeris, ut par sit centeno gutture niti ?
grande locuturi nebulas Helicone legunto,
si quibus aut Progues, aut si quibus olla Thyestae
fervebit, saepe insulso cenanda Glyconi ;
10 tu neque anhelanti, coquitur dum massa camino,
folle premis ventos, nec clauso murmure raucus
nescio quid tecum grave cornicaris inepte,
nec scloppo tumidas intendis rumpere buccas.
verba togae sequeris iunctura callidus acri,
15 ore teres modico, pallentis radere mores
doctus et ingenuo culpam defigere ludo.
hinc trahe quae dicis, mensasque relinque Mycenis
cum capite et pedibus, plebeiaque prandia noris.'
Non equidem hoc studeo, bullatis ut mihi nugis
20 pagina turgescat, dare pondus idonea fumo.
secreti loquimur ; tibi nunc hortante Camena
excutienda damus praecordia, quantaque nostrae
pars tua sit, Cornute, animae, tibi, dulcis amice,
ostendisse iuvat : pulsa, dinoscere cautus,
25 quid solidum crepet et pictae tectoria linguae.

his ego centenas ausim deposcere voces,
ut, quantum mihi te sinuoso in pectore fixi,
voce traham pura, totumque hoc verba resignent,
quod latet arcana non enarrabile fibra.
30   Cum primum pavido custos mihi purpura cessit
bullaque succinctis Laribus donata pependit;
cum blandi comites totaque inpune Subura
permisit sparsisse oculos iam candidus umbo;
cumque iter ambiguum est et vitae nescius error
35 deducit trepidas ramosa in compita mentes,
me tibi supposui: teneros tu suscipis annos
Socratico, Cornute, sinu; tum fallere sollers
apposita intortos extendit regula mores,
et premitur ratione animus vincique laborat
40 artificemque tuo ducit sub pollice vultum.
tecum etenim longos memini consumere soles,
et tecum primas epulis decerpere noctes:
unum opus et requiem pariter disponimus ambo,
atque verecunda laxamus seria mensa.
45 non equidem hoc dubites, amborum foedere certo
consentire dies et ab uno sidere duci
nostra vel aequali suspendit tempora Libra
Parca tenax veri, seu nata fidelibus hora
dividit in Geminos concordia fata duorum,
50 Saturnumque gravem nostro Iove frangimus una:
nescio quod, certe est, quod me tibi temperat astrum.
    Mille hominum species et rerum discolor usus;
velle suum cuique est, nec voto vivitur uno.
mercibus hic Italis mutat sub sole recenti

55 rugosum piper et pallentis grana cumini,
   hic satur inriguo mavult turgescere somno;
   hic campo indulget, hunc alea decoquit, ille
   in Venerem putris; sed cum lapidosa cheragra
   fregerit articulos, veteris ramalia fagi,
60 tunc crassos transisse dies lucemque palustrem
   et sibi iam seri vitam ingemuere relictam.
   at te nocturnis iuvat inpallescere chartis;
   cultor enim iuvenum purgatas inseris aures
   fruge Cleanthea. petite hinc puerique senesque
65 finem animo certum miserisque viatica canis!
   'Cras hoc fiet.' Idem cras fiet. 'Quid? quasi magnum
   nempe diem donas.' Sed cum lux altera venit,
   iam cras hesternum consumpsimus: ecce aliud cras
   egerit hos annos et semper paulum erit ultra.
70 nam quamvis prope te, quamvis temone sub uno
   vertentem sese frustra sectabere cantum,
   cum rota posterior curras et in axe secundo.
      Libertate opus est, non hac, ut, quisque Velina
   Publius emeruit, scabiosum tesserula far
75 possidet. heu steriles veri, quibus una Quiritem
   vertigo facit! hic Dama est non tressis agaso,
   vappa lippus et in tenui farragine mendax:
   verterit hunc dominus, momento turbinis exit
   Marcus Dama. papae! Marco spondente recusas
80 credere tu nummos? Marco sub iudice palles?
   Marcus dixit: ita est; adsigna, Marce, tabellas.
   haec mera libertas; hoc nobis pillea donant!
   'An quisquam est alius liber, nisi ducere vitam

cui licet, ut voluit ? licet ut volo vivere : non sum
85 liberior Bruto ?'  " Mendose colligis," inquit
stoicus hic aurem mordaci lotus aceto
"haec reliqua accipio; *licet* illud et *ut volo* tolle."
' Vindicta postquam meus a praetore recessi,
cur mihi non liceat, iussit quodcumque voluntas,
90 excepto si quid Masuri rubrica vetavit?'
Disce, sed ira cadat naso rugosaque sanna,
dum veteres avias tibi de pulmone revello.
non praetoris erat stultis dare tenuia rerum
officia atque usum rapidae permittere vitae:
95 sambucam citius caloni aptaveris alto.
stat contra ratio et secretam garrit in aurem,
ne liceat facere id quod quis vitiabit agendo.
publica lex hominum naturaque continet hoc fas,
ut teneat vetitos inscitia debilis actus.
100 diluis helleborum, certo conpescere puncto
nescius examen : vetat hoc natura medendi.
navem si poscat sibi peronatus arator,
luciferi rudis, exclamet Melicerta perisse
frontem de rebus.  tibi recto vivere talo
105 ars dedit, et veri speciem dinoscere calles,
ne qua subaerato mendosum tinniat auro ?
quaeque sequenda forent, quaeque evitanda vicissim,
illa prius creta, mox haec carbone notasti ?
es modicus voti ? presso lare ? dulcis amicis ?
110 iam nunc astringas, iam nunc granaria laxes,
inque luto fixum possis transcendere nummum,
nec glutto sorbere salivam Mercurialem ?

'haec mea sunt, teneo' cum vere dixeris, esto
liberque ac sapiens praetoribus ac Iove dextro,
115 sin tu, cum fueris nostrae paulo ante farinae,
pelliculam veterem retines et fronte politus
astutam vapido servas sub pectore vulpem,
quae dederam supra relego funemque reduco:
nil tibi concessit ratio; digitum exsere, peccas,
120 et quid tam parvum est? sed nullo ture litabis,
haereat in stultis brevis ut semuncia recti.
haec miscere nefas; nec, cum sis cetera fossor,
tris tantum ad numeros satyrum moveare Bathylli.
'Liber ego.'   Unde datum hoc sentis, tot subdite rebus?
125 an dominum ignoras, nisi quem vindicta relaxat?
'I puer et strigiles Crispini ad balnea defer!'
si increpuit, 'cessas nugator;' servitium acre
te nihil impellit, nec quicquam extrinsecus intrat,
quod nervos agitet; sed si intus et in iecore aegro
130 nascuntur domini, qui tu inpunitior exis
atque hic, quem ad strigiles scutica et metus egit
        erilis?
        Mane piger stertis.  'Surge!' inquit Avaritia 'heia
surge!'   Negas; instat 'Surge!' inquit.  "Non queo."
        'Surge!'
"Et quid agam?"   'Rogitas? en saperdam advehe
        Ponto,
135 castoreum, stuppas, hebenum, tus, lubrica Coa;
tolle recens primus piper ex sitiente camelo;
verte aliquid; iura.'   "Sed Iuppiter audiet."   'Eheu!
varo, regustatum digito terebrare salinum

contentus perages, si vivere cum Iove tendis!'
140 iam pueris pellem succinctus et oenophorum aptas
  'Ocius ad navem!' nihil obstat, quin trabe vasta
  Aegaeum rapias, ni sollers Luxuria ante
  seductum moneat 'Quo deinde, insane, ruis? quo?
  quid tibi vis? calido sub pectore mascula bilis
145 intumuit, quod non exstinxerit urna cicutae?
  tu mare transilias? tibi torta cannabe fulto
  cena sit in transtro, Veientanumque rubellum
  exalet vapida laesum pice sessilis obba?
  quid petis? ut nummi, quos hic quincunce modesto
150 nutrieras, pergant avidos sudare deunces?
  indulge genio, carpamus dulcia! nostrum est
  quod vivis; cinis et manes et fabula fies.
  vive memor leti! fugit hora; hoc quod loquor inde
      est.'
  en quid agis? duplici in diversum scinderis hamo.
155 huncine, an hunc sequeris? subeas alternus oportet
  ancipiti obsequio dominos, alternus oberres.
  nec tu, cum obstiteris semel instantique negaris
  parere imperio, 'rupi iam vincula' dicas;
  nam et luctata canis nodum abripit; et tamen illi,
160 cum fugit, a collo trahitur pars longa catenae.
  'Dave, cito, hoc credas iubeo, finire dolores
  praeteritos meditor.' crudum Chaerestratus unguem
  adrodens ait haec 'an siccis dedecus obstem
  cognatis? an rem patriam rumore sinistro
165 limen ad obscenum frangam, dum Chrysidis udas
  ebrius ante fores exstincta cum face canto?'

"Euge, puer, sapias, dis depellentibus agnam
percute." 'Sed censen plorabit, Dave, relicta?'
"Nugaris; solea, puer, obiurgabere rubra.
170 ne trepidare velis atque artos rodere casses!
nunc ferus et violens; at si vocet, haud mora, dicas:
*Quidnam igitur faciam? nec nunc, cum arcessat et
ultro*
*supplicet, accedam?* Si totus et integer illinc
exieras, nec nunc." hic hic, quod quaerimus, hic est,
175 non in festuca, lictor quam iactat ineptus.
ius habet ille sui palpo, quem ducit hiantem
cretata ambitio? vigila et cicer ingere large
rixanti populo, nostra ut Floralia possint
aprici meminisse senes: *quid pulchrius?* at cum
180 Herodis venere dies, unctaque fenestra
dispositae pinguem nebulam vomuere lucernae
portantes violas, rubrumque amplexa catinum
cauda natat thynni, tumet alba fidelia vino:
labra moves tacitus recutitaque sabbata palles.
185 tum nigri lemures ovoque pericula rupto,
tum grandes galli et cum sistro lusca sacerdos
incussere deos inflantis corpora, si non
praedictum ter mane caput gustaveris alli.

Dixeris haec inter varicosos centuriones,
190 continuo crassum ridet Pulfennius ingens,
et centum Graecos curto centusse licetur.

## SATURA VI.

Admovit iam bruma foco te, Basse, Sabino?
iamne lyra et tetrico vivunt tibi pectine chordae?
mire opifex numeris veterum primordia vocum
atque marem strepitum fidis intendisse Latinae,
5 mox iuvenes agitare iocis et pollice honesto
egregius lusisse senes.  mihi nunc Ligus ora
intepet hibernatque meum mare, qua latus ingens
dant scopuli et multa litus se valle receptat.
Lunai portum, est operae, cognoscite, cives!
10 cor iubet hoc Enni, postquam destertuit esse
Maeonides, Quintus pavone ex Pythagoreo.
hic ego securus vulgi et quid praeparet auster
infelix pecori, securus et angulus ille
vicini nostro quia pinguior, etsi adeo omnes
15 ditescant orti peioribus, usque recusem
curvus ob id minui senio aut cenare sine uncto,
et signum in vapida naso tetigisse lagoena.
discrepet his alius! geminos, horoscope, varo
producis genio.  solis natalibus est qui
20 tingat holus siccum muria vafer in calice empta,
ipse sacrum inrorans patinae piper; hic bona dente
grandia magnanimus peragit puer.  utar ego, utar,
nec rhombos ideo libertis ponere lautus,
nec tenuis sollers turdarum nosse salivas.
25 messe tenus propria vive et granaria, fas est,

emole; quid metuis? occa, et seges altera in herba est.
ast vocat officium: trabe rupta Bruttia saxa
prendit amicus inops, remque omnem surdaque vota
condidit Ionio; iacet ipse in litore et una
30 ingentes de puppe dii, iamque obvia mergis
costa ratis lacerae. nunc et de caespite vivo
frange aliquid, largire inopi, ne pictus oberret
caerulea in tabula. 'Sed cenam funeris heres
negleget, iratus quod rem curtaveris; urnae
35 ossa inodora dabit, seu spirent cinnama surdum,
seu ceraso peccent casiae, nescire paratus.
tune bona incolumis minuas? et Bestius urguet
doctores Graios: *Ita fit, postquam sapere urbi
cum pipere et palmis venit nostrum hoc maris expers;*
40 *fenisecae crasso vitiarunt unguine pultes.'*
Haec cinere ulterior metuas? At tu, meus heres
quisquis eris, paulum a turba seductior audi.
o bone, num ignoras? missa est a Caesare laurus
insignem ob cladem Germanae pubis, et aris
45 frigidus excutitur cinis, ac iam postibus arma,
iam chlamydes regum, iam lutea gausapa captis
essedaque ingentesque locat Caesonia Rhenos.
dis igitur genioque ducis centum paria ob res
egregie gestas induco; quis vetat? aude.
50 vae, nisi conives! oleum artocreasque popello
largior; an prohibes? dic clare! 'Non adeo,' inquis
'exossatus ager iuxta est.' Age, si mihi nulla
iam reliqua ex amitis, patruelis nulla, proneptis
nulla manet patrui, sterilis matertera vixit,

55 deque avia nihilum superest, accedo Bovillas
clivumque ad Virbi, praesto est mihi Manius heres.
'Progenies terrae?' Quaere ex me, quis mihi quartus
sit pater: haud prompte, dicam tamen; adde etiam
    unum,
unum etiam: terrae est iam filius, et mihi ritu
60 Manius hic generis prope maior avunculus exit.
qui prior es, cur me in decursu lampada poscis?
sum tibi Mercurius; venio deus huc ego ut ille
pingitur; an renuis? vin tu gaudere relictis?
'Dest aliquid summae.' Minui mihi; sed tibi totum est,
65 quidquid id est. ubi sit, fuge quaerere, quod mihi
    quondam
legârat Tadius, neu dicta repone paterna:
*Faenoris accedat merces; hinc exime sumptus.*
*quid reliquum est?* Reliquum? nunc, nunc inpen-
    sius ungue,
ungue, puer, caules! mihi festa luce coquetur
70 urtica et fissa fumosum sinciput aure,
ut tuus iste nepos olim satur anseris extis,
cum morosa vago singultiet inguine vena,
patriciae inmeiat vulvae? mihi trama figurae
sit reliqua, ast illi tremat omento popa venter?
75 vende animam lucro, mercare atque excute sollers
omne latus mundi, nec sit praestantior alter
Cappadocas rigida pinguis plausisse castata:
rem duplica. 'Feci; iam triplex, iam mihi quarto,
iam deciens redit in rugam: depunge, ubi sistam.'
80 Inventus, Chrysippe, tui finitor acervi.

# VITA A. PERSII FLACCI

## DE COMMENTARIO PROBI VALERII SUBLATA.

A. Persius Flaccus natus est pridie nonas Decembris
Fabio Persico L. Vitellio coss. decessit VIII kalendas
5 Decembris P. Mario Asinio Gallo coss.

natus est in Etruria Volaterris, eques Romanus, san-
guine et affinitate primi ordinis viris coniunctus. decessit ad octavum miliarium in via Appia in praediis
suis.

10 pater eum Flaccus pupillum reliquit moriens annorum fere sex. Fulvia Sisennia mater nupsit postea
Fusio equiti Romano et eum quoque extulit inter
paucos annos.

studuit Flaccus usque ad annum XII aetatis suae
15 Volaterris, inde Romae apud grammaticum Remmium
Palaemonem et apud rhetorem Verginium Flavum.

cum esset annorum XVI, amicitia coepit uti Annaei Cornuti, ita ut ab eo nusquam discederet. indu-
ctus aliquatenus in philosophiam est.

20 amicos habuit a prima adulescentia Caesium Bassum
poetam et Calpurnium Staturam, qui vivo eo iuvenis
decessit. coluit ut patrem Servilium Nonianum. cognovit per Cornutum etiam Annaeum Lucanum, aequae-
vum auditorem Cornuti. [nam Cornutus illo tempore

tragicus fuit sectae stoicae. sed] Lucanus adeo mira-
batur scripta Flacci, ut vix retineret se recitantem cla-
more, quin illa [esse] vera poemata diceret, etsi ipse
sua ludos faceret. sero cognovit et Senecam, sed non
ut caperetur eius ingenio. usus est apud Cornutum
5 duorum convictu virorum et doctissimorum et sanctissi-
morum, acriter tum philosophantium, Claudii Agathe-
meri, medici, Lacedaemonii, et Petronii Aristocratis,
Magnetis, quos unice miratus est et aemulatus, cum ae-
quales essent, Cornuti minores et ipsi.
10    idem etiam decem fere annos summe dilectus a Pae-
to Thrasea est, ita ut peregrinaretur quoque cum eo ali-
quando, cognatam eius Arriam habente uxorem.
    fuit morum lenissimorum, verecundiae virginalis,
formae pulchrae, pietatis erga matrem et sororem et
15 amitam exemplo sufficientis.
    fuit frugi et pudicus.
    reliquit circa HS vicies matri et sorori. scriptis ta-
men ad matrem codicillis Cornuto rogavit ut daret ses-
tertia, ut quidam, centum, ut alii volunt et argenti facti
20 pondo viginti et libros circa septingentos Chrysippi sive
bibliothecam suam omnem. verum Cornutus sublatis
libris pecuniam [sororibus, quas heredes frater fecerat]
reliquit.
    et raro et tarde scripsit. hunc ipsum librum inper-
25 fectum reliquit. versus aliqui dempti sunt ultimo libro, ut quasi finitus esset. leviter retractavit Cornutus
et Caesio Basso petenti, ut ipsi cederet, tradidit eden-
dum.

scripsit etiam Flaccus in pueritia praetextam † ve-
scio et hodoeporicon librum unum et paucos in so-
crum Thraseae [in Arriae matrem] versus, quae se
ante virum occiderat. omnia ea auctor fuit Cornu-
5 tus matri eius ut aboleret.

editum librum continuo mirari et diripere homines
coepere.

decessit autem vitio stomachi anno aetatis XXX.

sed mox ut a scholis et magistris divertit, lecto libro
10 Lucilii decimo vehementer saturas conponere instituit.
cuius libri principium imitatus est, sibi primo, mox omnibus detracturus cum tanta recentium poetarum et ora-
totum insectatione, ut etiam Neronem [illius temporis
principem] culpaverit. cuius versus in Neronem cum
15 ita se haberet 'auriculas asini Mida rex habet,' in eum
modum a Cornuto, Persio iam tum mortuo, est commu-
tatus 'auriculas asini quis non habet?' ne hoc Nero in
se dictum arbitraretur.

QUINTILIANUS X, 1, 94 multum et verae glo-
20 riae quamvis uno libro Persius meruit.

MARTIALIS IV, 9, 7
Saepius in libro numeratur Persius uno,
quam levis in tota Marsus Amazonide.

IOANNES LYDUS DE MAG. I, 41 Πέρσιος δὲ
25 τὸν ποιητὴν Σώφρονα μιμήσασθαι θέλων τὸ Λυκόφρονος
παρῆλθεν ἀμαυρόν.

# NOTES.

# NOTES.

## PROLOGUE.

ARGUMENT.—I never drank of Hippocrene, never dreamed on Parnassus. The maids of Helicon and the waters of Pirene are meat and drink for my masters—the acknowledged classics—not for me, a poor lay-brother, with my humble, homely song (1-7). Others succeed: the parrot with his Greek, the pie with her Latin. They have not dreamed on Parnassus either; but they have a teacher—the great master Belly—and Sixpence is their Phoebus Apollo. Hark how they troll forth their notes! (8-14).

Alas for me! no golden Muse, no silver sixpence inspires me. *Quis leget haec?*

---

This prologue is a survival of the dramatic element of the satire, as Casaubon has remarked. Peculiarly personal, the prologue is found in the earlier and in the later stages of art, in ballad literature and in reflective poetry. The spurious verses which precede the Aeneid—*Ille ego*—were intended to serve as a prologue, and prologues in prose and poetry are familiar to the readers of MARTIAL, STATIUS, AUSONIUS, and CLAUDIAN.

There is no good reason to doubt the genuineness of the prologue, or to attribute the authorship to CAESIUS BASSUS, the editor of PERSIUS, as Heinrich has done. Nor is there any sufficient ground for supposing that the prologue is fragmentary. The two parts—of seven verses each—do not hang well together, but the connection of the thought is not so remote after all. 'In the former part, PERSIUS ridicules the pretended source of the poetical inspiration of his time, in the latter he exposes its real origin' (Teuffel).

More open to debate is the relation of the prologue to the satires. Is it an introduction to all, or only to the first? It is true that the prologue seems to belong especially to the first. Both furnish us with a programme of the poet's views, with a confession of faith which consisted in a want of faith in the age; but as the First Satire itself contains a vindication of the poet's work, and forms an introduction to the other five satires, it is safer not to restrict the prologue to the narrower office.

D

It is needless to say that these verses have not lacked admirers and imitators. The latter half is parodied by Milton (*In Salmasii Hundredam*), and the line *magister artis ingenique largitor* is expanded by Rabelais (4, 59).

———

The metre is the *scazon* or *choliambus* (G., 755; A., 82, 2, *a*, R), and as the combination of different rhythms is one of the peculiarities of the earlier *satura*, it is not unlikely that PERSIUS followed an older pattern. In PETRONIUS, cap. 5, the choliambus is in like manner followed by the hexameter, but the analogy is not close. The choliambus, the invention of the great lampoonist HIPPONAX, is admirably adapted by its structure for the expression of disappointment, vexation, discontent. The march of the iambus is suddenly checked in the fifth foot, and the rapid measure violently tripped up. It is a mischievous metre, and betrays in its malice the Thersitic character of its inventor.

———

**1.** The allusion is to ENNIUS, the *alter Homerus*, who drank of Hippocrene (PROP., 3, 2 [4], 6), and dreamed that he had seen his great original on Parnassus (CIC., Ac. Pr., 2, 16, 51).—**fonte:** '*in* the spring.' The Latin Abl. often has a locative translation, when the conception is not necessarily or not distinctly locative. (G.,* 387.)—**prolui:** 'drenched' is designedly misused. The figure is *Litotes*. (G., 448, R. 2.) The greater the depression, the greater the rebound. *Non prolui labra* = *ne primoribus quidem labris attigi.*—**caballino:** *Fons caballinus*, 'hack's spring,' is a mock translation of *Hippocrene* = ἵππου κρήνη : the fountain opened by Pegasus with his hoof. *Caballus* is a comic equivalent of *equus*. Comp. JUVENAL's *Gorgonei caballi* (3, 118).

**2. bicipiti:** 'two-peaked.' Parnassus is called *biceps*, either because it appears to have two peaks from such common points of view as the entrance to the Corinthian Gulf (δικόρυμβος ὁ Παρνασός, LUCIAN, Char., 5), or because of the two tall cliffs (Ov., Met., 1, 316; 2, 221)—the Φαιδριάδες of DIODORUS (16, 28), the δίλοφος πέτρα of SOPHOCLES (Ant., 1126)—between which the Castalian spring takes its rise.—**somniasse:** sc. *me somniasse* (G., 527, R. 2; M., 401). With *memini* the Pres. Inf. is more common of Personal Recollection (G., 277, R; A., 58, 11, *b*), but the Perfect is also found when the action is distinctly recognized as a by-gone.

———

* G. = Gildersleeve's L. Grammar; A. = Allen and Greenough's; M. = Madvig's.

Comp. *saepe velut gemmas eius signumque probarem | per causam memini me tetigisse manum*, TIB., 1, 6, 26. Also Ov., Am., 3, 7, 25–6; A. A., 2, 169. The Perfect is especially appropriate here, as the balance of the period would seem to require *nec prolui nec* (*quod meminerim*) *somniavi;* and so Conington with correct instinct translates, 'never that I can remember.'

**3. sic:** οὕτως, 'just so,' 'without any warning, any preparation.'—**prodirem:** 'make my appearance' (as it were on the stage).

**4. Heliconidas:** The Muses. Comp. HESIOD (Theog., 1). Hermann prefers the epic form, *Heliconiadas.*—**-que—-que:** G., 478; A., 43, 2, *a.*—**pallidamque Pirenen:** Pirene is the fountain of Acrocorinthus, where Pegasus was broken in by Bellerophon. The poetic virtue of its water was a late discovery. *Pallidam*, attribute for effect. Comp. *pallida mors*, χλωρὸν δέος, and the like. The pallor of students and poets needs no illustration.

**5. remitto:** ἀφίημι, for the more usual *relinquo*, which is a common v. l. Kisselius (*Specimen criticum*, p. 51) cites CIC., De Orat., 1, 58: *tibi remittunt istam voluptatem et ea se carere patiuntur;* and TAC., Hist., 4, 11: *vim principis complecti, nomen remittere.*—**imagines:** 'busts' (set up in libraries, public and private). Comp. *ut dignus venias hederis et imagine macra*, JUV., 7, 29.—**lambunt:** more frequently used of flames.

**6. hederae:** Notice the plural, 'ivy wreaths,' G., 195, R. 6. The ivy, being sacred to Bacchus, formed the wreath of victors in scenic contests; thence transferred to poets generally.—**sequaces:** 'lissom, pliant.' PERSIUS seldom, if ever, uses a merely descriptive epithet, and hence some commentators have detected a sneer in these words, 'lackeying ivy belicks.'—**semipaganus:** 'poor half-brother of the guild' (Conington). The *paganus* is admitted to all the *sacra pagi* (*paganalia*); the *semipaganus* is a lay-brother. PERSIUS is not a *vates*, but a *semivates*. He is not initiated into what ARISTOPHANES calls the γενναίων ὄργια Μουσῶν, Ran., 356. Those who believe that the Satires of PERSIUS were aimed at Nero, see in *semipaganus*, 'half-educated,' as well as in the last seven verses, a deliberate disguise of the poet's real condition, as a man of culture and of wealth. They overlook the sneer at the class which he is not worthy to join.

**7. vatum:** with the same tone of derision as in the English equivalent, 'bards.'—**nostrum:** perhaps not simply = *meum*, but 'native, home-made.'

**8. expedivit:** *Expedire* and *conari* both imply difficulty (Jahn), but the difficulty is completely conquered in *expedire;* not so in *conari.* The parrot, if not a Greek (ψιττακός), is a Hellenized Hindoo (*bitak*), and has learned to utter glibly his familiar *Bonjour.* The magpie is an Italian, and not so deft. Others regard this interpretation, which is essentially Jahn's, as too subtle, and make *verba nostra*, which many prefer to *nostra verba*, simply equivalent to 'human speech.'—**chaere** = χαῖρε. Greek was the language of small talk, love talk, parrot-talk.

**10. magister artis ingenique largitor:** *Magister*, of that which is taught; *largitor*, of that which comes from nature's bounty; *-que* combines the two into an exhaustive unit (G., 478; A., 43, 3, *a*). The thought recurs in numberless forms. Comp. ἀ πενία, Διόφαντε, μόνα τὰς τέχνας ἐγείρει, THEOCR., 21, 1; *Paupertas omnes artis perdocet*, PLAUT., Stich., 1, 3. 23 (Jahn). Add χρεία διδάσκει, κἂν βραδύς τις ᾖ, σοφόν, EUR., fr. 709 (Nauck), and ALEXIS, fr. 205 (3, 479 Mein.), where the γαστήρ is expressly mentioned. Birds, it seems, were trained to talk by hunger.

**11. negatas:** (*a natura*).—**artifex sequi:** poetic syntax for *a. sequendi.* G., 424, R. 4. (comp. 429, R. 4); A., 57, 8, *f*, 3. A so-called Greek construction. See 1, 59. 70. 118; 5, 15. 24; 6, 6. 24.— **sequi** = *sectari*.—**voces:** (articulate) 'speech.'

**12. quod si:** 'Nay, if but.' Commentators on HORACE still indulge in remarks on the unpoetical character of *quod si*, copying Orelli on Od., 1, 1, 35. If *quod si* is prosaic, PROPERTIUS is to be pitied; he uses it at every turn.—**dolosi:** 'seductive, alluring.' PERSIUS does not deal much in 'general epithets;' hence δόλιον κέρδος (PIND., Pyth., 4, 140) is not a sufficient parallel.—**refulse-rit:** better every way than *refulgeat*, which Jahn accepts in his ed. of 1868. The Perf. Subj. is more vivid and more correct than the Present. *Re-* must not be overlooked. Like the English 'again,' it denotes the reversal of a previous condition. *Refulgere*, 'to catch the eye by its glitter,' 'to flash on the sight'—whereas it lay unnoticed before.—**nummi:** better translated as a coin. Comp. 'The Splendid Shilling,' 'The Almighty Dollar;' perhaps 'The Magic Sixpence.' Comp. Juv., 7, 8: *nam si Pieria quadrans tibi nullus in umbra* | *ostendatur*, etc.

**13. corvos poetas et poetridas picas :** 'Raven poets and poetess pies,' the substantive standing for an epithet, like *popa venter*, 6, 74. Which of the substantives is adjective to the other does not appear. For the *corvus*, Poe and Dickens will answer as well as Macrob., Sat. 2, 4. The male poet has a female counterpart in the magpie (*pica*). According to Ov. (Met., 5, 294, foll.), the daughters of Pierus, the Macedonian, were changed into magpies because they had challenged the Muses to a contest, and reviled the victorious goddesses. There seems to be an allusion to the literary ladies of the day, the blue-stockings of Juvenal's Satire (6, 434 foll.). See Friedländer, *Sittengeschichte*, 1, 481. *Poetridas* after Gr. analogy.

**14. cantare nectar :** a poetic extension of the cognate accusative = *nectareum carmen cantare* (G., 331 ; A., 52, 1, *b*). *Nectar* is copied from Pind., Ol., 7, 7 (νέκταρ χυτόν, Μοισᾶν δόσιν), and when combined with *Pegaseium* is sufficiently grandiloquent to be as absurd as it is intended to be. The old reading, *melos* (μέλος), with its faulty quantity, rarely finds a champion against *nectar*.

---

## FIRST SATIRE.

This Satire is an attack on the literature of the day as the efflorescence of the corruption of the times. The age is personified by a critical friend, but it is not always easy to determine when the poet is speaking and when the friend, or when the satirist is meeting an imaginary objection from some other imaginary quarter. The unreality of the whole dialogue is confessed with more candor than art in v. 44. Instead of a firm outline, we have a floating *quisquis es*.

Argument.—The poem opens with a line, which Persius recites to his man of straw, who forthwith urges him to abandon authorship (1–3). The poet acknowledges that he is at odds with his generation and expects no applause at their hands. But little does he care for their praise; let them prefer a Labeo to him. Their standard is not his standard. He is his own canon. He will not, can not follow the advice of his friend. He must obey the impulse of his temper and speak out (4–12).

Whether we write laborious verse or laborious prose—so the attack begins—it is all one; display and applause are the aim and object of both. The style is fustian; the delivery wanton; the theme prurient. The bard is little better than a bawd (13–23). And yet so deeply rooted is this love of praise that learning is loss, unless it be minted into golden opinions, and knowledge is naught until it be known of men. To be pointed out as a lion, to be used as a school classic—what glory! (24–30). Oh, yes! A glory shared by the dainty ditties, the mewling elegies of lisping, snuffling dandies, for this is what calls forth the approval of the after-dinner circle. Such is the praise that is to bless the poet even after death! (30–40). It is true that fame is not to be despised. No poet but feels his heart vibrate to praise. But the popular acclaim is not the ultimate standard. Mad epics, elegies thrown off in a surfeit, effusions of aristocratic easy-chairs are alike lauded. A man feeds the hungry and clothes the naked, and then asks for a candid opinion. Mockery of criticism! (40–62). The taste of the people relishes nothing but smooth verses—verses without flaw or break, faultless machine-verses—which answer any turn, and serve alike for satire, for eclogues, for heroic strains (63–75). Others, again, call themselves passionate pilgrims to the well of Latin undefiled, and linger over the obsolete magniloquence of PACUVIUS and ACCIUS. A fine *olla podrida*—this jumble of modern affectation and ancient trumpery (76–82). Bad as this is in literature, how much worse it is to find that the jargon of the *salon* has become the language of the courts, and that the manly Roman speech is dead. Even in a matter of life and death, the accused thinks more of his rhetorical than of his judicial sentence, and listens for a 'Pretty good,' as if that were the verdict (83–91). It will not do to say that great improvements have been made in the art of verse. Smooth are the verses and resonant, but at the cost of sense, of manly vigor. Once catch the trick, and any body can reel off such lines (92–106). Ears are ticklish, our satirist admits. Truth is an unwelcome rasp, and the cold shoulder of great men no toothsome meal. Police regulations are stringent. 'Commit no nuisance' is posted every where. Ah, well! It was otherwise in the time of Lucilius. That was a free world in which he craunched Lupus and Mucius. It was otherwise in the time of Horace. That was a gay world, in which he tickled while he taught. And is the poet not to mutter even? King Midas's barber told his master's secret to a ditch. Where can a ditch be found? Here in this book (107–121). Few readers can our author hope or desire—only such as have studied closely the great masters of the Attic sock, not such as ignorantly make a mock of Greek attire and Greek science, pride themselves on petty local honors, and rise to no higher conception of wit or fun than a dog-fight or a jibe at personal infirmity (122–134).

It has been well observed that this is the only Satire of PERSIUS in the strict sense of the term; the other five have rather the character of essays on moral themes.

One of the best commentaries on this poem is the famous 114th Epistle of SENECA.

The student of English literature will remember that Gifford's Baviad is an imitation of this piece.

———

**1-7.** At the very outset we encounter a difficulty in the distribution of the first lines between P. (Persius) and M. (Monitor, as the second interlocutor is usually called). The arrangement followed in the text may be explained thus:

P. (*is discovered absorbed in contemplation. He recites a line from his projected poem*).—'Vanity of vanities!'

M.—Who will read this stuff of yours?

P. (*wakes up*).—Do you mean that for me? Why, no one, of course.

M.—No one?

P.—Next to no one.

M.—A lame and impotent conclusion!

P.—Why so? Am I to fear that Polydamas and the Trojan dames shall make up their minds to give Labeo the preference over me? Stuff! Don't assent, when muddled Rome rejects a thing as light weight, and do not trouble yourself to get the faulty tongue of that pair of scales to work right, and look not outside of yourself for what you can find only within yourself.

**1. O curas hominum! O quantum est in rebus inane!** *Homines* and *res* are both used for 'the world,' sometimes singly, sometimes together. *Res* is often to be omitted in translation, or another turn given. *O quantum est in rebus inane*, 'Vanity of vanities'—a suitable Stoic text. There seems to be no allusion to LUCRETIUS's common phrase, *in rebus inane*.

**2. Quis leget haec?** a quotation from LUCILIUS, according to the scholiast. Jahn follows Pinzger in supposing that the quotation begins with *O curas hominum!* See, however, L. Müller, *Lucilius*, p. 194.

**3. vel duo vel nemo:** is more guarded, and hence (by Litotes) stronger than *nemo*. Comp. Gr. ἤ τις ἢ οὐδείς.

**4. ne mihi praetulerint:** an elliptical sentence, such as we

often find in final relations (A., 70, 3, *f*), in English as well as in
Latin (G., 688, R.). The sequence is not common in the classic
period, but see G., 512, R. Comp. PLAUT., Aul., 2, 3, 11; LIV.,
44, 22, and Weissenborn in loc. The Greek would be: μὴ προτι-
μήσωσι. — **Polydamas:** Some write *Pulydamas*, corresponding
with the Homeric form, Πουλυδάμας; but *Pŏlydamas* (Πωλυδάμας)
is the Sicilian Doric, like *pŏlypus* (πωλύπος). The allusion is to
a familiar passage in HOM., Il., 22, 100. 104. 5: Πουλυδάμας μοι
πρῶτος ἐλεγχείην ἀναθήσει— νῦν δ᾽ ἐπεὶ ὤλεσα λαὸν ἀτασθαλίῃσιν ἐμῇ-
σιν | αἰδέομαι Τρῶας καὶ Τρῳάδας ἑλκεσιπέπλους. These are the
words of Hector, as he steels his great heart to meet Achilles.
Polydamas is the counsellor who had urged him (18, 254) to
withdraw the Trojans into Troy, and Hector is ashamed to turn
back and encounter the rebuke of Polydamas and the reproaches
of his people. PERSIUS uses Polydamas as the type of the Roman critic, and by a familiar satiric stroke leaves out the Trojan
men, as if they were no men in Rome. Others understand
'Nero and his effeminate court.' The Homeric passage had been
well worn by ARISTOTLE and CICERO (Att., 2, 5, 1; 7, 1, 4; 8, 16,
2) before it came to PERSIUS. There is perhaps a side-thrust at
the pride of the old Roman families in their Trojan descent.
Comp. JUV., 1, 100: *iubet a praecone vocari | ipsos Troiugenas;* also
8, 181. See Friedländer, *Sittengesch.*, 1, 230.—**Labeonem:** the
ATTIUS (LABEO) of v. 50, an unfortunate translator of Homer, who
stuck close to the letter. The scholiast has preserved a line.
Ὠμὸν βεβρώθοις Πρίαμον Πριάμοιό τε παῖδας (Il., 4, 35) is rendered
thus: *crudum manduces Priamum Priamique pisinnos.* 'Raw
you'd munch both Priam himself and Priam's papooses.'

   **5. nugae:** The accusative is more common. Comp. G., 340,
R. 1.—**non accedas—nec quaesiveris:** *Non* and *nec,* where QUIN-
TILIAN's rigid rule (1, 5, 50) requires *ne* and *neve.* G., 266, R. 1;
A., 41, 2, *e.* Comp. 3, 73 and 5, 45.—**turbida:** 'muddle-headed'
(Conington). But comp. *Alexandrea turbida,* AUSON., Clar. Urb.,
3, 4.

   **6, 7. elevet:** 'reject as light.' The figure is taken from weigh-
ing, doubtless a common trope in the schools.—**examen:** (*filum,
ligula*) is the 'index, tongue, or needle' which is said to be *inprobum,* 'faulty,' 'wilful,' 'untoward,' because it does not move

freely or accurately on its pivot.—**trutina:** (Gr. τρυτάνη), a word
of doubtful etymology and loose application, means here ' a balance,' ' a pair of scales,' not, as the scholiast says, the *foramen*,
' fork' or ' cheeks,' in which the *examen* plays.—**castiges** = *percu-
tias* (Schol.) of the tap given to a hitching balance. Gesner, s. v.,
regards *castigare* here as equivalent to *conpescere* (5, 100), a view
which has a good deal in its favor. The notion is not ' do not
correct the popular standard,' but ' do not try to get an exact result by the popular standard (for your guidance).' Hermann
(*Lect. Pers.*, II., 9) follows those who understand the *examen* and
*trutina* of different instruments: *Noli examen tuum in populi trutina castigare.*\* So Pretor, who translates: ' Do not try to correct the erring tongue of your delicate balance by applying to
it a pair of ordinary scales.'—**nec te quaesiveris extra:** (*te*) ' Nor
look for yourself (what you can find only in yourself) outside
of yourself.' ' Be your own norm.' Others arrange: *nec quaesiveris extra te*, ' Nor ask any opinion but your own.'

**8-12.** The distribution followed is that of Jahn (1843), which
gives *nolo* (v. 11) to the interlocutor. The jerky, self-interrupting
discourse is supposed to be characteristic of the *petulante splene
cachinno.* ' What is the use of consulting Rome? Every body
there is an— If I might say what! If I might? Surely I may,
when I consider how old we are become, how grum we are, and
all the step-fatherly manner of our lives, since the days of " com-
moneys " and " alley tors." Indulge me. *It can not be.* What
am I to do? Nothing? But I am a man of laughter with a
saucy spleen.'

**8. nam Romae quis non?** The suppressed predicate is to be
supplied from the general scope of the passage. The sentence
is not completed in v. 121 (*auriculas asini habet*), for the simple
reason that PERSIUS did not write *quis non* in that passage,
but *Mida rex.*

---

\* No satisfactory treatment of this subject is accessible to me. The Greek
and Latin dictionaries are wildly at variance with one another and with the authorities. *Examen* seems to have been originally the strap by which the beam
was suspended—not from ΛΓ, but from ΛΡ. See ISIDOR., Orig., 16, 23, and comp.
*amentum (ammentum)*. Add LUCIL., 16, 14 (L. Müller). EUSTATHIUS's τρυτάνη
ἐπὶ ζυγοῦ ἡ τειρομένη τῷ βάρει τῶν ὄγκων points to the pivot (knife-edge) as the
first meaning of *trutina*.

D 2

**9. cum—aspexi:** *Cum* is equivalent to *postquam* here. G.,
567; A., 62, 3, *e.*—**canitiem:** 'premature old age,' 'loss of youthful freshness.' All through this satire the poet lashes old age,
as commentators have observed. So here, and 22. 26. 56. 79.
The 'hoary head' is not a 'crown of glory,' but a sign of de-
bauchery; the 'fair, round belly,' which is not uncomely in the
elderly justice, is nothing but a swagging paunch; the bald pate
is not a mirror of honor, but a mirror of dishonor; in short, 'no
fool like an old fool.' Especially severe is PERSIUS on the 'used-
up' man; and the affected moralizing of young men, who had
outlived their youth before they had had time to forget the
games of boyhood, drove him to satire. On the Neronian hypothesis, PERSIUS is endeavoring to masquerade as an old man.
—**nostrum istud vivere triste:** 'sour way of life.' This is a so-
called *figura Graeca*, which out-Greeks the Greeks. Good authors are very cautious in adding an attribute to the infinitive,
and do not go beyond *ipsum, hoc ipsum. Scire tuum*, v. 27; *ridere
meum*, v. 122; *velle suum*, 5, 53; *sapere nostrum*, 6, 38, can not be
rendered literally into the language from which they are supposed to be imitated. Nursery infinitives (3, 17) belong to a
different category.

**10. nucibus:** The modern equivalent is 'marbles.' The very
games survive. (See 3, 50.) It is hardly necessary to prove that
putting away such childish things means becoming a man. *Da
nuces pueris, iners | concubine: satis diu | lusisti nucibus*, CA-
TULL., 61, 127–9.

**11. patruos:** On the accusative, see G., 329, R. 1; A., 52, 1, *c.*
The *patruorum rigor* was proverbial. Owing to the legal position of the paternal uncle, who was often the guardian, it is the
*patruus*, not the *avunculus*, who is the type of severity. So the
cruel uncle of the ballad of the 'children in the wood' is the father's brother.

**12. quid faciam?** G., 258; A., 57, 6.—**sed:** (I know you want
me to do nothing), 'but' (I can't keep quiet) 'I am a laugher
born.'—**petulante:** literally, 'given to butting,' hence 'saucy'
—**splene:** The seat of laughter.—**cachinno:** a substantive, perhaps built by PERSIUS on the analogy of *bibo, epulo, erro*, etc.
Comp. *glutto*, 5, 112; *palpo*, 5, 176. Hermann, following Hein-

dorf, makes *cachinno* a verb, and reads : *tunc, tunc—ignoscite, nolo;
quid faciam sed sum petulante splene—cachinno,* ' Then—then—excuse me—I would rather not—what am I to do ?—I can't help
it—my spleen is too much for me—I must have my laugh.'
Jahn (1868) accepts *tunc, tunc—ignoscite, nolo,* but goes no further.

**13-23.** The battery opens.   Verse-wright and writer of prose
alike care for nothing except applause.   Follows a vivid picture
of a popular recitation.

**13. Scribimus inclusi :** Comp. *scribimus indocti,* etc.   Hor.,
Ep., 2, 1, 117.—**inclusi :** 'in closet pent ' (Gifford's Baviad), to
show the artificial and labored character of the composition in
contrast with the beggarly result.   Markland's ingenious conjecture, *inclusus numeris,* is not necessary.   Heinr. admires Markl.,
but retains *numeros* as a Greek accusative !—**numeros :** ' poetry ;'
**pede liber** = *pede libero,* ' foot-loose,' ' prose,' *soluta oratio.*

**14. grande :** ' vast,' ' grandiose.'   *Grandis* is always used with
intention, which our word ' grand ' sometimes fails to give.   See
1, 68 ; 2, 42 ; 3, 45. 55 ; 5, 7. 186 ; 6, 22.—**quod pulmo :** ' something vast enough to make a lung generous of breath pant in the
utterance of it.'   Jahn (1868) reads *quo* for *quod; quo* is not so
vigorous.—**animae praelargus :** a stretch of the adjectives of
fulness (G., 373, R. 6 ; A., 50, 3, *b*) ; *praelargus* = *capacissimus.*

**15. scilicet :** Ironical sympathy, ' O yes !'—**haec :** The position
is emphatic.—**populo :** ' to the public,' ' in public.'   The political force of *populus* has ceased.—**pexus :** ' with hair and beard
well dress'd.'   ' Combed ' hardly conveys the notion : say ' sham-
pooed.'—**togaque recenti :** ' fresh ' (from the fuller).

**16. natalicia sardonyche :** Jewelry reserved for great occasions.   The brilliancy of the sardonyx is a common theme.
*Rufe vides illum subsellia prima tenentem | cuius et hinc lucet sar-
donychata manus,* Mart., 2, 29, 1-2   **tandem :** shows impatience.—**albus** = *albatus* (comp. 2, 40 ; Hor., Sat., 2, 2, 61) on account of the *toga recens.*   So *niveos ad frena Quirites,* Juv., 10,
45.   Heinr. argues at length in favor of ' pale.'

**17. sede celsa** = *ex cathedra.*—**leges :** So Jahn (1868), despite
the MSS.   *Legens* may be explained at a pinch as *lecturus,* a com-
ma being put after *ocello;* Hermann combines with *pulmo,* and

comp. Juv., 10, 238 sq., where *os* stands for the owner of the same. Add *cana gula*, Juv., 14, 10. But *pexus* and *albus* make such a synecdoche incredible.—**liquido:** *quia liquidam vocem effi-cit.* Comp. Hor., Od., 1, 24, 3: *cui liquidam pater | vocem cum cithara dedit.* The attribute is put for the effect, as in *pallidam Pirenen*, Prol., 4. — **plasmate:** according to Quint., 1, 8, 2, a technical name for the professional training of the voice, a kind of rhetorical *solfeggio.* Others understand the *plasma* of a gargle to clear the throat.

**18. mobile collueris:** *Mobile* is predicative. Translate: 'after gargling your throat to suppleness by filtering modulation.'— **patranti ocello:** 'an eye that would be doing,' 'a leering, lustful eye.' Quint. (8, 3, 44) says of *patrare: mala consuetudine in obsce-num intellectum sermo detortus.* Comp. 'do' in Shaksp., Troil. and Cressida, 4, 2: Go hang yourself, you naughty, mocking uncle! You bring me to *do*, and then you flout me too. — **fractus =** *effeminatus*, 'debauched,' 'languishing,' κλαδαρός. Conington translates: 'with a languishing roll of your wanton eye.'

**19. neque more probo nec voce serena:** Litotes. See Prol., 1.

**20. ingentis Titos:** Comp. *celsi Rhamnes*, Hor., A. P., 342. Here, however, there is a reference to size of body (like *ingens Pulfennius*, 5, 190; *torosa iuventus*, 3, 86; *caloni alto*, 5, 95), for which Persius seems to have had a Stoic contempt. *Titi*, per-haps another form of *Tities*, the old Sabine nobility (Mommsen, *Röm. Gesch.*, B. 1, K. 4), of whom much aristocratic virtue might have been expected (*sanctos licet horrida mores | tradiderit domus ac veteres imitata Sabinos*, Juv., 10, 298-9). Instead of that we have great, hulking debauchees.—**trepidare:** 'quiver.' The word is used indifferently of pleasant and unpleasant agitation. The quavering measure thrills them so that they can not sit still. On the infinitive, see 3, 64.

**21. scalpuntur intima:** 'their marrow is tickled.' *Scalpere* is opposed to *radere*, 1, 107. Comp. 3, 114; 5, 15.

**22. tun:** *-ne* is often found in rhetorical questions.—**vetule:** 'you old reprobate,' 'you old sinner.'—**escas:** 'tidbits;' *escas col-ligere*,' 'cater.'

**23. quibus et dicas:** *Et* belongs to *cute perditus*, which is va-riously explained 'dropsical,' 'unblushing,' 'thoroughly diseased.' The context requires a tough subject, and 'hide-bound' or 'case-hardened' might answer as a rendering.—**ohe:** a reminiscence of Hor., Sat. 2, 5, 96 : *importunus amat laudari ; donec 'Ohe iam'* | *ad caelum manibus sublatis dixerit, urge,* | *crescentem tumidis infla sermonibus utrem,* which last line helps us to understand *cute perditus.* Persius, as is his wont, tries to improve on Horace, and makes his man inelastic.

**24-43.** M. Study is useless except to show what a man has in him.—P. A low ideal for a student.—M. Fame is a fine thing.—P. It would be a fine thing if it were not shared by every dinner-table poet.—M. You are too captious. It is a great thing to have written poems that are proof against trunk-maker and pastry-cook.

**24. Quo didicisse?** The exclamatory infinitive with involved subject. G., 534 (340) ; A., 57, 8, *g.*

**25. iecore:** the seat of the passions. Here 'heart' or 'breast' would seem to be more appropriate.—**caprificus:** the wild fig-tree sprouts in the clefts of rocks and cracks of buildings, which it rends in its growth. *Ad quae* | *discutienda valent mala robora fici,* Juv., 10, 145.

**26. En pallor seniumque:** 'So that's the meaning of your studious pallor (v. 124 ; 3, 85 ; 5, 62) and your (early) old age.' With *senium* comp. Hor., Ep., 1, 18, 47 : *inhumanae senium depone Camenae.* Persius mocks at the weariness to the flesh which the student has undergone for so paltry a result. This is the arrangement of Jahn (1843) and Hermann. Jahn (1868) follows Heinr. in giving the line to the remonstrant. *En,* originally an interrogative, is, after the time of Sallust, confounded with *em,* and combined with the nom. in the sense of *em,* which properly takes the accus. alone. So Ribbeck, *Beiträge zur Lehre von den latein. Partikeln,* S. 35.—**o mores:** Cicero's famous ejaculation. —**usque adeone:** *Usque adeone mori miserum est,* Verg., Aen., 12, 646 ; *usque adeo nihil est,* Juv., 3, 84.

**27. scire tuum nihil est,** etc. : 'And is thy knowledge nothing if not known' (Gifford). These jingles were much admired in antiquity. The passage from Lucilius, which Persius is said to have imitated, reads, according to L. Müller (fr. inc., 40, 73) : *ne dampnum faciam, scire hoc sibi nesciat is me.* A better example in Lucr., 4, 470.

**28. At:** objects. See G., 490; A., 43, 3, *b.*—**digito monstrari:** δακτύλῳ δείκνυσθαι (δακτυλοδεικτεῖσθαι). *Quod monstror digito praetereuntium,* HOR., Od., 4, 3, 22; *saepe aliquis digito vatem designat euntem,* Ov., Am., 3, 1. 19.—**hic est:** οὗτος ἐκεῖνος, in the well-known story of Demosthenes. CIC., Tusc. Dis., 5, 36.—**dicier:** On the form, see G., 191, 2; A., 30, 6, *e*, 4. So *fallier,* 3, 50.

**29. cirratorum:** 'curl-pates.' Jahn cites MART., 9, 29, 7: *Matutini cirrata caterva magistri.* School-boys wore their hair long, but PERSIUS does not waste his epithets, and 'youths of quality' are doubtless meant. Comp. the *lautorum pueros* of JUV., 7, 177.—**dictata:** 'Persius takes not only higher schools, but higher lessons, *dictata* being passages from the poets read out by the master (for want of books) and repeated by the boys' (Conington). Translate 'a lesson-book,' a 'school classic.'

**30. Ecce:** introduces a satiric sketch of 'classic poets at work.'—**inter pocula:** 'over their cups.' Poems were read at table by an ἀναγνώστης, as lives of the saints are still read in religious houses.

**31. Romulidae:** Comp. *Titos,* v. 20; *trossulus,* v. 82; *Romule,* v. 87.—**dia:** θεῖα, an affected word. 'Let us hear,' say the company, 'what his charming verses are about' (Pretor). Conington renders: 'What news from the divine world of poesy?'

**32. hyacinthia laena:** The dandies of the day wore upper garments of military cut and gay colors. A similar military dandyism on the part of non-military men is observable in the Macedonian period. Comp. χλαμυδηφόροι ἄνδρες, THEOCR., 15, 6, with the commentators.

**33. rancidulum quiddam:** 'affected stuff,' 'namby-pamby trash.'—**balba de nare** = *de nare balbutiens,* 'with a nasal lisp,' 'with a snuffle and a lisp' (Conington). *Balbus* is especially used of the introduction of an aspirate, and 'lisp,' which involves a spirant, is only approximate. Comp. θαῦμα μέγα, *inquid balba,* LUCIL., 6, 20, with L. Müller's note.—**locutus:** Perf. Part. where we should expect a Present. G., 278, R.

**34. Phyllidas Hypsipylas:** Phyllis, fearing that she had been deserted by her lover, Demophon, hanged herself, and was changed into an almond-tree (Ov., Her., 2). Hypsipyle of Lem-

nos, after bearing two children to Jason, was forsaken by him
(Ov., Her., 6). These doleful themes (*plorabilia*) were popular in
PERSIUS's time. The plural is contemptuous in Latin as in En-
glish.

**35. eliquat:** 'filters.' Every rough particle is strained out so
as to make the voice 'liquid.' The passage from APUL., Flor., p.
351, Elm., cited by Jahn, *canticum videtur ore tereti semihianti-
bus in conatu labellis eliquare*, indicates a cooing position of the
lips, in which the mouth simulates a colander.—**supplantat:**
ὑποσκελίζει (LUCIL., 29, 50, L. M.), 'trips up.' To judge by HOR.,
Sat., 2, 3, 274, *balba feris annoso verba palato*, of which the language of PERSIUS seems to be an exaggeration, the sounds im-
pinge upon the roof of the mouth instead of coming out boldly—
a kind of lolling utterance.—**tenero :** adds another shade : the
tripping is light, for the roof is sensitive; 'minces his words
as though his mouth were sore' (Pretor).

**36. adsensere viri:** Observe the Epic vein. *Adsensere omnes*,
VERG., Aen., 2, 130; *adsensere dii*, Ov., Met., 9, 259 (Jahn). *Viri*,
'heroes.'—**non- ?—non- ?** On the form of the question, see G., 455 ;
A., 71, 1, R.

**37. levior cippus:** Sufficiently familiar is the old wish, SIT ·
TIBI · TERRA · LEVIS, which, like the modern R · I · P ·, was
promoted to the dignity of initials (S · T · T · L · ).—**ossa:** *Patrono
meo ossa bene quiescant,* PETRON., 39.

**38. manibus** = *cineribus,* 'remains' (Conington). On this 'ma-
terialism,' see Tylor, *Primitive Culture,* 2, 24 foll.

**40. nascentur violae :** 'Lay her i' the earth | and from her
fair and unpolluted flesh | may *violets spring.*' SHAKSP., Hamlet,
5, 1.—**'Rides' ait :** As in HOR., Ep., 1, 19, 43. *Ait* is used like
*inquit* (G., 199, R. 3), without any definite reference.—**nimis un-
cis | naribus indulges :** 'you are too much given to hooking,
curling your nose.' *Naribus uti,* HOR., Ep., 1, 19, 45; *naso
adunco,* HOR., Sat., 1, 6, 5.

**41. an :** when used alone is more or less rhetorical, and is intended to force a conclusion involved in the foregoing ; 'What ?'
'So then ?' G., 459 ; A., 71, 2, *b.* PERSIUS's use of it is instructive: v. 87 ; 2, 19. 26 ; 3, 19. 27. 61 ; 5, 83. 125. 163. 164 ; 6, 51. 63.
—**velle meruisse :** See G., 275, 2 ; A., 53, 11, *d,* for the tense of

*meruisse.* The Perf. after *velle* is legal rather than Greek. Comp.
v. 91, *qui me volet incurvasse querela.* So HOR. (Sat. 2, 3, 187),
mimicking the legal tone: *ne quis humasse velit Aiacem, Atri-
da, vetas? cur?* Other Perf. Infinitives with varying motives are
found: 1, 132; 2, 66; 4, 7. 17; 5, 24. 33; 6, 4. 6. 17. 77.

**42. os populi:** 'popular applause,' 'a place in the mouths of
men' (Conington). Comp. the phrase *in ore esse.*—**cedro digna:**
Cedar oil was used to preserve manuscripts. *Speramus carmina
fingi | posse linenda cedro,* HOR., A. P., 331–2.

**43. nec scombros nec tus:** The fear of the mackerel is a stroke
of CATULLUS, 95, 8, which Milton imitates, Ep., 10: *gaudete scom-
bri.* Comp. MART., 4, 86, 8. For *tus,* comp. HOR., Ep., 2, 1, 269:
*deferar in vicum vendentem tus et odores | et piper et quicquid char-
tis amicitur ineptis.* The modern equivalent is the grocer or the
pastry-cook.

**44-62.** The poet gives up his dramatizing and speaks in his
own person. 'I am not indifferent to fame, but I reject a standard which approves such stuff as Labeo's, such ditties as "persons of quality" dictate after dinner, a standard which makes a
hot dish the test of poetic fervor, and covers a multitude of poetic sins with a cast-off cloak. If you had eyes in the back of
your head, you would see that all this praise is for value received.'

**44. dicere feci:** G., 527, R. 1; A., 70, 2.

**45. non ego:** 'I do not decline your praise—no, not I.' G.,
447; A., 76, 3, *d.* Comp. 2, 3; 3, 78; and HOR., Ep., 1, 19, 37,
*non ego ventosae plebis suffragia venor.*—**si forte quid aptius exit:**
'if I chance to turn out (off) a rather neat piece of work.' *Exit*
may mean 'to leave the shop' (*ex officina exire,* CIC., Parad., pr.
5), or 'to leave the potter's wheel,' as *urceus exit,* HOR., A. P., 22
(Jahn). Conington translates 'hatch' on account of *rara avis.*
Κακὸν ᾠόν. The passage is imitated by QUINT., 12, 10, 26.

**46. quando:** gives the reason for his saying *si forte.* There is
no necessity of writing *quanquam,* but the translation 'although'
is not unnatural, as causative particles are often adversative.
Comp. *cum* and Gr. ἐπεί.—**rara avis:** proverbial as in the famous
line of JUV., 6, 165.

**47. laudari metuam:** So HOR., *metuens audiri,* Ep., 1, 16, 60;

*metuit tangi,* Od., 3, 11, 10. In prose the construction is less common with *metuo* than with *vereor.* G., 552, R. 1; M., 376, Obs. —**cornea:** 'of horn.' The metaphorical use seems to be novel. Comp. Hom., Od., 19, 211: ὀφθαλμοὶ δ' ὡς εἰ κέρα ἕστασαν ἠὲ σίδηρος.—**fibra:** 'heart.' See 5, 29.

**48. recti finemque extremumque:** 'the ultimate standard.' Conington renders ' be-all and end-all.'

**49. euge, belle:** like *decenter* (v. 84), are current expressions of approbation at public readings. *Euge,* 'bravo!' *belle,* 'well said!' *decenter,* 'pretty fair!' Martial gives us a list of popular comments (2, 27, 3–4): *Effecte! graviter! st! nequiter! euge! beate! | hoc volui!*—**excute:** a favorite word with Persius as with Seneca, Ep., 13, 8; 16, 7; 22, 10; 26, 3; De Ira, 3, 36 (Jahn). The metaphor is taken from shaking clothes in order to get out any thing that may be concealed in them—Gr., ἐκσείειν. We should say 'analyze.'

**50. quid non intus habet:** The figure is kept up. ' What is not covered up in that beggarly rag of a *belle?*'—**non** = *nonne.* G., 445 and R.; A., 71, 1.—**Atti:** See v. 4.—**Ilias ebria:** Comp. *ebrius sermo,* Sen., Ep., 19, 9.

**51. veratro:** white hellebore (*album multum terribilius nigro,* Plin., H. N., 25, 5, 21), a strong emetic, which students took 'to quicken their wits.' The modern *veratrum* is a different drug. —**elegidia:** contemptuous, ' bits of elegies' on such themes as Phyllis and Hypsipyle. *E.* a Greek word not in Greek lexicons, like *poetridas,* Prol., 13.—**crudi:** with their dinners undigested and their brains muddled.

**52. dictarunt:** ' extemporize.'—**lectis:** ' sofas.' The ancients wrote in a recumbent posture far more frequently than we do.

**53. citreis:** ' of citron wood,' 'wood of the thyia' (*Thyia articulata,* African Arbor Vitae, Plin., 15, 29). The fabulous cost of tables of this material is well known. Cic., Verr., 4, 17, 37.— **scis:** ' you know how.' *Scire* in this sense is related to *posse,* as Fr. *savoir* to *pouvoir,* a traditional distinction.—**calidum:** ' hot-and-hot' (Pretor).—**ponere:** 1. ' serve up;' 2. ' cause to serve up,' ' treat to.' *Heri non tam bonum posui et multo honestiores cenabant,* Petron., 34.—**sumen:** a dainty dish in the eyes of Greek and Roman. Comp. *vulva nil pulchrius ampla,* Hor., Ep., 1, 15,

41; Plut., Sanit. Praec., 124 F; Alciphr., Ep., 1, 20; and the joke in Alexis, fr. 188 (3, 473 Mein.).

**54. comitem horridulum trita donare lacerna :** This is the kind of patronage that galled Lucian (De Merced. Cond., 37), who mentions the paltry present of an ἐφεστρίδιον ἄθλιον ἢ χιτώνιον ὑπόσαθρον. On the word *comitem*, see 3, 7. *Horridulum comitem*, ' shivering beggar of a companion,' ' poor devil in your suite.' For the custom, comp. Hor., Ep., 1, 19, 37 : *Non ego ventosae plebis suffragia venor | impensis cenarum et tritae munere vestis.*

**56. qui pote ?** *Pote* is an archaism for *potis.* Both *potis* and *pote* are used as predicates without regard to number and gender.— **vis dicam :** G., 546, R. 3 ; A., 70, 3, *f*, R. *Vis* does not wait for an answer. See 6, 63.—**nugaris :** ' you are à twaddler ' (Conington).—**calve :** Persius calls up his *vetulus* (v. 22) again, and gives him a huge ' bombard ' of a belly. Nero had a *venter proiectus*, and some editors fancy that Nero's person is aimed at here, and Nero's poetry in the verses that follow. See Introd., xxxvi.

**57. aqualiculus :** (said properly to mean ' a pig's stomach ') ' paunch,' ' cloak-bag of guts,' Shaksp.—**protenso sesquipede :** Comp. the Greek proverb : παχεῖα γαστὴρ λεπτὸν οὐ τίκτει νόον. Even M. Martha is forced to say : *Le trait n'est ni spirituel ni poli* (*Moralistes Romains*, p. 147). For the justification, see v. 128. Jahn (1843) reads *propenso.*

**58. Iane :** Janus, who sees both ways, is secure from being laughed at behind his back.—**ciconia pinsit** *= pinsendo ludit.* The fingers of the mocker imitate the clapping of the stork's bill. *Pinsit*, ' pounds,' because the *ciconia levat ac deprimit rostrum dum clangit*, Isidor., Orig., 20, 15, 3. ' Pecks at ' is not correct ; ' claps ' is nearer. What seems to be meant is mock applause.

**59. auriculas :** The imitation of ass's ears by the hands belongs to universal culture.—**imitari mobilis** *= ad imitandum m.* G., 424, R. 4 ; A., 57, 8, *f*.—**albas :** on account of the white lining. Ov., Met., 11, 176 : *aures—villis albentibus implet.*

**60. linguae :** The thrusting out of the tongue in derision is as common now as it was then.—**canis Apula :** Apulia was the δίψιον Ἄργος of Italy. *Siticulosae Apuliae*, Hor., Epod., 3, 16.— **tantae :** So Jahn and Herm. ' Tongues big enough to represent the thirst of an Apulian hound' (Pretor). Jahn compares for the construction, Luc., 1, 259 : *quantum rura silent, tanta quies.* Conington considers *tantum* ' much neater,' and makes *quantum sitiat* =*quantum sitiens protendat,* ' a length of tongue protruded like an Apulian dog in the dog-days.'

**61. vos, o patricius sanguis :** Hor., A. P., 291 : *vos, o | Pompilius sanguis.* The Nom. for the Vocative in solemn address. G., 194, R. 3 ; A., 53, *a.*—**fas est** =*fatum est,* ' it is ordained.'

**62. occipiti :** Notice the exceptional Abl. in *i.* Comp. Auson., Epigr., 12, 8 : *occipiti calvo es,* and *capiti,* v. 83.—**posticae :** chiefly of the back part of a building : ' back-stairs ' (Conington).— **occurrite :** ' turn round and face ' (Conington and Pretor).— **sannae :** ' flout,' ' gibe,' ' fleer,' μῶκος.

**63-82.** Persius takes up the thread which Janus had rudely snapt : ' We have heard the bounden praise of dependants. What does the town say ? Why, they admire the smooth flow of the verse, the grand style. If they find these requisites, little do they care about theme or order of development ; the 'prentice hand that bungles an eclogue, undertakes an epic—nay, jumbles eclogue and epic—Bravo, poet ! all the same. Another mania is the passion for the old poets, a Pacuvian revival. What is to be expected when all this bubble-and-squeak language is the daily food of our children and the dear delight of lecture-halls ?'

**63. Quis** =*qui.* G., 105 ; A., 21, 1, *a.*—**quis enim :** *Enim,* like γάρ ; ' why, what else ?' ' of course.' G., 500 ; A., 43, 3, *d.*

**64. nunc demum :** as if something marvellous had been accomplished.—**severos :** ' captious, critical.'

**65. effundat :** ' suffers to glide smoothly,' a harsh expression. —**iunctura :** The image is that of the joining of pieces of marble, as in an *opus tessellatum.* Comp. Lucil., fr. inc., 10, 23 (L. M.) : *quam lepide* λέξεις *conpostae, ut tesserulae, omnes | arte pavimenti atque emblemati' vermiculati.* The poet is compared with an artisan, not with an artist. He knows how to fit the pieces together so perfectly as to present a continuous smooth surface to the pressure of the most exacting nail. Comp. v. 92.—**tendere versum :** ' to lay off a verse,' as a carpenter lays off his work. The propriety of the word *tendere* is heightened, if we remember that the hexameter was called the *versus longus.*

**66.** Carpenter-like, the versewright stretches his ruddled line (*rubrica*), sights it (*oculo derigit uno*), and springs it. The modern carpenter uses chalk instead of ruddle, but the red pencil may be regarded as a survival of color. For references, see Rost's Passow, s. v. στάϑμη. For the spelling *derigat*, remember that *dirigere* is 'to point in different directions;' *derigere* 'in one.'—**ac si derigat:** On the sequence, see G., 604; A., 61, 1, R.

**67. sive:** seldom used alone; here for *vel si.*—**in mores, in luxum, in prandia regum:** a kind of anticlimax. *In* does not necessarily, though it does naturally, denote hostility. The *prandium* was originally a very simple meal. The Stoic model is set up in SENECA, Ep. 83, 6: *Panis deinde siccus et sine mensa prandium, post quod non sunt lavandae manus.* The *manger sur le pouce* became in time the *déjeuner à la fourchette* (*calidum prandium*, PLAUT., Poen., 3, 5, 14), and then the *déjeuner dinatoire* (*prandia cenis ingesta*, SEN., N. Q., 4, 13, 6). *Regum*, 'grandees,' 'nabobs,' belongs to *prandia* alone.

**68. res grandis:** 'sublimities.'

**69. heroas:** used as an adjective.—**sensus:** 'sentiments.'—**adferre:** 'parade,' 'bring on parade.' On the Inf., see 3, 64.

**70. nugari graece:** 'dabble in Greek verses,' a phase of fashionable education, no more peculiar to Nero than to HORACE (Sat. 1, 10, 31).—**ponere lucum:** 'put before our eyes,' 'paint,' 'describe.' *Lucus*, a favorite poetic theme. Jahn thinks of the grove in which Mars and Rhea Silvia met, JUV., 1, 7. Perhaps young poets tried their skill on groves, as young draughtsmen on trees.

**71. artifices:** With *artifices ponere* comp. *artifex sequi*, Prol., 11. —**rus saturum:** 'lush, teeming country.'—**corbes—focus—porci:** all 'properties' of country life.

**72. fumosa Palilia faeno:** The festival called *Palilia*, in honor of Pales (from the same radical as *pa-sco*), was celebrated on the anniversary of the founding of Rome, April 21st. It was a day reeking (*fumosa*) with bonfires of hay (*faenum*), over which the peasants leaped, doubtless 'to appease the evil spirit by a pretended sacrifice' (Pretor). The dictionaries will furnish the *loci classici*. The other form, *Parilia*, is due to 'dissimilation.' Comp. *meridies* for *medidies*.

**73. unde:** 'the source of;' loosely used to show connection.— **Remus:** not unfrequently takes the place of his longer brother, whose oblique cases do not fit well into dactylic verse. So *turba Remi*, Juv., 10, 73; *reddat signa Remi*, Prop., 4, 6, 80; and the other examples in Freund.—**sulco:** '*with*' and '*in* the furrow.' See Prol., v., 1.—**terens:** 'wearing bright' (Conington), 'furbishing.' König compares: *sulco attritus splendescere vomer*, Verg., Georg., 1, 46.—**dentalia:** 'share-beams,' Verg., Georg., 1, 171, with Conington's note.—**Quinti:** Cincinnatus, Liv., 3, 26.

**74. cum dictatorem induit:** So Jahn (1843). Decidedly the easiest reading, but the best in connection with *terens*. In his ed. of 1868, Jahn reads *quem dictatorem*. Hermann objects to the expression, and insists on *dictaturam*, appealing in his preface to Plin., H. N., 18, 3, 20, for *dictaturam* in the sense of *vestem dictatoriam*. Surely, to 'robe dictator' and to 'robe with the dictatorship' are not far apart, and the former is the more striking expression.—**trepida:** 'flurried.' See v. 20.—**ante boves:** is supposed to give local coloring, and to bring before us the 'slow, bovine gaze' of the astonished cattle.

**75. tua aratra:** Poetic plural.—**euge poeta:** Here the applause comes in. Mr. Pretor considers the words from *corbes* to *tulit* 'a quotation, perhaps from one of Nero's poems.'

**76. est nunc:** Persius attacks the *antiquarii* in imitation of Horace. The older Latin poets have long been restored to their rights. Accius and Pacuvius hardly need defenders. Hermann makes the sentence interrogative.—**Brisaei:** 'Bacchic.' *Brisaeus* was an epithet of Bacchus, transferred to the poet of Bacchus, who was perhaps too devoted a worshipper of the god. There was a famous saying of Cratinus, who was in like manner called ταυροφάγος, a surname of Bacchus: ὕδωρ δὲ πίνων οὐδὲν ἂν τέκοι σοφόν, fr. 186 (2, 119 Mein.). Comp. Hor., Ep., 1, 19, 1.—**venosus:** For the figure, comp. Tac., Dial. 21. The 'standing out of the veins' refers not so much to the 'shrinking of the flesh in old age' (Conington), as to the scrawniness of the person. So Tacit. uses *durus et siccus* of Asinius Pollio (l. c.), Gr. ἰσχνός. 'Angular,' 'hard-lined,' is about what is meant. Others prefer 'thick-veined,' 'turgid.'—**liber:** of a play, Quint., 1, 10, 18; Prop., 4 (3), 21, 28 (Jahn).—**Acci:** also written *Atti* (584–650? A. U. C.).

CICERO calls him *gravis et ingeniosus poeta, summus poeta* (pr. Planc., 24, 59; Sest., 56, 120); HOR., *altus* (Ep., 2, 1, 56); Ov., *animosi oris* (Am., 1, 15, 19). PACUVIUS said that the compositions of ACCIUS were *sonora quidem et grandia sed duriora paulum et acerbiora.*

**77. Pacuvius:** nephew of Ennius (534–622 A. U. C.). His great model was SOPHOCLES.—**verrucosa:** 'warty,' intended to be a climax of ugliness.—**moretur:** 'fascinates,' 'enthralls.' *Fabula—valdius oblectat populum meliusque moratur*, HOR., A. P., 321.

**78. Antiopa:** imitated from a lost play of EURIPIDES. The fragments have been collected by Ribbeck, *Tr. Lat. Reliq.*, p. 62; comp. p. 278. Antiope, as the mother of Amphion and Zethus, and the victim of Dirce, is famous in literature and in art (the *Toro Farnese*).—**aerumnis cor luctificabile fulta:** 'who props her dolorific heart on teen' (Gifford). Jahn defends the conception as truly poetical, apart from the obsolete language. 'The only stay of her sad heart is sorrow.' The words are doubtless taken from the play itself, of course in different order. *Aerumna* was out of date as early as the time of QUINTILIAN (8, 3, 26), who protests against the use of it. As to *luctificabile*, if we go by the fragments, it is ACCIUS, rather than PACUVIUS, that indulges in such formations as *horrificabilis, aspernabilis, tabificabilis, execrabilis, evocabilis.*

**79. lippos:** of the eyes of the mind. Comp. 2, 72.

**80. sartago:** literally 'a frying-pan,' 'hubble-bubble' (Conington), 'gallimaufry,' 'galimatias,' 'olio' (Gifford), 'olla podrida.'

**81. dedecus:** The language is disgraced and degraded by this mixture of old and new. PERSIUS would not have enjoyed Tennyson's resuscitations. See Introd., xxiv.—**in quo:** 'at which.'

**82. trossulus:** an old name of the Roman knights, of disputed origin. It was afterward used in derision. Jahn compares the German *Junker*.—**exsultat:** ἀναπηδᾷ, 'jumps up in delight.'—**per subsellia:** Jahn understands the 'benches' or 'forms' in court; others, perhaps more correctly, the seats in the lecture-hall. There is a climax. First, private teaching; next, public lectures; thirdly, practical life, to which we come in the following verse.—**levis:** the position is emphatic, 'the smug, woman-ish creature.' *Levis* is *levigatus.* Ancient literature is full of al-lusions to this effeminate παράτιλσις.

**83. nilne:** stronger than *nonne,* 'not a blush of shame.'—**ca-piti:** rarer Ablative in *i.* Neue gives examples (*Formenlehre,* 1, 242). The simple Abl. is found with *pellere,* even in prose, and the Dative, which some prefer, would be forced.—**cano:** See note on v. 9.

**84. quin optes:** G., 551; A., 65, 1, *b.*—**tepidum:** 'lukewarm,' *decenter* being faint praise. 'In good taste' (Conington). Gr. πρεπόντως.

**85. 'Fur es:'** The accuser puts his point plainly enough; in three letters, as the Romans would say.—**ait:** Comp. v. 40.—**Pe-dio:** Jahn thinks it likely that this Pedius is not HORACE's man (Sat., 1, 10, 28), but one Pedius Blaesus, condemned under Nero, TAC., Ann., 14, 18; Hist., 1, 77. PERSIUS knew more about HORACE than about the *causes célèbres* of his own day.—**rasis an-tithetis:** commonly rendered 'polished antitheses.' With *radere* comp. the Gr. διεσμιλευμέναι φρουντίδες, ALEXIS, fr. 215 (3, 483 Mein.). But the figure may possibly be taken from the careful removal of overweight in either scale of the balance. The an-titheses are scraped down to an exact equipoise.

**86. doctas figuras:** *Doctus,* Scaliger's correction, which re-quires, moreover, a period at *figuras,* is unnecessary. *Doctas figu-ras,* like *artes doctae, dicta docta, doli docti. Figurae,* σχήματα, em-braces 'tropes.'—**posuisse** = *quod posuerit* G., 533; A., 70, 5, *b.*

**87. an:** 'what?' 'can it be that?'—**Romule:** bitter, like *Titi, Romulidae, trossulus.* Comp. CATULL., 29, 5. 9.—**ceves:** 'Wag the tail' keeps within bounds of possible translation.

**88. men moveat?** So *men moveat cimex Pantilius,* HOR., Sat., 1, 10, 78. The sentiment is that of the well-worn *si vis me flere, dolendum est | primum ipsi tibi,* HOR., A. P., 102. *Moveat* sc. *Pe-dius.*—**quippe:** is often ironical, 'good sooth.'—**protulerim:** The Perf. Subj. in a sentence involving total negation.

**89. cantas?** 'you sing, do you?'—**fracta te in trabe pictum:** Shipwrecked men appealed to charity by carrying about pictures of the disaster which had overtaken them. Comp. 6, 32. *Si fractis enatat exspes | navibus, aere dato qui pingitur,* HOR., A. P.,

20, and Juv., 14, 302.  *Trabe* is the wreckéd vessel as it appears
in the picture, although it is possible that the painting may have
been put on a broken plank of the ship, in order to heighten the
pathos.  So Jahn.

**90. ex umero :** We say 'on the shoulder,' from a different
point of view.  G., 388, R. 2.—**nocte paratum :** 'got up over-
night.'

**91. plorabit :** an imperative future.—**volet:** Observe the greater exactness of the Latin expression.  G., 624; A., 27, 2.—**incurvasse :** See v. 42, and add Liv., 28, 41, 5; 30, 14, 6; 40, 10, 5,
and the *S. C. de Bacanalibus* (passim).

**92-106.** ' But,' rejoins the impersonal personage, whom Persius always has at hand, ' we have made great advances in art.
Contrast this verse and that verse with the roughness of the
Aeneid !'—' The Aeneid rough ?  Well, what is smooth ?  [*He
gives a specimen of fashionable poetry.*]  If we had an inch of our
sires' backbone, such drivel would be impossible.  And as for
art—it is as easy as spitting.'

I have followed the distribution as presented in Hermann.
Jahn gives vv. 96, 97 to Persius, 98–102 to the interlocutor, the
rest to Persius.  It is impossible to discuss all the arrangements
that have been suggested for this passage.

**92. decor :** Gr. χάρις.—**iunctura :** is used as in v. 64, of ' smooth-
ness,' ' harmonious sequence,' the even surface without a break.
See Quint., 9, 4, 33.  All the specimen verses that follow avoid
mechanically the offences against *iunctura* that Quintilian
enumerates, and do not avail themselves of the license which he
accords to a *grata neglegentia*.  There is no elision, no synaloepha,
in any of them.  As these fashionable verses have been held up
to derision by the satirist, commentators have been busy in hunt-
ing out defects, and translators have vied with each other in
absurd renderings.  But Jahn has wisely warned us against an
over-curious search into the supposed faults of these verses, which
Vossius pronounced superior to any thing in the compositions
of the critic himself.  It is enough for us to know that to the
ear of Persius the lines lacked masculine vigor.  The multipli-
cation of diaereses, the length of the words, the careful avoid-
ance of elision, the dainty half-rhyme of *bombis* and *corymbis*, the

jingle of *ablatura* and *flexura*, may be cited as confirmations of the view of PERSIUS, but, with the exception of the desperate verse 95, the diction is in keeping with the theme. If *adsonat Echo* is not ridiculous in OVID (Met., 3, 505), it is not ridiculous here; and one surely needs to be told that *reparabilis* is not a happy adjective for Echo, who is always 'paying back' and making good.

**93. cludere versum :** like *concludere versum* (HOR., Sat., 1, 4, 40), is ' round a verse ' (Conington), rather than ' close a line.'— **didicit:** What is the subject ? ' Our man,' ' our poet,' the lover of *decor et iunctura?* So most commentators. Heinr. makes *Attis* the subject. The personification of *iunctura* would not be too harsh for PERSIUS.—**Berecyntius Attis:** It suffices to refer to CATULL., 63. Berecyntus, a mountain in Phrygia.

**94. Nerea:** god of the sea, the water. In modern Gr. νερόν is ' water.' The use, which Conington calls ' grotesque,' is almost as ' grotesque ' as *Vulcanus* for ' fire.' The scholiast thinks of Arion's dolphin. Bacchus's dolphin is as likely.

**95. sic costam longo subduximus Appennino:** With the close of the verse, comp. Ov., 2, 226 : *Aeriaeque Alpes et nubifer Appenninus;* and Haupt's note. ' We filched a rib from the long Apennine.' The interpretations are all unsatisfactory. The scholiast sees in the removal of the rib from the mountain a metaphor for the removal of a syllable from the hexameter. The only point worthy of notice in this remark is the emphasis laid on the spondaic verse. The *Graii nugari soliti* doubtless used spondaic verses more freely than the model Latin poets (comp. CATULL., 64). Some understand the words to refer to a forced march (*putavi tam pauca milia subripi posse*, SEN., Ep., 53, 1) ; others to the device attributed to Hannibal in crossing the Alps (*montem rumpit aceto*, JUV., 10, 153). It is all idle guess-work, without a context; but, guess for guess, the expression would suit a ' Titanomachia,' and the rib might answer for a weapon, as once a jaw-bone did. The jingle of the verse is like VERG., Aen., 3, 549 : *cornua velatarum obvertimus antennarum*, quoted by the scholiast.

**96. Arma virum!** ' Compare with these elegant verses *Arma virum;* what a rough affair !' Not only were the opening words

E

of a poem used to indicate the poem itself—Μῆνιν ἄειδε the Iliad, Ἄνδρα μοι ἔννεπε the Odyssey, *Arma virum* the Aeneid—but the first verses were considered peculiarly significant. So the metrical structure of the first verse of the Iliad is very different from that of the first verse of the Odyssey. *Arma virum*, etc., with its short words and its frequent caesurae, was harsh to the ear of the interlocutor, and is compared with the rough, cracked bark of the cork-tree.—**spumosum et cortice pingui:** 'frothy and fluffy' (Conington). As usual, PERSIUS works out his comparison into minute details.

**97. vegrandi subere:** So Jahn, instead of *praegrandi subere.* Do not translate 'huge, overgrown bark' (Conington), but '. dwarfed, stunted cork-tree.' See Ribbeck (*Beiträge zur Lehre von den lateinischen Partikeln*, S. 9), who has discussed *ve* and this verse at some length. Both Conington and Pretor admire the metaphysics of Jahn, who has 'explained, after FESTUS and NONIUS, *vegrandis* as *male grandis*, so as to include the two senses attributed to it by GELL., 5, 12 ; 16, 5, of *too small* and *too large*.' But *ve-* means separation (Vaniček, *Etym.Wb.*, S. 166) ; *ve-cor-s*, 'out of one's mind ;' *ve-sanu-s*, 'out of one's sound senses ;' *vegrandi-s*, 'shrunken,' 'dwarfed,' 'undergrown' (if the word is admissible). For the growth of the cork-tree, R. refers to PLIN., N. H., 16, 8, 13 : *suberi minima arbor—cortex tantum in fructu, praecrassus ac renascens atque etiam in denos pedes undique explanatus.* Some of the best commentators give these two verses (96 and 97) to PERSIUS, and consider *Arma virum* as an invocation of the shades of VERGIL, 'as HORACE, A. P., 141, contrasts the opening of the Odyssey with *Fortunam Priami cantabo.*' *Hoc* is supposed to refer to the specimen verses. Ribbeck also (l. c.) regards the swollen, light bark of the low cork-tree as the image of the *genus tumidum et leve*, as opposed to the *grande et grave.* —**coctum :** 'thoroughly dried.'

**98. Quidnam igitur :** *Igitur* is not unfrequently used in questions, as our 'then.' So *quidnam igitur censes?* JUV., 4, 130. But, unless the question is a rejoinder, it is not very appropriate. 'If the Aeneid is rough, give us something really soft,' would be a fit reply to *Arma virum*, etc., in the mouth of the objector. Conington, who gives 96–98 to PERSIUS, connects thus : 'If these are your specimens of finished versification, give us something peculiarly languishing.'—**laxa cervice:** the attitude of the *mobile guttur*, v. 18.

**99. Torva mimalloneis:** PERSIUS can not wait for a specimen, and gives one himself. This is much more dramatic than the arrangement, which makes the respondent cite the verses. The verses are attributed to Nero by the scholiast, and in fact Nero is said to have composed a poem on the Bacchae, DIO., 61, 20. The theme is so common that no conclusion is to be drawn from that statement. Mr. Pretor, who understands by *iunctura* 'a resetting of old verses,' regards 99–102 as a weak *réchauffé* of CATULL., 64, 257 seqq., and compares TAC., Ann., 14, 16.—**Torva:** 'grim.' So *torvumque repente | clamat*, VERG., Aen., 7, 399 (of Bacchanalian madness).—**mimalloneis:** from Mimas, on the coast opposite Chios. With the whole verse comp. *multis raucisonos efflabant cornua bombos*, CATULL., 64, 264, and LUCR., 4, 544.

**100. vitulo superbo:** variously caricatured as 'the haughty, the scornful calf.' No such effect could have been produced by the original. Comp. ταῦροι ὑβρισταί, EUR., Bacch., 743 (Jahn); γαυροτέρα μόσχω, THEOCR., 11, 21 ; *equae superbiunt*, PLIN., 10, 63. The Bacchanal rending of animals is familiar.—**ablatura:** On this free use of the future participle, see G., 672 ; A., 72, 4.

**101. Bassaris:** a Bacchante. Jahn cites a Greek epigram (ANTH. PAL., 6, 74), which shows how close a resemblance may be due simply to community of theme.—**lyncem:** 'The lynx was sacred to Bacchus as the conqueror of India.'

**102. euhion:** Gr. εὑιον, Accus. of εὑιος (commonly but falsely spelled *Evius*), *Euhius*, Bacchus.—**reparabilis:** Actively, as HORACE's *dissociabilis*, Od., 1, 3, 22 ; 'renewing,' 'restoring,' 'reawakening.' So Ov., Met., 1, 11, of the moon: *reparat nova cornua.*—**adsonat:** 'chimes in.'

**103. testiculi vena ulla paterni:** '*Honestius expressit*, Ov., Her., 16, 291 : *si sint vires in semine avorum*.' 'If we had one spark of our fathers' manhood alive in us' (Conington).

**104. delumbe:** 'backboneless,' 'marrowless.' Comp. ἰσχιορρωγικός.—**saliva:** Spittle is 'foolish rheum' as well as tears.

**105. in udo est Maenas et Attis :** 'Your Maenas and your Attis —it drivels away.'

**106. nec pluteum caedit,** etc.: *Pluteus*, which is commonly rendered 'desk,' is, 'according to the scholiast, the back-board of the *lecticula lucubratoria*,' or studying-sofa, such as Augustus indulged in, SUET., Aug., 78; comp. v. 53. 'The man lies on his couch after his meal, listlessly drivelling out his verses, without any physical exertion or even motion of impatience' (Conington). PERSIUS underrates the artistic finish, as he has overdrawn the moral conclusion.—**demorsos:** 'bitten down to the quick.' *Et in versu faciendo | saepe caput scaberet vivos et roderet ungues*, HOR., Sat., 1, 10, 70.

**107-121.** M. But what is the use of offending people? We must not tell the truth at all times. You will have a cool reception at certain great houses. Nay, the dog will be set on you.—P. Well! I make no struggle. Every thing is lovely. No nuisance, you say. All right. Boys, let us go somewhere else. But there was LUCILIUS—he wielded the lash, he gnawed the bones of his victims. There was HORACE—he probed his friend's heart and punched him in the ribs, and had the town dangling from the gibbet of his tip-tilted nose. And I am not to say— Bo! Not all to myself? Not with a ditch for my confidant? Nowhere? Nowhere, you say? But I will. I have found a place—a ditch. It is my book. Here, book, is my great secret: 'All the world's an ass.' What a relief!

**107. quid:** What case?—**radere:** 'rasp.'—**mordaci vero:** *Verum* is so completely a substantive that there is no difficulty about *mordaci vero* (comp. G., 428, R. 2). Much bolder is *generoso honesto*, 2, 74; *opimum pingue*, 3, 32.

**108. vidĕ:** like *cavĕ*, and other iambic Imperatives. G., 704, 2; A., 78, 2, *d.*—**sis** = *si vis*, to soften the Imperative, 'pray do.' —**maiorum tibi forte:** HOR., Sat., 2, 1, 60: *O puer ut sis | vitalis metuo et maiorum ne quis amicus | frigore te feriat. Maiores =* 'grandees.'

**109. limina frigescant:** like the modern slang, 'leave one out in the cold.' *Limen* is used in many Latin turns where 'threshold' would be too stately in English. Mrs. Gamp would render: 'the great man's cold doorsteps will settle on your lungs.'—**canina littera:** 'R is for the dog,' SHAKSP., Romeo and Jul.; 'A dog snarling R,' BEN JONSON. See Dictionaries, s. v. *hirrire*. Gr.

ἀραρίζειν. An allusion to the familiar *cave canem.* 'The snarl is that of the great man' (Scholiast). Conington compares *ira cadat naso*, 5, 91. The obvious interpretation is the right one. 'There is a sound of snarling in the air,' refers simply to the great man's dog, which will be set on the unwelcome satirist.

**110. per me:** 'for all I care,' ἐμοῦ γ᾽ ἕνεκα, a familiar use of the preposition *per: per me habeat licet*, PLAUT., Mercat., 5, 4, 29. **—equidem:** Not for *ego quidem*, although this opinion affected the practice of CICERO, HORACE, VERGIL, QUINTILIAN, the younger PLINY. SALLUST, like VARRO, combines *equidem* with every person. So Ribbeck (l. c. S. 36), who derives *equidem* from *e* interj. and *quidem.* Conington tries to save the rule here by making the expression equivalent to *equidem concedo.* Another exception is found 5, 45, where C. goes through the same legerdemain: *non equidem dubites*, 'I would not have you doubt.'—**alba:** 'lovely,' 'whitewash them as much as you please.'

**111. nil moror,** etc.: The whole line, indeed the whole passage, is strongly conversational in its tone. *Nil moror*, 'I don't wish to be in your way, to spoil sport.' Comp. TER., Eun., 3, 2, 7, and Gesner, s. v. *moror.*—**bene:** Comp. CIC., Fam., 7, 22: *bene potus.* See also note on 4, 22.—**mirae res:** 'wonders of the world' (Conington), 'miracles of perfection.'

**112. hoc iuvat?** 'I hope that is satisfactory.'—**veto quisquam faxit oletum:** 'commit no nuisance.' Observe the legal tone. *Quisquam*, on account of the negative idea. The negative *ne* is omitted after *veto* as often after *caveo.* G., 548, R. 2; A., 57, 7, *a. Faxit*, a disputed form. G., 191, 5; A., 30, 6, *e.*

**113. pinge duos anguis:** 'a sign of dedication rather than of prohibition' (Pretor). The dedication involves the prohibition. This is one of the innumerable phases of serpent-worship. For the serpent, as the symbol of the *genius loci*, which is Greek as well as Latin, see VERG., Aen., 5, 95, and the commentators. The reading *pinguedo sanguis* of some of the best MSS. may be mentioned, *animi causa.*

**114. secuit:** 'cut to the bone.'—**Lucilius:** The *loci classici* are HOR., Sat., 1, 4, 6; 1, 10, 1; 2, 1, 62; JUV., 1, 19, 165. The *testimonia de Lucilio* have been collected and annotated by L. Müller, LUCIL., p. 170 seqq.; p. 288 seqq.

**115. Lupe, Muci:** L. Cornelius Lentulus Lupus Cons. A. U. C. 598, and P. Mucius Scaevola Cons. A. U. C. 621, Juv., 1, 154.— **genuinum:** 'Breaking the back-tooth' shows the eagerness with which the satirist gnawed the bones of his victims. Comp. Petron., 58 : *venies sub dentem,* 'you will be "chawed" up.'

**116.** A deservedly admired characteristic of Horace.—**vafer:** a hard word to catch. *Vafer* crowns the formidable list of synonyms in the well-known passage of Cic., Off., 3, 13, 57 : *versuti, obscuri, astuti, fallacis, malitiosi, callidi, veteratoris, vafri,* 'a shuffler, a hoodwinker, a trickster, a cheat, a designing rascal, a cunning fox, a blackleg, *a sly dog.*' The indirectness of *vafer* may sometimes be rendered by 'politic,' 'adroit.' 'Rogue' is a tolerable equivalent.—**amico:** is much happier than *amici* would be ; it makes the friend a party to the game. *Horatius qui ridendo verum dicit* (Sat., 1, 1, 24) *tam leniter vitia tangit, ut ipse, quem tangit, amicus rideat et poetam, qui dum ludere videtur intima aggreditur, lubens admittat et excipiat* (Jahn, after Teuffel).—**admissus:** 'gets himself let in,' 'gains his entrance' (Conington, after Gifford).

**117. praecordia:** 'heartstrings.'

**118. excusso:** Persius would not be Persius, if he did not give us a problem even in his best passages. *Excusso naso* stronger than *emunctae naris,* Hor., Sat., 1, 4, 8 (Jahn). According to Heinr., *excusso = sursum iactato,* like *excussa brachia,* Ov., Met., 5, 596, which seems to suit *suspendere.* Conington renders, 'with a sly talent for tossing up his nose and catching the public on it,' doubtless with reference to 'tossing in a blanket,' a pastime not unknown to the ancients : *Ibis ab excusso missus in astra sago,* Mart., 1, 3, 8. Comp. Suet., Otho, 2 ; Cervantes, Don Quijote, 1, 17; and on the *sagatio,* see Friedländer, *Sittengesch.,* 1, 25. As the blanket is drawn tight in order to effect the elevation of the person tossed, we may combine with this figure the old version of an 'unwrinkled nose,' a nose that is 'kept straight' (*exporrectus*) by the owner to disguise his merriment (*ac si nihil tale ageret*). But this is over-interpretation, the besetting sin of the editors of Persius.—**callidus suspendere:** On the construction, see Prol., 11.—**naso:** *Naso suspendis adunco,* Hor., Sat., 1, 6, 5. Comp. 2, 8, 64.

**119. men:** On *ne* in rhetorical questions, see v. 22.—**nec clam**

—nec cum scrobe: 'neither to myself nor with a hole in the ground for my listener.' The negative in *nefas* is subdivided by *nec—nec*, G., 444, R. Others supply *fas*, G., 446, R.—nusquam: The answer of the critic, Jahn (1843). In the ed. of 1868 he writes with Hermann, *nusquam?* as a part of PERSIUS'S question. The arrangement in the text seems to be more in accordance with PERSIUS'S fashion of anticipating an answer (ἀνϑυποφορά). 'Nowhere? you say.'—scrobe: Allusion to the story of Midas and his barber, for which no reader will need to be referred to Ov., Met., 11, 180 seqq.

**121. quis non habet?** According to the *Vita Persii*, the poet had written *Mida rex habet*, intended for King Populus. Cornutus, afraid that Nero would take the fling to himself, changed the words to *quis non habet?* The story is not very consistent with the theory that PERSIUS went so far as to ridicule Nero's poetry.

**122. ridere meum:** See v. 9.—nulla: G., 304, R. 2.—vendo: 'I am going to sell;' familiar present for future; hence = *vendito*.

**123. Iliade:** Probably the Iliad of Labeo. Homer's Iliad would be too extravagant.—audaci quicumque, etc.: The poet distinctly points to the mordant Old Attic Comedy as his model; yet there is little trace of direct imitation of the worthies whom he cites, and the interval of conception is abysmal.—adflate: PERSIUS, like some other Roman poets, goes beyond reasonable bounds in the use of the Vocative as a predicate. G., 324, R. 1; A., 35, *b*. The Greeks were cautious, and in VERGIL the Vocative can be detached and felt as such, but not here, nor in 3, 28. — Cratino: the oldest of the famous comic triumvirate: *Eupolis atque Cratinus Aristophanesque poetae*, HOR., Sat., 1, 4, 1. CRATINUS was the Archilochus of the Attic stage, hence *audax*. See the famous characteristic in ARISTOPHANES, Eq., 527.

**124. iratum Eupolidem:** The epithet is borne out by the fragments.—praegrandi cum sene: ARISTOPHANES. The adjective refers to his greatness: 'the old giant.' *Sene* is not to be pressed. Men who come before the public early are often called old before their time. Hannibal calls himself an old man when he was only in his forty-fourth year, LIV., 30, 30. Others understand *sene* as a compliment to an 'ancient' author. Instead of ARISTOPHANES, Heinrich and others suppose that LUCILIUS is

meant. Comp. Hor., Sat., 2, 1, 34 : *vita senis*, although Lucilius
was only about forty-five at the time of his death—but see L. Müller, *Lucilius*, p. 288.—**palles:** 'study yourself pale over.' The
combination with the Accusative is bold, but not bolder than
other cognate Accusatives. 'Gain a Eupolidean pallor' ='a pallor due to Eupolis.' For different phases of *pallere* with Accus.,
see 3, 43. 85 ; 5, 184.

**125. decoctius:** The figure is from wine that is 'boiled down,'
'well refined.' Not 'opposed to the *spumosus* of v. 96' (Conington), as is shown by *coctum*, v. 97.—**audis:** 'have an ear for'
(Conington).

**126. inde** =*ab iis*, 'by these' (G., 613, R. 1 ; A., 48, 5), 'by the
study of these,' dependent on *vaporata*.—**vaporata:** 'steamed,'
hence 'cleansed,' 'refined' (Jahn). Comp. *purgatas aures*, 5, 63 ;
*aurem mordaci lotus aceto*, 5, 86.—**lector mihi ferveat:** *Mihi* really depends on *ferveat*, though it may be conveniently translated
by 'my' with *lector*. 'Let my reader be one who comes to me
with his ears aglow from the pure effluence of such poetry.'

**127. non hic:** *Hic* is different in tone from *is*, more distinctly
demonstrative, and hence more distinctly contemptuous.—**in
crepidas:** The simple Accusative with *ludere* is the regular construction. *Crepidae*, a part of the Greek national dress. Comp.
Suet., Tib., 13 : *redegit se [Tiberius], deposito patrio habitu, ad pal-
lium et crepidas.* Hence *fabulae crepidatae* of tragedies with
Greek plots.—**Graiorum:** the rarer and more stilted form for
*Graecorum*, perhaps by way of rebuking the impertinence of this
stolid would-be wag.

**128. sordidus:** 'low creature,' 'dirty dog.' Himself vulgar,
he can not understand refinement of manners or attire.—**qui
possit:** Casaubon reads *poscit* to match *gestit*. But Indicative
and Subjunctive may well be combined, the former of a fact, the
latter of a characteristic : 'a man who— and a man to—.' So in
the famous line : *sunt qui non habeant, est qui non curat habere*,
Hor., Ep., 2, 2, 182.—**lusce:** 'Old One-eye' (Conington). The
lowness of the wit is evident. In v. 56 the poet appears to break
his own rule, but baldness and corpulence are in his eyes badges
of vice, not simple misfortunes.

**129. aliquem:** G., 301.—**Italo:** 'provincial.'—**supinus** =*su-*

*perbus.* The head is thrown back with the chin in the air, a familiar stage attitude. Others render 'lolling at his ease.'

**130. fregerit:** G., 541; A., 63, 2.—**heminas iniquas:** 'short half-pint measures.' This was the duty of the aedile.—**Arreti:** Arretium in Etruria. So JUVENAL takes Ulubrae as the type of a small provincial town: *vasa minora | frangere pannosus vacuis aedilis Ulubris*, 10, 102.

**131. abaco:** The *abacus* was a slab of marble or other material which was covered with sand (*pulvis*), for the purpose of drawing mathematical figures or making calculations (Jahn). Or *pulvere* may be dissociated from *abaco*, and then *abacus* would be a counting-board, *pulvis*, the sand on the ground (*eruditus pulvis*, CIC., N. D., 2, 18, 48), familiar from the story of the murder of Archimedes.—**metas:** 'cones.'

**132. scit:** as if this were a feat. Comp. v. 53.—**risisse:** γελάσαι, 'to have his laugh at,' one of the Perfect Infinitives mentioned in note on v. 41.—**vafer:** ironical. —**gaudere paratus:** *Paratus*, as a Participle from *parare*, takes the Infinitive with ease. The grammars generally treat it as an exceptional Adjective. Here *paratus* is οἶος; 'Just your man to have a fit of glee.' Comp. PETRON., 43: *paratus fuit quadrantem de stercore mordicus tollere.*

**133. Cynico barbam:** 'a Cynic's beard for him.' G., 343, R. 2. *Vellunt tibi barbam lascivi pueri*, HOR., Sat., 1, 3, 133 (of a Stoic). The beard was the badge of a philosopher.—**nonaria:** so called because women of that class were not allowed to ply their trade before the 'ninth hour'—'callet,' 'trull.'—**vellat:** because dependent; otherwise *gaudet si vellit.* G., 666; A., 66, 2. The Cynic philosopher and the *nonaria* (ὁ καὶ ἡ κύων) belong to each other by elective affinity, ALCIPHRON, 3, 55, 9. See an amusing parallel between philosopher and courtesan in the same sophist, 1, 34; and on the worst specimens of the 'Capuchins of antiquity,' as the Cynics have been called, comp. Friedländer, *Sittengesch.*, 3, 572.

**134. edictum:** 'play-bill,' after SEN., Ep., 117, 30. Others, 'the business of the courts,' the praetor's court being a favorite lounging-place.—**prandia:** See v. 67.—**Calliroen:** possibly one of the *elegidia procerum* (v. 51), after the order of Phyllis and Hypsipyle (v. 34). Comp. Ov., Met., 9, 407, Rem. Am., 455–6.

E 2

Others suppose that PERSIUS meant a *nonaria*. See note on 6, 73, and comp. PLUTARCH, Quaest. Conv., 3, 6, 4. With this gracious permission, Casaubon compares the edict of HOR., Ep., 1, 19, 8: *Forum putealque Libonis | mandabo siccis, adimam cantare severis.*

---

## SECOND SATIRE.

THE theme of this Satire is the Wickedness and Folly of Popular Prayers. The true philosopher is the only man that knows how to pray aright, and the Stoic is your only true philosopher. Compare, on the subject of prayer, the Second Alcibiades ascribed to PLATO.

ARGUMENT.—Macrinus, you may well salute your returning birthday. Your wishes on that day of wishes are pure, whereas most of our magnates pray for what they dare not utter aloud. Any one can hear their requests for sound mind and good report, but the petitions for the death of an uncle, a ward, a wife, the prayer for sudden gain, are mere whispers (1–15). Strange that, in order to prepare for such impieties as these, men should go through all manner of lustral services, and trust to the ear of Jove what they would not breathe to any mortal (15–23). Strange that men should fancy because Jove is not swift to strike the sinner dead that he may be insulted with safety, or easily bought off by a lot of greasy chitterlings (24–30).

Pass from wicked to foolish prayers. Grandam and aunt would have skinny Master Hopeful a wealthy nabob, would have him make a great match. Girls are to scramble for him, and roses spring up beneath his feet. Silly petitions! Refuse them, Jupiter (31–40). Nor less silly are those prayers whose fulfilment the suppliant himself defeats—prayers for a hale old age, despite rich made-dishes (41–43); prayers for wealth, while the worshipper expends his whole substance in sacrifice (44–51).

The trouble lies in this, that men judge the gods by themselves. Because gold brings a joyous flutter to their hearts, they think to sway the gods by gold, and change to gold the vessels of the sanctuary. The gods are measured by our 'accursed blubber,' that flesh which corrupts all that it handles. Yet the flesh tastes what it touches, and enjoys the ruin which it has wrought. But what can a pure god do with our gold? To him it is a spent toy, an idle offering. Let us give the gods honest and upright hearts, and a handful of meal will suffice to gain their blessing (52–75).

---

Although the colors of the piece pale before the rhetorical glare of

Juvenal's Tenth Satire, which treats of a kindred theme—the ' Vanity of
Human Wishes '—the philosophical commonplace is handled with considerable vigor, and with all the picturesque detail of the author's style.
And Montaigne, who, as a moralist, quotes PERSIUS very often, has
garnished the 56th essay of his First Book with copious extracts from
this Satire.

**1-15.** Macrinus, your prayers are pure, you need no private
audience of the gods. Not so the petitions of many of our foremost men. Far different is what they say and what they whis-
per, when they come before the gods in prayer.

**1. Hunc diem :** The birthday was always a high-day in Rome,
as elsewhere. In French, *fête* is a synonym of birthday.—**Macrine :** ' Plotius Macrinus, the scholiast says, was a learned man,
who loved PERSIUS as his son, having studied in the house of
the same preceptor, Servilius. He had sold some property to
PERSIUS at a reduced rate ' (Conington).—**meliore :** sc. *solito.*
G., 312, 2 ; A., 17, 5.—**lapillo :** The Scythians used to drop into a
quiver a stone for every day, white for the good and black for
the bad, and when life was over the stones were counted. There
is a similar story of the Thracians, PLIN., H. N., 7, 40, 41 (Jahn).
The phrase ' white stone ' is so common that one passage will
suffice as a parallel : *Felix utraque lux diesque nobis | signandi
melioribus lapillis,* MART., 9, 52, 4.

**2. labentis :** not simply an *epitheton ornans,* ' the gliding years,'
but ' the years as they glide away.' *Eheu, fugaces, Postume, Postu-
me | labuntur anni,* HOR., Od., 2, 14, 1.--**apponit :** ' puts to
your account.' Comp. *quem fors dierum cumque dabit lucro | ap-
pone,* HOR., Od., 1, 9, 15. Each day lived may be a day gained
or a day lost. Comp. also HOR., Od., 2, 5, 15.—**candidus :** λευκὴ
ἡμέρα, λευκὸν εὐάμερον φάος, SOPH., Ai., 709. Comp. CATULL., 8, 3 :
*fulsere vere candidi tibi soles.*

**3. genio :** ' The tutelary Deity, or " guardian angel," who was
supposed to attend on every individual from the cradle to the
grave. Its cultus was strictly materialistic, and should be compared with the offerings of meat, drink, and clothes which were
made to the *manes* of the dead. Comp. CENSORIN., De Die Nat.,
3 ; SERV. ad VERG., Georg., 1, 302 ; HOR., Ep., 2, 2, 187 : *scit
Genius, natale comes qui temperat astrum | naturae deus humanae,*

*mortalis in unum | quodque caput, vultu mutabilis albus et ater.* In character it was the reflex of the man (comp. Sat. 6, 48, where it represents the *felicitas* of the emperor); it might be humored and appeased by proper attention, more especially by sacrifice (comp. 5, 151), or irritated and made baneful by neglect (comp. 4, 27; Juv., 10, 129). From these latter passages it would appear to represent the *alter homo*, or second self.' So Pretor. The *genius* is the divine element which is born with a man, and when he dies becomes a *lar*, if he is good; if he is wicked, a *larva*, or a *lemur.* Departed *genii* were called *manes*—'good fellows'— doubtless with a view to propitiation.—**non tu:** Comp. 1, 45.— **emaci:** 'chaffering, haggling.' Prayer was often conceived as bargain and sale. See v. 29, and PLATO, Euthyphro, 14 E (Jahn). By the *prece emaci* is meant the *votum*, or vow, the εὐχή, and not the προσευχή, as GREGORY of Nyssa puts it (De Orat., Ed. Paris. a. 1638, Tom. 1, p. 724 D). Casaubon compares HOR., Od., 3, 29, 59: *ad miseras preces | decurrere et votis pacisci.*

**4. seductis:** Comp. *paulum a turba seductior audi*, 6, 42.— **nequeas:** G., 633; A., 65, 2.

**5. at bona pars:** Comp. HOR., Sat., 1, 1, 61: *at bona pars homi- num.*—**libabit:** Gnomic or sententious future. See 3, 93. Jahn comp. Juv., 8, 182: *quae | turpia cerdoni Volesos Brutumque dece- bunt.* 'That which is done is that which shall be done.' The other reading, *libavit* (gnomic Perfect), is not so good. See G., 228, R. 2, and Dräger, *Histor. Synt. der lat. Sprache*, § 127.

**6. haud cuivis:** Comp. *non cuivis homini contingit*, HOR., Ep., 1, 17, 36.—**humilis:** 'that keep near the ground,' 'groundling,' hence 'low.' PERSIUS delights in rare epithets.

**7. aperto vivere voto:** Comp. MART., 1, 39, 6: *si quis erit recti custos, mirator honesti | et nihil arcano qui roget ore deos.*

**8. Mens bona:** Comp. HOR., Ep., 1, 16, 59.—**Mens bona, fama, fides:** are commonly considered to be the things prayed for. They are possibly persons prayed to. 'Such notions as Welfare (*salus*), Honesty (*fides*), Harmony (*concordia*), belong to the old- est and holiest Roman divinities' (Mommsen).—**hospes:** 'a stran- ger,' 'any body.'

**9. o si:** On this form of the wish, see G., 254, R. 1; A., 57, 4, *b.  O si* may be considered an elliptical conditional sentence, but as the ellipsis is emotional it must not be supplied. Such an apodosis as scholars are prone to understand for the Greek (καλῶς ἂν ἔχοι) *bene sit*, would change the *wish* into a *thought*. In this passage the apodosis, which is involved in *praeclarum funus*, comes limping in as an afterthought.

**10. ebulliat:** is slang. Comp. *tam bonus Chrysanthus animam ebulliit*, PETRON., 42 (*nos non pluris sumus quam bullae*, ibid.); SEN., Apocolocynt., 4. Conington renders 'go off.' 'Kick the bucket' would be worthy of PERSIUS. *Ebulliat* must be read *ebulljat* (G., 717). The best MSS. have *ebullit*, but such a Sub-junctive would be more than doubtful (G., 191, 3; Neue, *Formenl.*, 2, 339).—**praeclarum funus:** Either 'that would be a grand funeral,' or 'that would be a corpse worth seeing.' In the for-mer case the man of prayer tries to salve his conscience by prom-ising his uncle (comp. 1, 11) a 'first-class funeral.' Comp. *f u n u s egregie factum laudet vicinia*, HOR., Sat., 2, 5, 105. In the latter, he is welcoming the death of the crabbed old man. For *funus*, in this connection, Jahn compares PROP., 1, 17, 8: *haecine parva meum f u n u s harena teget?* The half-light of the passage is well suited to the paltering knavery of the prayer.

**11. sub rastro,** etc.: HOR., Sat., 2, 6, 10: *O si urnam argenti fors quae mihi monstret, ut illi | thesauro invento, qui mercennarius agrum | illum ipsum mercatus aravit, dives amico | Hercule.*

**12. Hercule:** This is Hercules πλουτοδότης, to whom the Ro-mans consecrated a tithe of their gains. Mommsen and others dissociate this Hercules from the Greek ʹΗρακλῆς. According to Casaubon and the schol. (v. 44), Hermes (Mercury) is the bestow-er of windfalls found on the way, Hercules the patron of sought treasures.—**pupillum:** 'The Twelve Tables provided that where no guardian was appointed by will, the next of kin would be guardian, and he would of course be heir' (Conington, after Jahn).

**13. inpello:** 'whose kibe I gall,' 'whom I tread hard upon.' —**expungam:** 'get him out' (of his place in the will).—**namque:** gives an explanation, which serves at once to heighten and to excuse the hope. 'You see he is in a bad way already. He is going to die at any rate, and death would really be a relief to all parties.'—**scabiosus:** 'scrofulous.'—**acri | bile:** δριμεῖα χολή, Casaubon, who compares Juv., 6, 565 : *consulit ictericae lento de funere matris.*

**14. tumet :** Comp. *turgescit vitrea bilis*, 3, 8 ; *mascula bilis* | *intumuit*, 5, 145.—**Nerio :** Nerius is the usurer in Horace, Sat., 2, 3, 69. Persius borrows his names from Horace, as Horace borrows his from Lucilius—progressive bookishness, of which there are several examples. Comp. Pedius, 1, 85 ; Craterus, 3, 65 ; Bestius, 6, 37.—**conditur :** So Jahn (1868) and Hermann. Jahn (1843) reads *ducitur* with many MSS. *Ducitur* is not to be explained of 'being carried out to burial' (Servius ad Verg., Georg., 4, 256), but in its ordinary sense of 'being married.' Nerius has got rid of two wives, and 'is actually marrying a third.' *Conditur* is best supported by MS. authority, and gives a sufficiently good sense. Hermann quotes, in support of *conditur*, Mart., 5, 37, where a man survives the loss of a rich wife, and γυναῖκα θάπτειν κρεῖττόν ἐστιν ἢ γαμεῖν, Chaeremon, ap. Stobaeus, Sermon., 88, 22. Among the wishes in Lucian's Icaromen., 25, we find ὦ θεοί, τὸν πατέρα μοι ταχέως ἀποθανεῖν (comp. v. 10), and εἴθε κληρονομήσαιμι τῆς γυναικός, which is the key of this verse. On the use of the Dative, see G., 352, R. 1 ; A., 51, 4, *c.*

**15, 16.** These are the impious prayers that must be prefaced by pious observances.

**15. in gurgite mergis :** G., 384, R. 1 ; A., 56, 1, *c*, R.

**16. bis terque :** δὶς καὶ τρίς. G., 497.—**flumine :** Prol., 1. The lustral use of the bath, the pollution of the night, the peculiar virtue of running water, are common to Scriptural and classical antiquity. Lev., chap. 15. *Illo* | *mane die, quo tu indicis ieiunia nudus* | *in Tiberi stabit*, Hor., Sat., 2, 3, 290 ; *Ter matutino Tiberi mergetur et ipsis* | *verticibus timidum caput abluet*, Juv., 6, 523 ; *Ac primum pura somnum tibi discute lympha*, Prop., 4, 10, 13. For parallels, see Tylor, *Primitive Culture*, 2, 388.

**17-30.** With a sudden dramatic turn, Persius pins his omnipresent Second Person to the wall by an ironical question touching his conception of the divine character. 'What do you think of God ? What can you think of God when you confide to him wishes that you would conceal from a Staius ? Are you so bold because God is so slow ? Are you so bold because God's favor is so cheaply bought ?'

**17. minimum est,** etc. : Ironical.—**scire laboro:** So Hor., Ep., 1, 3, 2, and *nosse laboro*, Sat., 2, 8, 19.

**18. estne ut:** On this periphrasis, see G., 558; A., 70, 4, *a*. *Si est, patrue, culpam ut Antipho in se admiserit*, Ter., Phormio, 2, 1, 40. Comp. Hec., 3, 5, 51; 4, 1, 43; Adelph., 3, 5, 4; Hor., Od., 3, 1, 9.—**cures:** *Curare*, with Inf. usually has a negative (3, 78) or equivalent, as here.

**19. 'cuinam?' cuinam?** The first *cuinam* is the question of the other man, the second the echo of Persius. Comp. Ar., Ach., 594: ἀλλὰ τίς γὰρ εἶ; Δ. ὅστις; πολίτης χρηστός.—**vis:** Comp. 1, 56.—**Staio:** Staius can not be identified—*homuncio nobis ignotus* (König)—and, as Jahn admirably remarks, it makes no difference who he was, whether Staienus, as the scholiast says (Cic., Verr., 2, 32, 79; pro Cluentio, 7, 24, 65), or an average Philistine, or a typical scoundrel. The name was a common one. Jones is measured with Jupiter.—**an scilicet haeres:** 'what? are we to suppose that you are hesitating?'

**20. quis:** may be for *uter*. Comp. Cic., Att., 16, 14, 1; Fam., 7, 3, 1; Caes., B. G., 5, 44. 'Which of the two is the better judge?' And this is the more satisfactory rendering if Staius is a neutral character. If he is a villain, 'who would be a better judge' or 'better as a judge,' is more suitable.

**21. inpellere:** 'smite' (Verg., Georg., 4, 349; Aen., 12, 618), a rather strong word for *humilis susurros*. Pretor renders 'quicken;' Conington, 'have an effect on.' 'Reach' is about what is meant. With the thought of the passage, comp. Sen., Ep., 10, 5, cited by Casaubon: *Nunc quanta dementia est hominum? Turpissima vota diis insusurrant: si quis admoverit aurem, conticescent; et quod hominem scire nolunt, deo narrant.*

**22. agedum:** *Agedum hoc mi expedi primum*, Ter., Eun., 4, 4, 27. *Dum* shows impatience. 'Be at it,' or 'be done with it,' as the case may be.—**clamet:** *Dic—clamet = si dicas- -clamet.* G., 594, 4; A., 60, 1, *b*.

**23. sese non clamet:** *Iovem* would make the joke clearer, but Persius would have had to pound his desk and bite his nails to get *Iovem* in. 'Because he could swear by no greater, he sware by himself,' Hebr., 6, 13. König compares Hor., Sat., 1, 2, 17: *Maxime, quis non, | Juppiter, exclamat simul atque audivit?*

**24.** 'The guilty worshipper is in a grove (*lucis*, v. 27) during a thunderstorm; the lightning strikes not him but one of the sacred trees, and he congratulates himself on his escape—without reason, as PERSIUS tells him. The circumstances are precisely those used by LUCRETIUS to enforce his skeptical argument, 6, 390 and 416' (Conington).

**25. sulpure sacro:** 'lightning.' Comp. the Greek ϑεῖον, once innocently derived from the Adjective ϑεῖος.—**tuque domusque:** Comp. JUV., 13, 206: *cum prole domoque.* The editors cite the oracle in HEROD., 6, 86, 3: πᾶσαν | συμμάρψας ὀλέσει γενεὴν καὶ οἶκον ἅπαντα.

**26. fibris:** the extremities of the liver, λόβοι.—**Ergenna:** an Etruscan name. The Etruscans were great bowel-searchers (*haruspices*) and lightning-doctors.

**27. lucis:** local Abl. and poetic Plural.—**bidental:** According to a law of Numa, whosoever was struck dead by lightning was buried where he fell, and the spot was inclosed. The place was called *puteal*, from the resemblance of the inclosure to a well-curb, or *bidental*, because of the *oves bidentes* (sheep with upper and lower teeth, hence 'full grown') sacrificed in the consecration of the spot, which was invested with a holy horror (*triste*), and might not even be looked at (*evitandum*). Here *bidental* is transferred from the place to the person: 'a trophy of vengeance' (Conington), 'a monument of wrath' (Gifford). *Triste bidental*, HOR., A. P., 471.

**28. idcirco:** Emphatic resumption.—**vellere** = *vellendam.* G., 424, R. 4; A., 57, 8, *f.* On the phrase *vellere barbam*, comp. 1, 133. Jupiter was always represented as bearded, γενειήτης, LUCIAN, Sacrif., 11. 'Jove, will nothing wake thee? | Must vile Sejanus *pull thee by the beard* | ere thou wilt open thy black-lidded eyes | and look him dead?' BEN JONSON, Sejan., 4, 5.

**29. aut:** Another (negatived) case. See G., 460, R.; A., 71, 2. —**quidnam est, qua mercede** = *quanam mercede;* unusual. Not dissimilar, CAES., B. G., 5, 31: *Omnia excogitantur quare nec sine periculo maneatur et languore militum et vigiliis periculum augeatur.*

**30. emeris:** Jahn compares *praebere* and *dare aurem*, to which Conington adds *commodare*, HOR., Ep., 1, 1, 40.—**pulmone:** for the larger, *lactibus* for the smaller intestines (γαλακτίδες). 'The details are mentioned contemptuously' (Conington). Comp. Juv., 6, 540; 10, 354; 13, 115.

**31-40.** Thus far we have had wicked prayers; now we have specimens of silly prayers, of old wives' wishes.

**31. Ecce:** *transitioni servit* (Casaubon). See 1, 30. The showman puts in a new slide, and says 'Look here.'—**avia aut matertera:** The doting fondness of grandmothers, aunts, and nurses is proverbial. Their affection is not tempered by responsibility; hence their indiscretion. *Matertera* is the mother's sister, as *amita* (whence 'aunt') the father's; but, significantly enough, there is not the same moral distinction as between *patruus* and *avunculus* (whence 'uncle').—**metuens divum:** δεισιδαίμων. G., 374, R. 1; A., 50, 3, *b.*—**cunis:** Dat. is more picturesque than Abl.

**32. exemit:** The Perf. brings the scene before us, and makes it particular instead of generic.—**uda:** 'slobbering.'

**33. infami digito:** The middle finger (Juv., 10, 53) being used in mocking and indecent gesture, was considered on that very account to have more power against fascination. The notion still survives, and is embodied in coral 'amulets' or 'charms' (*breloques*) manufactured at Genoa.—**lustralibus:** The lustral day for a girl was the eighth, for a boy the ninth. Such a day would be the day for vows and prayers. On the corresponding Gr. ἀμφιδρόμια, see the Classical Dictionaries.—**ante:** adverbial, 'first of all.'—**salivis:** Spittle has manifold medical and magical virtues among all nationalities. Comp. Plin., H. N., 28, 4, 22; Juv., 9, 112; Petron., 131. The Plural is poetical, perhaps intimating abundance.

**34. expiat:** 'charms against mischief' (Conington).—**urentis:** 'blasting,' 'withering,' μαραίνοντας.—**oculos:** If the belief in the 'evil eye' is not too well known and too widely spread to need illustration, comp. Verg., Ecl., 3, 103; Hor., Ep., 1, 14, 37. On the philosophy of the evil eye, see Plutarch, Quaest. Conv., 5, 7. —**inhibere perita:** On the construction, see Prol., 11.

**35. manibus:** We say 'in,' Prol., 1. Translate 'arms,' as often. —**quatit:** Il., 6, 474: αὐτὰρ ὅ γ' ὃν φίλον υἱὸν ἐπεὶ κύσε πῆλέ τε χερσίν, | εἶπεν ἐπευξάμενος Διί τ' ἄλλοισίν τε θεοῖσιν. 'Dances,' 'dandles.'—**spem macram:** 'the skinny hope.'

**36. Licini :** Licinus, originally slave and steward of Caesar, then set free and made procurator of Gaul, where he acquired immense wealth by extortion. Comp. Juv., 1, 109 : *Ego possideo plus | Pallante et Licinis.*—**Crassi :** a still more familiar synonym for wealth, Cic., Att., 1, 4, 3. The two combined in Sen., Ep., 119, 9 : *Quorum nomina cum Crasso Licinoque numerantur.* —**mittit :** ' transports,' ' wafts ' (Pretor) ; ' packs off' (Conington), is not in keeping with the mock-lyrical tone of the passage.

**37. hunc :** δεικτικῶς. König comp. Catullus, 62, 42 : *Multi illum pueri, multae optavere puellae.* On *optet*, comp. G., 281, Exc. 1 ; A., 49, 1, *d.*—**rex et regina :** Comp. 1, 67. ' My lord and [my] lady' (Conington). As the prayer is extravagant, Pretor thinks that the words are to be taken literally, and Conington inclines to the same opinion. But there is no objection to *regina* for *domina* in itself, Mart., 10, 64.

**38. rapiant** = *diripiant,* ἁρπάζοιεν. ' May the girls have a scramble for him.' The sexes are to be reversed in his honor. Casaubon comp. : *Editum librum continuo mirari homines et diripere coeperunt,* Vita Persii.—**rosa fiat :** Casaubon comp. Claud., Seren., 1, 89 : *Quocumque per herbam | reptares, fluxere rosae.* A fairytale wish. Comp. Theocr., 8, 41 ; Verg., Ecl., 7, 59.

**39. ast** = *at* + *set.* G., 490, R.—**nutrici :** *Quid voveat dulci nutricula maius alumno,* Hor., Ep., 1, 4, 8. With the sentiment of the passage Casaubon comp. Sen., Ep., 60, 1 : *Etiamnum optas quod tibi optavit nutrix aut paedagogus aut mater? Nondum intellegis quantum mali optaverint?*

**40. albata :** ' clad in white,' the proper attire of worshippers, Tibull., 2, 1, 13 ; Plaut., Rud., 1, 5, 12 (Jahn). Hence ' though she ask it with every requisite form ' (Conington). See v. 15.

**41-51.** From wicked wishes we have passed to silly wishes, from silly we now pass to insane. Men pray for health and pray for wealth, and all the while are doing their utmost to break down their health and squander their wealth.

**41. nervis :** ' thews,' ' sinews.'—**senectae :** may depend on *poscis opem* or on *fidele* (Casaubon's view), ' to stand you in stead in old age ' (Conington), or ' to stand your old age in stead.' The latter is the more forcible.

**42. esto :** ' so far, so good ' (Conington).—**grandes patinae,**

etc.: Comp. Hor., Sat., 2, 2, 95: *Grandes rhombi patinaeque | grande ferunt una cum damno dedecus.* Jahn (1868) reads *pingues.*
—**tuccetaque crassa**: According to the Schol., ' beef steeped in a thick gravy, which enables it to keep a year.' 'Rich gravies' (Conington) ; ' rich forced meats' (Pretor). ' Rich potted meats.'
—**his** = *his precibus, votis.*—**vetuere**: Perf. to show that ' the mischief is already done' (Pretor). It is not a general Perfect. Comp. 32.

**44. rem struere**: The Biblical ' heap up riches.' Hor., Sat., 1, 1, 35 : *acervo | quem struit.*—**caeso bove**: An expensive sacrifice. Comp. Gr. βουϑυτεῖν.—**Mercurium**: See note on v. 11. An allusion to Mercury, or rather Hermes, as the God of Flocks and father of Pan, is barely possible.

**45. arcessis** = *in auxilium vocas* (Jahn). Conington's ' serve a summons on' is a caricature. Comp. Ov., Fast., 4, 263, and Petron., 122. *Accerso* is a rarer form than *arcesso*, and to be reserved for state occasions, according to Brambach.—**fibra**: See v. 26.—**da fortunare** = *ut fortunent.*—**fortunare**: used absolutely, as in Afranius, v. 84 (Ribbeck). *Fortuno* a *vox sollemnis* in prayers (Jahn).—**Penatis**: Gods of the Basket and Store.

**46. quo, pessime, pacto**: Hor., Sat., 2, 7, 22: *quo pacto, pessime?*

**47. iunicum** = *iuvencarum.* Observe the extravagance of the sacrifice, and compare with the expression Catull., 90, 6 : *omentum in flamma pingue liquefaciens.*

**48. extis et ferto**: Comp. vv. 30, 45. *Fertum (a ferendo)*, a kind of sacrificial cake or pudding, *libi genus, quod crebrius ad sacra obmovebatur* (Jahn).

**49. et tamen**: *at tamen* (Hermann), on which see 5, 159.

**50-51.** Casaubon sees in this passage an imitation of Hesiod, O. et D., 369: δειλὴ δ' ἐνὶ πυϑμένι φειδώ (*sera parsimonia in fundo est*, Sen., Ep., 1, 5). I have followed the old reading, which makes *nummus* the subject. The personification is in Persius's vein, as Schlüter correctly remarks. Comp. *tacita acerra*, v. 5 ; *gemuerunt aera*, 3, 39 ; *sapiens porticus*, 3, 53 ; *modice sitiente lagoena*, 3, 92. *Nummi* are nursed as children, 5, 149 ; there is a kind of personification in *dolosi nummi*, Prol., 12, and literature is full of personified coins, of ' nimble sixpences,' ' slow shillings,' 'adventurous guineas.' Add: *ac velut exhausta redivivus pullulet arca | nummus*, Juv., 6, 363. Paley (ap. Pretor) suggests that *nequiquam* may be considered the exclamation of the *nummus*. This gives so happy a turn that I am almost tempted to put it in the text. It is the familiar story of 'the bottom dime,' set to the familiar tune of the 'Last Rose of Summer.' Jahn makes the numbskull, not the *nummus*, the subject, and reads in his ed. of 1843:

*Nequiquam fundo*, suspiret, *nummus in imo!*

In his ed. of 1868 he follows Hermann, who reads:

Nequiquam *fundo*, suspiret, *nummus in imo!*

Pretor prints:

*Nequiquam: fundo*, suspiret, *nummus in imo!*

The scholiast hesitates. All much more prosaic and much less satisfactory.—**suspiret:** See G., 574, R.; A., 62, 2, *d*.

**52-75.** With a sudden start Persius strikes at the root of the matter—the false conception of the divine character. 'Thou thoughtest,' saith God, 'that I was altogether such a one as thyself,' Ps. 50, 21. Because you love gold, you fancy that God loves gold, and judge of His Holiness by your corruption. God demands a pure heart, and not 'thousands of rams.' This is a plane on which the highest expressions of the most various religions meet, so that Hebrew, Greek, and Christian hold almost identical discourse. M. Martha (*Moralistes Romains*, p. 134) recognizes 'a progress' in thoughts, which are immemorial in their antiquity.

**52. creterras:** preferred by Jahn (1868) and Hermann to *crateras*, in which the Acc. Sing. of the Greek word κρατήρ seems to be taken as the stem (G., 72, R. 2). See Hor., Od., 3, 18, 7: Sat., 2, 4, 80. Comp. also *statera* and *panthera*. G. Meyer (*Beiträge zur Stammbildung* in Curtius, *Studien*, 5, 72) questions the Accus. origin.—**argenti:** The context indicates the material, which in prose would be *ex argento* or *argentea* (G., 396; A., 54, 2). The Genitive should give us the contents as in v. 11, *argenti seria*. Comp. Juv., 9, 141: *argenti vascula puri*.—**incusa:** 'is a translation of ἐμπαιστά (Casaubon), ἐμπαιστικὴ τέχνη being the art of embossing silver or some other material with golden ornaments (*crustae* or *emblemata*).  Hence *crateras argenti incusaque dona* is probably a hendiadys' (Conington).  *Chrysendeta*, or parcel-gilt plate (Pretor).—**pingui:** ' thick,' not a generic epithet.

**53. dona:**  Predicate.—**pectore laevo:** Jahn strangely follows Casaubon in understanding *pectore laevo* as *mente laeva.*  Comp. VERG., Ecl., 1, 16 : *si mens non laeva fuisset.*  The side of the heart is meant.  König comp. *laeva parte mamillae | nil salit Arcadico iuveni,* JUV., 7, 159.

**54. excutiat:**  In his ed. of 1868 Jahn has abandoned the harsh *excutias* of 1843, which leaves *laetari praetrepidum cor* to take care of itself, with *laetari* as an histor. Inf. of habit.  Comp. VERG., Georg., 1, 200 ; 4, 134; Aen., 4, 422 ; 7, 15.—**guttas:** 'Your heart in an eager flutter of excited joy would drive the life-drops from your left breast.'  So Pretor, who adds that PERSIUS alludes to the faintness produced by any violent excitement.  Comp. VERG., Georg., 3, 105 : *cum spes arrectae iuvenum exsultantiaque haurit | corda pavor pulsans.*  With *guttas* comp. ' As dear to me as are the ruddy *drops* that visit this sad heart,' SHAKSP.  Jahn understands 'tears,' Heinrich 'sweat' (comp. JUV., 1, 167: *tacita sudant praecordia culpa*).  In the latter case we should expect *ut,* as Schlüter observes.—**laetari praetrepidum:** ' over-hasty to rejoice ' (Conington).  For the construction, comp. Prol., 11, and HOR., Od., 2, 4, 24 : *cuius octavum trepidavit aetas | claudere lustrum.*  On the meaning of *trepidum,* see 1, 20.

**55. illud, quod:** 'that strange fashion that,' instead of the impersonal construction with the Inf. with a different shade of meaning (G., 525 ; A., 70, 5) - **sublit:** On the quantity of the final syllable, see G., 705, Exc. 4; A., 84, *g,* 5.—**auro ovato:** Comp. *triumphato auro,* Ov., Ep. ex Ponto, 2, 1, 41 (Jahn).  An allusion to the ' unjust acquisition of the gold offered to Heaven ' seems to be too modern, despite JUV., 8, 106.

**56. nam:** ' for instance.'  G., 500, R. 1.—**fratres aenos:** ' brazen brotherhood ' (Gifford).  There are various interpretations : 1. The gods generally (Jahn).  2. The fifty sons of Aegyptus, whose statues stood in the portico of the Palatine Apollo over against those of the fifty Danaides, PROP., 2, 31, 1 seqq.; Ov., Trist., 3, 1, 59 seqq. (Scholiast).  3. The Dioscuri.  The first explanation is the best.  All the gods might appear in vision, but some were more famous for such appearances than others. The very existence of the statues of the sons of Aegyptus is problematical, and their connection with dreams inexplicable (Jahn). As for the Dioscuri, they were notoriously beardless youths, apart from the fact that *qui mittunt* points to more than two (Casaubon).

**57. pituita:** trisyllabic, as in HOR., Sat., 2, 2, 76 ; Ep., 1, 1, 108. *Pituita,* 'phlegm,' 'gross humor.' 'That *pituita* was supposed to mark a heavy, cloudy intellect, is clear from the meaning of the opposite expression, *emunctae naris'* (Pretor). See also the commentators on HOR., ll. cc.

**58. aurea barba:** CIC., N. D., 3, 34, 83 : *Aesculapii Epidaurii barbam auream demi iussit [Dionysius], neque enim convenire barbatum esse filium cum in omnibus fanis pater imberbis esset.*

**59. vasa Numae:** called *capedines* and *simpuvia.*—**Saturnia aera:** Old coinage, according to Schol., Casaubon, and Jahn. The earliest coinage is said to have been stamped on one side with the head of Janus, the coiner, on the other with a ship, in honor of Saturn's arrival in Italy. It is best to translate loosely by 'brass' or 'bronze,' as the explanation is far from certain.— **inpulit:** 'kicked out.'

**60. Vestalis urnas:** always of earthenware.—**Tuscum fictile:** 'Etruscan pottery.' 'Etruscan' both by reason of its origin and its use in Etruscan ritual.

**61. O curvae:** A passionate apostrophe, which reminds M. Martha of Bossuet.—**in terris:** So Jahn and Hermann. We should expect *in terras,* but the Abl. is more forcible as denoting the fixity rather than the tendency of the position.—**caelestium inanes:** On the Gen., see G., 373, R. 6 ; A., 50, 3, *c.* Jahn quotes HOR., Od., 3, 11, 23 : *inane lymphae | dolium fundo pereuntis imo.*

**62. quid iuvat hoc:** So Jahn. *Hos,* Hermann's reading, is not necessary, though natural. *Hoc* often anticipates the contents of a dependent clause, as here with the Inf., 5, 45 ; *ut* with Subj., 5, 19.—**templis inmittere mores:** is more than 'the opposite to v. 7 : *tollere de templis.' Inmittere,* 'turn loose upon,' like so many *hostes, sicarii,* etc. *Mores,* 'courses of life.'

**63. bona dis:** Brachylogy. 'What is good in the eyes of the gods.'—**ducere:** 'infer.'—**scelerata pulpa:** 'sinful, pampered flesh' (Conington).  *Pulpa* is the Stoic σάρξ, σαρκίδιον, in a stronger form.  M. Martha (l. c. p. 133, note) says that the Christian σάρξ (*caro*) is borrowed from the language of philosophy.  Others only note the coincidence.  *Pulpa* may be rendered ' blubber.'

**64. haec:** sc. *pulpa.*—**sibi :** ' to suit its taste.'—**corrupto :** The oil is spoiled by the spice, Verg., Georg., 2, 465 : *Alba nec Assyrio fucatur lana veneno | nec casia liquidi corrumpitur usus olivi.*

**65. Calabrum :** ' The beauty of the Calabrian fleece consisted in its perfect whiteness,' which is destroyed by the dye.—**coxit :** here in a bad sense, as we often use ' cook,' ' doctor.'—**vitiato :** The *murex* is spoiled as well as the *vellus;* both have violence done to their natures.  Comp. Juv., 3, 20 : *ingenuum violarent marmora tofum.*  On the hard treatment of the *murex*, or κάλχη, see St. John, *Manners and Customs of Ancient Greece*, 3, 225 foll.

**66. bacam :** ' pearl,' literally ' berry.'  The transfer is explained by Auson., Mos., 70 : *albentes concharum germina bacas. Diluit insignem bacam*, Hor., Sat., 2, 3, 241.—**rasisse :** Perf., like the Greek Aor. Inf.  See 1, 42.

**67. massae :** ' ore.'—**crudo de pulvere :** ' from their primitive slag ' (Conington).

**68. vitio utitur :** ' gets some good out of its sin.'—**nempe :** G., 500, R. 2.

**70. pupae :** The ancients dedicated to the gods what they had done with.  So when the girl was ripe for marriage, she hung up her dolls.  The sailor hangs up his clothes, Hor., Od., 1, 5, 16; the lover his harp, Od., 3, 26, 3.  The Sixth Book of the Greek Anthology is full of examples.  An ingenious friend suggests that the practice of publishing a list of commentators in editions of the classics is a survival of this usage.

**71. quin damus :** See G., 268 ; A., 57, 7, *d.*—**lance :** ' sacrificial plate,' ' paten.'  Ov., Ep. ex P., 4, 8, 39 : *nec quae de parva dis pauper libat acerra | tura minus grandi quam data lance valet* (Jahn).

**72. Messallae propago :** Lucius Aurelius Cotta Messalinus (Schol.), an unworthy son of M. Valerius Messalla Corvinus.  See Tac., Ann., 6, 7.  He was a notorious debauchee in the reign of Tiberius.—**lippa :** alludes to the effect of his excesses.  Comp. 5, 77.

**73. conpositum:** ' in just balance,' 'well blended' (Conington).
—**ius fasque:** ' duty to God and man' (Conington).—**recessus |
mentis:** φρενῶν μυχός, THEOCR., 29, 3 (Jahn).

**74. incoctum:** 'thoroughly imbued.'—**generoso honesto:**
' with the honor of a gentleman.' See note on *mordaci vero*, 1,
107.

**75. cedo:** Notice the quantity. G., 190, 4; A., 38, 2, *f.* *Cĕ-
do*, 'give here,' 'let.' For the construction: *cedo ut bibam*,
PLAUT., Most., 2, 1, 26 ; *cedo ut inspiciam*, Curc., 5, 2, 54.—**admo-
vere:** a sacrificial word.—**farre litabo:** Comp. HOR., Od., 3, 23,
19 : *mollivit aversos Penatis | farre pio et saliente mica.* *Litare* is
the Greek καλλιερεῖν, ' offer acceptably.' The sentiment may be
illustrated without end. Comp. θυσία μεγίστη τῷ θεῷ τό γ' εὐσεβεῖν,
MEN., Mon., 246, and EUR., fr. 329 and 940 (Nauck).

---

## THIRD SATIRE.

ARGUMENT.—The Satire opens dramatically. A young Roman of the
upper classes is discovered asleep, snoring off the effects of yesterday's
debauch. To him one of his familiars, half companion, half tutor, who
rouses him by telling him that the sun is already high in the heavens,
and it is time to be up. The young fellow bawls for his servants, brays
for them, and makes a show of going to work. But nothing suits him.
He curses the ink because it is too thick, then he curses it because it is
too thin, and finally swears at pen and ink both. 'You big baby,' ex-
claims the monitor. 'Do you expect me to study with such a pen?'
asks the young man with a whine. 'Don't come to me with your puling
nonsense, you dab of untempered mortar, you unformed lump of clay.
You are lazing away the time, when every minute is of moment, when
the potter's wheel should fly faster and faster, and deft hands should
mould the vessel of your life (1–24). But I see you think that you have
already attained perfection. You are satisfied with your position in
life, move in a good circle. Tell that to the profane vulgar. I know
you, every inch of you. Shame on you, that you, with your training,
should live like a brutish creature, who does not know what a rich jewel
he is flinging away, who sinks without a struggle in the slough of vice,
whose soul dies and makes no sign. But you, who know better, will
have a dire fate. No worse doom could Jove himself bring down on
cruel tyrants than the vain yearning for lost virtue, which they can
never hope to regain. Nay, worse than the brazen bull of Phalaris and

the pendent sword of Damocles is the consciousness of sin, the pallor that blanches not the cheek only, but the very heart (25–43). You are past the age of childhood, and have not the excuse of tender years. If you were a child, I could understand your behavior. I remember my own childhood, how hateful and unprofitable task-work alternated with frivolous play, how I dodged the learning of the piece I had to speak, how I had no thought for any thing save dice and marbles and tops (44–51). But you have reached a higher level. You know the great norms of life, the doctrines of the Porch; you understand the distinctions of Right and Wrong. Pshaw! As I live, you are snoring still. Wake up, I say, and tell me—have you any aim in life? Or are you nothing better than a boy following sparrows with a pinch of salt?' (52–62).

Here the poet drops the dramatic form, deserts the individuality of the student, and makes his exhortation general, reserving, of course, the right to pick out at will any member of his congregation for rebuke. He mounts the pulpit and begins to preach. His text is:

'Be wise to-day; 'tis madness to defer.' Go back to the first princi- ples of all true philosophy, the constitution of the universe, the posi- tion of man in that universe, the great laws of Ethic as derived from the great laws of Physic. In brief, study your Stoic catechism. Do not allow yourself to be diverted from higher study by success in the lower ranges of life. You lawyer there, for instance, do not let hams and sprats, the gifts of thankful clients, seduce you from the ambrosia of true philosophy (63–76).

But hark! some one is talking out in church. It is the voice of the unsavory centurion.

'I have got all the sense I want. I would not be for all the world one of your painful philosophers, with head tucked down, eyes riveted on the ground, mumbling and muttering a lot of metaphysic trash—*chi- maera bombinans in vacuo*—and the rest of the scholastic stuff. What! get pale for that? What! miss my breakfast for that!'

Great applause in the galleries, and a rippling reduplication of laugh- ter from the muscular humanity of the period (77–87).

A sudden turn, or rather a sudden return to the figure of v. 63. The connection, if there be a connection, seems to be this:

Such men as the centurion are hopelessly lost, have already 'imbodied and imbruted.' Like Natta, they are unconscious of their moral ruin. But there are those who, half-conscious of their condition, consult a physician of the soul, a spiritual director. The state of this class is set forth in a dramatic parable. A man feels sick, goes to see a doctor, fol- lows his advice for a while, gets better, and then, despite all remon- strance, violates the plainest rules of diet and falls dead (88–106).

But before our preacher can make the application, he is interrupted by an impatient hearer, perhaps none other than the yawning youth,

F

whose acquaintance we made in the beginning of the Satire. Whoever he is, he is so literal that he does not understand the drift of the apologue.

'Sick! Who's sick? Not I. No fever in my veins. No chill in hands or feet.'

'But,' says our resolute moralist, 'the sight of money, the meaning smile of a pretty girl, makes your heart beat a devil's tattoo. Coarse flour shows that you are mealy-mouthed, and tough cabbage brings out the ulcer in your throat. Kindle the fire of wrath beneath the cauldron of your blood, and Orestes is sane in comparison' (107–118).

---

According to Jahn, this Satire is aimed at those that have received a thorough training in ethics, but, owing to the weakness of human nature, fail to follow the true guide of life; and, although well aware of their short-comings, imitate the example of those brutish souls whose sins are excused by their ignorance. In short, the Satire is an expansion of the old theme — *Video meliora proboque.*

Knickenberg (*De Ratione Stoica in Persii Satiris Apparente*, p. 16 seqq.) maintains that in conformity with Stoic doctrine, it is not so much the weakness of human nature as imperfect knowledge—the *inscitia debilis* of v. 99—that is the source of the vices which the author lashes in the present Satire. According to the Stoic, virtue is knowledge, and the snoring youth, with his half-knowledge, which keeps him from rising to the height of virtue, is the pattern of the false philosophy of the time.

But PERSIUS is not an expounder of the Stoic philosophy, as a system, any more than SENECA is; and commentators have attributed to him a profounder knowledge of philosophy than he had, certainly a profounder knowledge than it would have been artistic to show. PERSIUS repeats the catechism of the sect, expands some of their favorite theses, elaborates some of their pet figures, and finds fault with his fellow-students in the lofty tone which he had caught from his teachers. A glaring paradox, such as we find in 5, 119, he is but too happy to reproduce, but the subtle analysis for which the Stoics were famous does not appear in his poems.

---

The Satire is said by the Scholiast to be imitated from the Fourth Book of LUCILIUS.

**1-24.** A young student is roused by one of his companions, who, after meditating on his snoring form (1–4), remonstrates with him against lying abed so long. Yawning and headachy, he attempts to go to work, calls his servants testily, has his writing materials brought, swears at them, and is rebuked by his sage friend for his babyishness, and urged to make use of this golden season of life.

**1. Nempe:** The opening is made very lively by the use of *nempe*, which implies a preceding statement, and thus plunges at once into the thick of the dialogue. 'And so'—a clear imitation of HOR., Sat., 1, 10, 1. Comp. the English use of 'and' in the first verse of lyrics, and the common stage trick of beginning a scene with conjunctions: FARQUHAR, Beaux' Stratagem, 2, 2: '*And* was she the daughter of the house?' CIBBER, The Provoked Wife, 5, 4: '*But* what dost thou think will come of this business?' This effect is lost by bringing in the *comes* at v. 5, as some do.— **mane:** Substantive, the Abl. of which, *mane* (*mani*), is in more common use as an Adverb.—**fenestras:** 'windows,' here for 'window-shutters.'

**2. extendit:** 'makes wider,' 'makes seem wider,' a familiar optical effect.—**rimas:** 'chinks' (between the shutters).

**3. stertimus:** Ironical First Person, excluding the speaker.— **indomitum:** 'heady,' 'unmanageable' (Conington). Falernian was a strong wine: *ardens*, HOR., Od., 2, 11, 9; *severum*, Od., 1, 27, 19; *forte*, Sat., 2, 4, 24. Add LUCAN, 10, 162: *Indomitum Meroe cogens spumare Falernum.*—**quod sufficiat:** 'what ought to be enough.' G., 633; A., 65, 2.—**despumare:** 'work off,' 'carry off the fumes of' (Conington). *Despumare* is a technical term 'skim' (VERG., Georg., 1, 296), like 'rack' in English.

**4. quintā dum linea tangitur umbrā:** where we should expect *quintā linea umbrā*, by what is called Hypallagē. Conington compares AESCHYL., Ag., 504: δεκάτῳ σε φέγγει τῷδ' ἀφικόμην ἔτους. See Schneidewin's note.—**dum:** 'while,' 'whereas,' 'and yet.' Comp. G., 572, R.; A., 72, 1, *c.*—**linea:** of the sun-dial. The fifth hour (about 11 o'clock) was the time of the *prandium*, according to AUSON., Ephem. Loc. Ordin. Coqui, 1, 2 (Casaubon): *Sosia, prandendum est, quartam iam totus in horam | sol calet: ad quintam flectitur umbra notam.* In HORACE's time breakfast was after 10 (Sat., 1, 5, 25). The sophist ALCIPHRON implies that 12 was the hour in his day (3, 4, 1).

**5. en quid agis?** Comp. *en quid ago?* VERG., Aen., 4, 534. In lively questions the present is often used as a future, as: *Quoi dono lepidum novum libellum?* CATULL., 1, 1.—**siccas:** proleptic

or predicative, to be combined with *coquit*. Conington renders
'is baking the crops dry,' but *coquere* is too common in this sense
for such a translation, a criticism which applies to a very large
proportion of Conington's picturesque versions. *Coquere* is the
regular word for 'ripen'—Gr. πέσσω—VARRO, R. R., 1, 7, 4 ; 54, 1.
Tr. 'is ripening hard' (in the broiling sun).—**insana canicula :**
'the mad dog-star' is, of course, the 'mad dog's star' (Conington).
Comp. HOR., Od., 3, 29, 18 ; Ep., 1, 10, 16.

**7. comitum :** *Comes* is a wide term, embracing fellow-students
and tutors. The Greek word is οἱ συνόντες. See LUCIAN's famous tract, περὶ τῶν ἐπὶ μισϑῷ συνόντων (de mercede conductis).

**8. aliquis :** 'somebody,' 'τις,' of a servant. *Aperite aliquis
actutum ostium*, TER., Adelphi, 4, 4, 46. Ὥσπερ ἐν οἴκῳ ἔνιοι δε-
σπόται προστάττουσι, Ἴτω τις ἐφ' ὕδωρ, Ξύλα τις σχισάτω, XEN.,
Cyr., 5, 3, 49.—**nemon ?** on the rhetorical *-ne*, see 1, 22.—**vitrea
bilis :** a medical term, ὑαλώδης χολή, according to Casaubon.
Comp. *splendida bilis*, HOR., Sat., 2, 3, 141.

**9. findor :** 'I'm splitting,' the exclamation of the impatient
youth. The old reading, *finditur*, 'he' or 'it' (*bilis*) 'is splitting,'
has little MS. authority. Others read *findimur*.—**Arcadiae pecu-
ria :** The asses of Arcady were famous in antiquity.—**rudere :**
with *u* long only here and AUSON., Epigr., 76, 3.

**10. iamque liber :** The distribution of these articles is not
without its difficulty. According to some, *liber* is the author to
be explained by the teacher ; *chartae*, the papyrus for rough notes ;
*membrana*, the parchment for a more careful transcript. According to others, '*liber* is the author out of which the lesson or thesis is to be transcribed, and *membrana* the parchment wrapper
for preserving the loose sheets, as the work progresses' (Pretor).
—**bicolor :** used either of the two sides of the skin—the one
from which the hair had been scraped, yellow, the other white
(Casaubon), or, more probably, of the custom of coloring the
parchment artificially (Jahn).—**capillis :** is commonly taken for
*pilis*, a rare use. The hair side of the skin was carefully smooth-
ed with pumice-stone. *Arida modo pumice expolitum*, CAT., 1, 2 ;
*cui pumex tondeat ante comas*, TIB., 3, 1, 10. The old explanation, according to which *positis capillis*=*capillis ornatis sive
pexis* (Plum), has found an advocate in Schlüter. The young

man is supposed to have dressed his hair before he goes to work.

**11. nodosa harundo** $=calamus$ of the next verse.

**12. querimur:** In his ed. of 1868 Jahn has abandoned *queritur* (1843) here and in v. 14. Comp. *stertimus*, v. 3.—**calamo:** In prose, *de calamo*.

**13. nigra sepia:** 'The blackness of the liquor,' Conington, who says correctly that *nigra* is emphatic. *Sepia*, 'juice of the cuttle-fish,' used for ink. Comp. AUSON., Epist., 4, 76; 7, 54 (Jahn).

**14. fistula** $=harundo$. The nib of the pen was badly slit. Comp. *nec iam fissipedis per calami vias | grassetur Cnidiae sulcus harundinis*, AUSON., Epist., 7, 49–50.

The whole period is very awkward, and is not improved by Jahn's *sed* for *quod* in v. 13. Mr. Pretor suspects a *duplex recensio*, and brackets v. 13. In any other author I should suggest *dilutasque nimis* for *dilutas querimur*, v. 14 (Mp. *querimus*).

**15. ultra miser** $=miserior$.—**hucine rerum:** *Hucine* is archaic and colloquial. On *rerum*, see G., 371, R. 4; A., 50, 2, *d*. Comp. 1, 1 for the translation.

**16. tenero columbo:** a pet name for children (Schol.). *Columbus* is 'the house-pigeon,' *palumbus* 'the wood-pigeon.' Some of the best MSS. read *palumbo*, which Bentley on HOR., Od., 1, 2, 10, prefers. Notice further that nurses often feed their babies pigeon-fashion.—**regum pueris:** 'aristocratic babies,' 'babies of quality' (Conington). *Regum* as in 1, 67.—**pappare:** (*papare*, Jahn, 1843) Infin. for Substantive, 'pap.' Such Infinitives are hardly parallel with *vivere triste* (1, 9), and belong rather to the *verba togae*. They may be called nursery Infinitives. Comp. TITIN. (ap. CHARISIUM, 1, p. 99 P.), v. 78 Ribb.: *Date illi biber, iracunda haec est.* Comp. the Greek τὸ πιεῖν, τὸ φαγεῖν, THEOCR., 10, 53; ANTHOL. PAL., 12, 34, 5. The Scholiast calls *pappare* and *lallare* '*voces mutilas*.'—**minutum:** 'chewed fine,' 'minced.'

**18. iratus:** 'in a pet.'—**mammae:** exactly our 'mammy;' depends on *lallare*, not on *iratus*.—**lallare:** like *pappare*, 'lullaby.' 'Pettishly refusing to let mammy sing you to sleep' (Conington) —'to go by-bye for mammy.'

**19. studeam:** G., 258; A., 57, 6. The absolute use of *studere* is post-Augustan. *Desidioso studere torqueri est*, SEN., Ep. M., 71, 23.—**Cui verba:** sc. *das?*

**20. succinis:** 'sing to an instrument or second to a person,' 'hence to sing small' (Conington), 'come whimpering, whining with.'—**ambages:** 'beating about the bush,' 'shuffling excuses.' *Quando pauperiem, missis ambagibus, horres*, HOR., Sat., 2, 5, 9.— **tibi luditur:** *Tua res agitur*, 'it is your game,' 'your stake,' 'your affair.'—**effluis amens:** with a sudden change of figure. The dissolute young man is compared to a cracked jar, from which all the noble 'wine of life' (SHAKSP., Macbeth, 2, 3) is escaping. The passage in TER., Eun., 1, 2, 25, which is often cited in this connection: *Plenus rimarum sum; huc atque huc perfluo* refers to 'a leaky vessel,' one who can not keep a secret.

**21. contemnere:** A sudden desertion of the metaphor, unless *contemnere* be a technical term, like ἀποδοκιμάζειν, 'reject on test.' CICERO combines *conterere et contemnere, contemnere et reicere, contemnere et pro nihilo putare*. The Scholiast thinks that the word is an unhappy reminiscence of HOR., Sat., 2, 3, 14: *contemnere miser.*—**sonat vitium** = *sono indicat vitium. Sonat vitium*, like *sapit mare*, 'sounds flawy,' 'has a flawy ring.' The Schol. comp. VERG., Aen., 1, 328: *nec vox hominem sonat.*—**maligne:** 'ill-naturedly,' 'grudgingly,' of that which falls short of what was expected. *Maligne respondet*, 'gives a short answer,' 'a dull sound.'

**22. viridi** = *crudo*, 'untempered.' The material is ill-mixed and the crock ill-baked (*non cocta*).

**23.** 'Persius steps back, as it were, while pursuing the metaphor,' is Conington's droll defence of PERSIUS's ὕστερον πρότερον. Common critics would say that PERSIUS had bungled the figure. —**properandus et fingendus:** not necessarily equivalent to *propere fingendus*. Comp. JUV., 4, 134: *argillam atque rotam citius properate*.

**24-43.** PERSIUS: 'I know what you are going to say. You have a fair estate, you have nothing to dread, you have good connections, you have a good position. Away with these baubles. I know you yourself. You live no higher life than the dullest sensualist, who knows not what he is losing; but the time will come when you will be roused to the consciousness of your loss, and your soul must be tortured with the expectation of impending ruin and the carking of hidden sin.'—**rure pater-no:** G., 412, R. 1 ; A., 55, 3, *c*, R.

**25. far modicum:** *Modicum* with a sneer. The young man keeps up a show of Stoic moderation.—**salinum—patella:** two articles of plate, to which every respectable family aspired. Compare the apostle-spoons and the caudle-cup of the Elizabethan period. The *salinum* and the *patella* were exempt, when all other gold and silver plate was called for to meet the necessities of the state.—**purum et sine labe:** literally and metaphorically.

**26. quid metuas:** *ex animo iuvenis.* The young man is supposed to ask *quid metuam?* See v. 19. 'I have nothing to fear on the score of poverty.'—**cultrix foci:** The *patella* was used in the worship of the Lares. Conington preserves the possible double sense of 'inhabitant' and ' worshipper,' by rendering ' a dish for fireside service.'—**secura:** 'that knows no fear' (of want).

**27. hoc satis?** This is very well, but is it enough?—**an dece-at:** The connection is not very plain, and Jahn thinks that another person is apostrophised. PERSIUS is attacking the same man, now as to his fortune, now as to his family. That this is not clearly brought out, is simply his own fault.—**ventis:** 'with airs' (Pretor). See 4, 20.

**28. stemmate:** Abl. as a whence-case. 'Comp. JUV., 8, 1-6 ; SUET., Nero, 37. These *stemmata* were genealogical trees or tables of pedigree, in which the family portraits (*imagines*) were connected by winding lines. Comp. *stemmata vero lineis discurrebant ad imagines pictas,* PLIN., H. N., 25, 2, and *multae stemmatum flexurae,* SEN., de Benef., 3, 28 ' (Pretor, after Jahn).—**Tusco:** The Etruscans were great sticklers for family, as PERSIUS well knew. Comp. HOR., Od., 3, 29, 1 ; Sat., 1, 6, 1 ; PROP., 4, 9, 1. Your aristocratic philosopher can afford to be disdainful of birth. A Stoic commonplace: *si quid est aliud in philosophia boni, hoc est quod stemma non inspicit,* SEN., Ep., 44, 1.—**ramum =** *lineam.*—**millesime:** ' a thousand times removed ' (Pretor). On the case, 1, 123. Conington recognizes a side-thrust, and compares Savage's ' No *tenth* transmitter of a foolish face.'

**29. censoremne:** So Casaubon. Jahn (1868) reads -*que*, thus abandoning the reading which is best supported by MSS., but utterly unsupported by grammar, *-ve*. The careless use of *vel* after *ve* is one of those slips that are simply incredible, nor can *-ve—vel* be successfully defended by connecting the latter close- ly with *trabeate*. Pretor explains, 'because you have a censor in your family, or are yourself a knight of distinction (sc. *quodve censorem tuum salutas vel quod ipse trabeatus es* '). Heinr.'s con- jecture, *fatuum*, with a reference to the censorship of Claudius, is itself almost fatuous. If we are to resort to conjecture, Heinr.'s other suggestion, *vetulum*, would be mild. Jahn explains this line (after Niebuhr) of the *municipales equites*, 'Because you are a great man in your own provincial town.' Comp. 1, 129. 'In any case the allusion is to the annual *transvectio* of the *equites* be- fore the censor, who used to review them (*recognoscere*) as they defiled before him on horseback. If *censorem* is understood of Rome, *tuum* will imply that the youth is related to the Emperor, like JUVENAL's Rubellius Blandus, 8, 40; otherwise it means " your local censor " ' (Conington).—**trabeate :** The *trabea* is the official dress of the *equites*. Comp. 1, 123.

**30. ad populum phaleras :** ' The *phalerae* included all the trap- pings of the horse and rider. They were on occasion much orna- mented with metal, and POLYBIUS (6, 23) says that they were given as rewards of merit to cavalry soldiers' (Pretor, after Jahn). ' To the mob with your trappings, your stars and garters.'—**intus et in cute :** 'inside and out ;' a rough equivalent. *In cute* (Gr. ἐν χρῷ) means ' closely ' (' to a dot, a T '). See Lexx. s. v. χρῶς.

**31. non pudet :** ' You are not ashamed ?' (you ought to be). See G., 455. — **discincti :** Comp. *discinctus aut perdam nepos*, HOR., Epod., 1, 34 (Schol.). The *discinctus* is 'a man of loose habits.'—**Nattae :** taken at random from HOR., Sat., 1, 6, 124.

**32. stupet :** ἀναισθητεῖ (Casaubon). He is ' past feeling,' his conscience is benumbed, is 'seared with a hot iron.'—**fibris in- crevit opimum pingue :** ' his heart is overgrown with thick col- lops of fat ' (Conington). The Scriptural parallels are familiar : Psa., 119, 70; Matt., 13, 15; John, 12, 40. The Delphin ed. comp. TERTULL., de Anima, 20 : *Opimitas impedit sapientiam*. On *opimum pingue*, comp. 1, 107.

**33. caret culpa :** Perhaps because the Stoic would not hold

him responsible, EPICTET., Diss., 1, 18. Conington well remarks that Casaubon's quotation from MENAND., Mon., 430—ὁ
μηδὲν εἰδὼς οὐδὲν ἐξαμαρτάνει—does not meet the case. In MENAN-
DER we have to do with 'a sin of ignorance' against others.
Here the sin is against the man's own nature. Possibly *culpa* is
=*conscientia culpae.*—**rursum non bullit :** ' he makes no bubbles,'
'makes no further struggles,' ' he is down among the dead men.'

**34-43.** The terrors of remorse.

**36. velis :** 'deign.' *Velle* gives a reverential turn to the wish.

**37. moverit :** Perf. Subj. Attraction of mood. G., 666; A.,
66, 2.—**ferventi tincta veneno :** The *gelidum venenum* chills, this
poison fires the blood. Comp. ALCIPHR., 1, 37, 3 : ϑερμότερον
φάρμακον, of a love potion. *Occultum inspires ignem fallasque
veneno*, VERG., Aen., 1, 688. *Tincta* is a reminiscence of the
shirt of Nessus and the bridal-gift of Medea to Glaucé.

**38. intabescant :** belongs to the same sphere of comparison.
*Intabescere*, κατατήκεσθαι, is hopeless pining for a lost love.
Comp. THEOCR., 1, 66 ; 11, 14. For the figure, see Ov., Met., 3,
487 : *ut intabescere flavae | igne levi cerae—solent, sic attenuatus
amore | liquitur.*—**relicta :** sc. *virtute.* Conington comp. VERG.,
Aen., 4, 692 : *quaesivit caelo lucem ingemuitque reperta. Relicta
=quod reliquerint.*

**39. anne** =*an.*—**Siculi iuvenci :** Every one has heard of the
brazen bull made by Perillus for Phalaris of Agrigentum, CIC,
Off., 2, 7, 26, and the sword of Damocles, in the next verse, is a
proverb in English. Comp. HOR., Od., 3, 1, 17 ; CIC., Tusc. Dis., 5,
21, 61.—**aera :** poet. Plur. Vivid personification and identifica-
tion.

**40. auratis laquearibus** =*de a. l. Laquearibus*, 'sunken panels
(*lacus*) between the cross-beams of the ceiling.' See VERG., Aen.,
1, 726.—**ensis :** a poetic word, ' glaive,' ' brand.'

**41. purpureas cervices :** Damocles was arrayed in royal purple ; hence *purpureas* (Casaubon). Others apply the expression to
tyrants generally. Comp. HOR., Od., 1, 35, 12 : *purpurei tyranni.*

**42. imus :** Better to have a sword hanging by a hair over your
neck than yourself to be hanging above an abyss of misery. The
commentators refer to Tiberius's letter to the senate (TAC., Ann., 6,
6 ; SUET., Tib., 67), by way of illustrating the shuddering perplexi-

ty of the sinful tyrant.—**dicat:** The subject is loosely involved.—
**intus | palleat:** This 'not very intelligible expression' (Coning-
ton) is paralleled by SHAKSP., Macb., 2, 2 : 'My hands are of your
color, but I shame | to wear a heart so *white.*'

**43. quod:** dependent on the notion of fear contained in *pallere.*
G., 329, R. 1 ; A., 52, 1, *a.*—**proxima uxor:** 'the wife at his side,'
'the wife of his bosom.'—**nesciat:** 'is not to know.'

**44-51.** You have not the excuse of an unenlightened conscience, nor have you the plea of the ignorance of boyhood.
Boys will be boys. I was a boy myself, played boyish tricks,
loved boyish sports. My training was bad, my behavior only to
be justified by my training.

**44. parvus:** 'as a small boy:' *Memini quae plagosum mihi
parvo | Orbilium dictare,* HOR., Ep., 2, 1, 70.—**olivo:** The boy
would tip (*tangere*) his eyes with oil, in order to make believe, by
the use of the remedy, that he was suffering from the disease.
For the anointing of sore eyes, see HOR., Sat., 1, 3, 25 ; Ep., 1,
1, 29.

**45. grandia:** 'sublime.' *Grandia verba* is the American 'tall
talk.'—**nollem:** Iterative conditional. G., 569, R. 2 ; A., 59, 5, *b.*
—**morituri Catonis:** Such compositions were very much in
vogue as rhetorical exercises. Comp. JUV., 1, 16 (oration to
Sulla, advising a withdrawal from public life) ; 7, 161 (speech
made for Hannibal). SENECA (Ep., 24, 6) does not seem to regard the theme of Cato's death as threadbare.

**46. discere:** better than *dicere.* The boy shirks the learning
rather than the speaking, and the sore eyes would be a better
excuse for the one than for the other.—**non sano:** Comp. PE-
TRON., cap. 1 ; TAC., Or., 35, on this system of training. Hermann
reads *et insano.*—**laudanda** = *quae laudaret,* the free adjective use
of the Gerundive, which is more common in later times.

**47. quae pater audiret:** JUV., 7, 166 : *ut totiens illum pater
audiat.*—**sudans:** from excitement; hardly 'in a glow of per-
spiring ecstasy' (Conington). *Sudans* is thrown in maliciously
as a comment.

**48. iure:** εἰκότως, 'and well I might.'—**etenim:** is καὶ γάρ.
Theoretically the predicate of the preceding sentence is to be repeated with the *et.* Practically it is often best to leave *et* un-

translated.  G., 500, R. 2 and 3;  A., 43, 3, *d.*—**senio,** etc.: 'The game was played with four *tali*, which, unlike the *tesserae*, were rounded on two sides, while the other four faces were marked with one, three, four, or six pips, and called respectively *unio, ternio, quaternio, senio.*  The *canis* was the worst throw, when all four *tali* showed single pips (Ov., A. A., 2, 206;  Trist., 2, 474; MART., 13, 1, 6;  PROP., 4, 8, 46), and the *Venus* the best, when all the faces turned up were different (LUCIAN, Amor., p. 415);  or else, for it varied upon occasion, when all showed sices.  The ace was a losing throw and the sice a winning one, when the pips were counted' (Pretor, after Jahn).  PERSIUS wanted to know the value of each throw, what one brought in (*ferret*) another swept off (*raderet*).

**49. scire erat in voto:** *Hoc erat in votis,* HOR., Sat., 2, 6, 1.

**50. angustae collo non fallier orcae:** The allusion is to a game at *nuces*, called τρόπα, or 'cherry-pit.'  ''Tis not for gravity to play at *cherry-pit* with Satan,' SHAKSP., Twelfth N., 3, 4.  Fr. *à la fossette.*  Comp. RABELAIS, 1, 2.  The modern equivalent of *nuces* is marbles, and the modern τρόπα is 'pitch-in-the-hole,' or 'knucks.'  Instead of the hole in the ground (βόθρος), the ancients used a small jar (*orca*), and to enhance the difficulty of getting in, the neck of this jar was made narrow (*collo angustae orcae* = *angusto collo orcae*, by Hypallagê, v. 4).  So the modern hole admits but one marble.  Comp. [Ov.] Nux, 85, 86: *Vas quoque saepe cavum spatio distante locatur,* | *in quod missu levi nux cadat una manu.*—**fallier:** like *dicier*, 1, 28.

**51. nou quis** = *et ne quis.*  G., 546.  '*Et [erat in voto] ne quis callidior [esset].*'—**buxum:** 'top,' because made of 'boxwood.'  Comp. VERG., Aen., 7, 382: *volubile buxum.*—**torquere:** See Prol., 11, and 1, 118.

**52.** You have had a better training.  You have reached years of discretion.  You know Right from Wrong.—**curvos** = *pravos.*  Comp. *scilicet ut possem curvo dinoscere rectum,* HOR., Ep., 2, 2, 44, and PERSIUS, 4, 12;  5, 38.

**53. quaeque docet:** *Quae* depends by Zeugma on some notion involved in *deprendere*, such as *tenere.*  G., 690;  M., 478, Obs. 4. —**sapiens porticus:** Comp. *sapientem barbam,* HOR., Sat., 2, 3, 35; *eruditus pulvis,* CIC., N. D., 2, 18, 48.—**bracatis inlita Medis:** The στοὰ ποικίλη, the resort of Zeno and his school, was adorned with paintings by Polygnotus and others.   One of these paintings represented the battle of Marathon, hence 'the wise Porch bepainted with the trouser'd Medes.'   *Inlita* perhaps contemptuous, not necessarily 'frescoed.'   The *bracae* (ἀναξυρίδες, ϑύλακοι), a mark of barbaric luxury and display.   Comp. PROP., 4, 3, 17 : *Tela fugacis equi et bracati militis arcus* and *Persica braca*, Ov., Tr., 5, 10, 34 (Freund).—**quibus:** Neuter.   *Quibus et = et quibus.* Trajection, G., 693.—**detonsa:** 'close-cropped,' for so the Stoics wore their hair, although they let their beard grow long (ἐν χρῷ κουρίαι), LUC., Hermot., 18 ; Vit. Auct., 20.   Comp. JUV., 2, 15 : *supercilio brevior coma.*

**55. invigilat:** 'rather tautological after *insomnis. Nec capiat somnos invigiletque malis*, Ov., Fast., 4, 530' (Conington).   Positive and negative sides of an action are more frequently combined in Latin and Greek than in English, and 'sleepless vigil' would not be strange even in English.—**siliquis:** 'pulse.' HOR., Ep., 2, 1, 123 : *vivit [vates] siliquis et pane secundo.*—**grandi polenta:** 'mighty messes of porridge;' coarse, thick stuff (Macleane). '*Polenta*, ἄλφιτα, "pearl barley," a Greek, not a Roman dish (PLIN., H. N., 18, 19, 28), mentioned as a simple article of diet by Attalus, SENECA's preceptor (Ep., 110, 18) ' (Conington, after Jahn).

**56. Samios** = Pythagorean, from Pythagoras of Samos.   'And the letter, which is disparted into Samian branches, has pointed out to you the steep path whose track is on the right.'—**diduxit:** as demanded by the sense against the MSS., which have *deduxit.*—**littera:** The letter Y, or rather its old form Y, was selected by Pythagoras to embody the immemorial image of the two paths (HESIOD, O. et D., 287–292), so familiar in the apologue of Hercules at the cross-roads (XEN., Comm., 2, 1, 20), and alluded to again by our author, 5, 34.   Hence this letter was called the Pythagorean; AUSON., Id., 12, de litt. monos., 9 : *Pythagorae bivium ramis patet ambiguis Y* (comp. also Id., 15, 1 : *quod vitae sectabor iter?*)   Hence the *rami Samii* above.   'The stem stands for the unconscious life of infancy and childhood, the diverging branches for the alternative offered to the youth, virtue or vice' (Conington).

**57. surgentem:** The path to the right is the *surgens callis* of

PERSIUS, the ὅρθιος οἶμος of HESIOD. The character itself points upward, and the right-hand path is a clear-cut line (*limes*), so that there is no mistaking the road, unless you are bent on following Shakspeare's 'primrose path of dalliance,' instead of 'the steep and thorny path to heaven.'

**58. stertis adhuc:** The preacher finds his audience still snoring, despite his eloquence. As *stertis* can not be divorced from what follows, it is better to take it as an exclamation than as a rhetorical question.—**laxumque caput,** etc. : 'Your head a-lolling with its coupling loose, yawns a yawn of yesterday with jaws unhinged at every point.' The head is *laxum* on account of its weight. Comp. καρηβαρεῖν, ALCIPHR., 3, 32, and MENAND., fr. 67 (4, 88 Mein.).

**59. oscitat hesternum:** 'Yawning off yesterday' (Conington); the yawn is yesterday's yawn, because it comes from yesterday's debauch, ALEXIS, fr. 277 (3, 515 Mein.).—**undique:** 'from all points of the compass' (Conington), 'an intentional exaggeration for *utraque parte.*'—**malis:** Jahn's *malis?* (1843) is not good. The description is too minute for the interrogative form.

**60. est aliquid:** Ironical; hence the expectation of a negative answer is suppressed. G., 634, R. 1 ; A., 65, 2, *a.*—**quo** = *in quod.* Schlüter combines with *tendis arcum.*—**in quod:** The other reading, *in quo*, is unsatisfactorily defended by Hermann and Pretor.

**61.** 'A wild-goose chase' is the corresponding English expression for the Latin *corvos sequi,* the Greek ἰὰ πετόμενα διώκειν. 'Each word is carefully selected. Thus the chase is a random one (*passim*), the object worthless (*corvos*), the missile any thing that comes first to hand' (Pretor, after Jahn). Jahn refers further to AESCHYL., Ag., 394 (Dind.) : διώκει παῖς ποτανὸν ὄρνιν. Familiar is EURIP. : πτηνὰς διώκεις, ὦ τέκνον, τὰς ἐλπίδας.

**62. ex tempore:** 'for the moment,' 'at the beck of the moment,' 'by the rule of the moment' (Conington).

**63-76.** A general preachment begins. Wake up, you snorer. Wake up, all you snorers. You are all sick, or all threatened with sickness. Do not postpone the remedy until it is too late. That remedy is to be found in the principles of true wisdom ; in other words, in the doctrines of the Stoic creed. Before the sermon is finished, the preacher notices an unfriendly stir in his audience, and is punching a member of his congregation when he is interrupted.

**63. helleborum:** The black hellebore this time (1, 51). The black was good for dropsy, PLIN., H. N., 25, 5, 22. It was the great 'purger of melancholy.'—**cutis aegra tumebit:** Comp. vv. 95, 98.—**venienti occurrite morbo:** Every one will remember the well-worn Ovidian *Principiis obsta*, R. A., 91. The comparison of moral with physical disease was a favorite topic with the Stoics, who overdid it, according to CIC., Tusc. Dis., 4, 10, 23.

**64. poscentis:** Elsewhere PERSIUS uses after *video* the less vivid Infinitive, 1, 19. 69; 3, 91. On the difference, see G., 527, R. 1; A., 72, 3, *d*. So after *facio*, 1, 44.

**65. quid opus:** G., 390, R. ; A., 52, 3, *a.* — **Cratero:** More bookishness. Craterus was a famous physician of the time of CICERO. HOR., Sat., 2, 3, 161.—**magnos promittere montis:** A proverbial phrase, which survives in several modern languages : Fr. *monts et merveilles;* Germ. *goldene Berge versprechen.* Jahn compares TER., Phormio, 1, 2, 18 : *modo non montis auri pollicens;* Heinr., SALL., Cat. 23 : *maria montisque polliceri coepit.*

**66. discite o:** To remove the hiatus, Barth suggested *io*, Guyet *vos.* HOR., Od., 3, 14, 11 : *male ominatis*, is not a parallel for the hiatus, even if the reading be correct, and the parallel in CATULL., 3, 16, is conjectural. — **causas cognoscite rerum:** Comp. VERG., Georg., 2, 490: *Felix qui potuit rerum cognoscere causas*, and *sapientia est rerum divinarum et humanarum causarumque scientia*, CIC., Off., 2, 2, 5. On the connection of the different articles of this catechism, see Knickenberg, l. c. p. 35 seqq. *Discite* is the exhortation to the study of philosophy. *Causas cognoscite rerum* bids us pursue what the Stoics called Physic, for without a knowledge of nature there can be no knowledge of duty. Ethic is based on Physic ; τέλος ἐστὶ τὸ ὁμολογουμένως τῇ φύσει ζῆν (STOB., Ecl., 2, 132). See Long's *Antoninus*, p. 56. The constitution of nature once understood, we shall know what we owe to God, what to ourselves, what to mankind, what things are good, what evil. *Quid fas optare* refers to our duty to God, *quem te deus esse iussit* to our duty to ourselves, *patriae carisque propinquis* to our duty to our neighbors. But nothing is more evident than the absence of any logical development. Comp. with the whole passage, SEN., Ep., 82, 6 : *sciat quo iturus sit, unde ortus, quod illi bonum, quod malum sit, quid petat, quid evitet, quae sit illa ratio quae appetenda ac fugienda discernat, qua cupiditatum mansuescit insania, timorum saevitia conpescitur.*

**67. quid sumus:** The independent form with the Indicative is more lively; the regular dependent form with the Subjunctive comes in below, v. 71.  G., 469, R. 1; A., 67, 2, *d*.—**quidnam** = *quam vitam.*   G., 331, R. 2;  A., 52, 3, *a*, N. — **victuri:** The use of the Participle in an interrogative clause is unnatural in English (G., 471). The future Participle of purpose is late or poetical (G., 673; A., 72, 4, *a*).   'And what the life that we are born to lead.'—**ordo:** According to Heinr. and Jahn *ordo* is used with reference to the position in the chariot-race, so that the comparison begins here, and not at *metae.*   SOPH., El., 710 : στάν-τες δ᾿ ἵν᾿ αὐτοὺς οἱ τεταγμένοι βραβεῖς | κλήροις ἔπηλαν καὶ κατέστησαν δίφρους.   But as τάξις (*ordo*) is a Stoic term, it is not unlikely that the use of the word suggested the figure, which came in as an after-thought.   The Stoic preacher, as well as the Christian, finds it necessary to repeat himself in slightly different forms, and we must not look for a sharp distinction between *ordo quis datus* and *humana qua parte locatus es in re*, between *quidnam victuri gignimur* and *quem te deus esse iussit.*

**68. quis** = *qui*.  So 1, 63.   G., 105 ;   A., 21, 1, *a*.—**qua et unde:** where (how) it lies and from what point to begin, 'where to take it' (Conington).   Herm.'s *quam* is not so good.—**metae flexus:** 'turn round the goal.'   The difficulty of rounding the goal in a chariot race is notorious.   See Il., 23, 306 foll. ;  SOPH., El., 720 foll., and the commentators on PLATO, Io, 537.   With the expression *metae flexus* Jahn comp. STAT., Theb., 6, 433 : *flexae —metae.   Mollis*, 'gradual,' 'easy.'   So CAES., B. G., 5, 9 : *molle litus*, of a gently sloping shore.

**69. quis modus argento:** The Sixth Satire deals with a similar theme.—**quid fas optare:** the argument of the Second Satire. —**asper nummus:** 'coin fresh from the mint,' 'rough from the die,' SUET., Nero, 44.  So Jahn.   Others consider this distinction too subtle, and make *a. n.* simply equivalent to 'coined silver,' as opposed to 'silver plate,' *argentum.*   Conington suggests the meaning, 'What is the use of money hoarded up and not circulated (*tritus*)?' Comp. HOR., Sat., 1, 1, 41 foll., 73 : *nescis quo valeat nummus? quem praebeat usum?*

**70. carisque propinquis:** HOR., Sat., 1, 1, 83.

**72. locatus:** 'posted,' τεταγμένος, 'a military metaphor' (ARRIAN, Diss., 1, 9, 16 ; M. ANTON., 11, 13).—**humana re:** 'humanity,' *inter homines.*

**73. disce, nec invideas:** sc. *discere,* according to Jahn. *His te quoque iungere, Caesar | invideo,* LUCAN., 2, 550, like φθονεῖν : μὴ φθόνει μοι ἀποκρίνασθαι τοῦτο, PLAT., Gorg., 489 A. PERSIUS singles out one of his audience, who is tempted away from philosophy by his gains as an advocate. Others, less satisfactorily, suppose that the lawyer is outside of the congregation. On *nec invideas,* see 1, 7.—**multa fidelia putet :** 'Many a jar of good things is spoiling ;' 'The details are contemptuous. There is a coarseness in fees paid in kind' (Conington). Comp. JUV., 7, 119.—**pinguibus Umbris :** 'fat' in every sense, in figure, in fortune, and in wit. In MART., 7, 53, an Umbrian sends by eight huge Syrian slaves a miscellaneous lot of presents, value 30 nummi—a proceeding due as much to stupidity as to stinginess (*parcus Umber,* CAT., 39, 11). The appearance of the Umbrians was not prepossessing, if we may judge by OVID's portrait of an Umbrian dame (A. A., 3, 303–4).

**75. et piper et pernae:** The *piper* is not the Indian, but the inferior Italian (PLIN., H. N., 12, 7, 4 ; 16, 32, 59) (Meister). *Pernae,* a stock present. Comp. *siccus petasunculus et vas | pelamydum,* JUV., 7, 119. To supply *putet* with *piper* is not satisfactory, and we must take refuge in Zeugma. Pretor is for dropping v. 75, and sees in PERSIUS's awkwardness traces of a *duplex recensio,* as in vv. 12–14.—**Marsi :** For the simplicity of the Marsians, Jahn compares JUV., 3, 169 ; 14, 180.

**76. mena :** 'sprat,' cheap sea-fish of some sort. 'You have not yet come to the last sprat of the first barrel' (Conington).—**defecerit :** As *non quod* more commonly takes the Subjunctive, the shifting to the Subjunctive from the Indicative, after *nec invideas,* is not strange. G., 541, R. 1 ; A., 66, 1, *d,* R.

**77-85.** The discourse is cut short by a military man, who, with the dogmatism of his class (*vieux soldat, vieille bête*), sets down all philosophers as a pack of noodles. The lines of the picture

which he draws are familiar to every student of manners. 'PER-
SIUS hates the military cordially (comp. 5, 189–191) as the most
perfect specimens of developed animalism, and consequently most
antipathetic to a philosopher. See Nisard, *Études sur les Po-
ëtes Latins* [1, 3ᵉ éd. 273–277 ; Martha, *Moralistes Romains*, p. 141].
HORACE merely glances at the education their sons received, as
contrasted with that given him by his father, in spite of narrow
means, Sat., 1, 6, 72. JUVENAL has an entire satire on them (16),
in which he complains of their growing power and exclusive
privileges, but without any personal jealousy' (Conington). PER-
SIUS is so bookish that I suspect Greek influence. Comp. κομψὸς
στρατιώτης, οὐδ' ἐὰν πλάττῃ θεός, | οὐδεὶς γένοιτ' ἄν, MENAND., fr. 711
(4, 277 Mein.). See Introd., xx.

**77. de gente:** G., 371, R. 5 ; A., 50, 2, *e*, R. 1. *Gente*, 'tribe,'
'crew.'—**hircosa:** 'Rammish' is not too strong, opposed to *un-
guentatus* in a fragment of SEN., ap. GELL., 12, 2, 11 (cited by Jahn).
The unsavory soldier and the perfumed dandy are alike foes to
the simplicity of the Stoic school. Your old soldier prided himself on his stench, as would appear from the dainty anecdote in
PLUTARCH, Mor., 180 C: ὦ βασιλεῦ, θάρρει καὶ μὴ φοβοῦ τὸ πλῆθος
τῶν πολεμίων, αὐτὸν γὰρ ἡμῶν τὸν γράσον οὐχ ὑπομενοῦσι.—**centurionum:** The rank is higher, but the intellectual level is that
of the typical German *Wachtmeister*.

**78. Quod sapio satis est mihi:** Jahn (1868) ; *Quod satis est sapio mihi*, Jahn (1843), Herm. With the latter reading the words
*quod satis est = satis* must bo taken together, and a little more
stress is laid on *mihi*. The general sense is the same. Comp.
PLATO, Phaedr., 242 C: ὥσπερ οἱ τὰ γράμματα φαῦλοι ὅσον ἐμαυτῷ
μόνον ἱκανός, with a very different tone.—**non ego:** 'no—not I.'
See 1, 45.—**curo:** 'care,' i. e., 'want.' See 2, 18.

**79. Arcesilas:** Arcesilaus, the founder of the New Academy,
flourished about 300 B.C. His great advance on Socrates was his
knowing that he did not even know that he knew nothing, CIC.,
Acad., 1, 12, 45. Solon flourished about 600 B.C. Our hircose
friend is made to jumble his samples.—**aerumnosi Solones:** Notice the contemptuous use of the Plural. *Aerumnosus*, κακοδαίμων,
'God-forsaken,' 'poor devil,' is a strange epithet for Solon, but
we have to do with an ignoramus and a jolter-head.

**80. obstipo capite :** 'with stooped head,' 'bent forward,' κεκυ-
φότες. HOR., Sat., 2, 5, 92 : *Davus sis comicus atque | stes capite
obstipo, multum similis metuenti.*   Comp. the description of
Ulysses in Il., 3, 217 foll.—**figentes lumine terram :** Jahn quotes
a parallel from STAT., Silv., 5, 1, 140.   More common forms are
*figere lumina terra, in humo, in terram.*   'They bore the ground
with their eyes,' 'look at it as if they would look through it.'
Casaubon comp. PLAT., Alcib. II., 138 A.   Add LUCIAN, Vit. Auct.,
7 ; ARISTAENET., 1, 15.

**81. murmura :** Imitated by AUSON., Id., 17, 24 : *murmure con-
cluso rabiosa silentia rodunt.*—**rabiosa :** 'Mad dogs do not bark.'
—**silentia :** Poetic Plural ; very common.—**rodunt :** 'biting the
lips and grinding the teeth.'   'Whether *murmura* and *silentia*
are Accusatives of the object, or cognates, is not clear' (Conington).   'Chewing the cud of mumbled words and mad-dog silence' is very much in the vein of PERSIUS.   Comp. *rarus sermo
illis et magna libido tacendi,* JUV., 2, 14.

**82. exporrecto trutinantur :** The lips are thrust out (a sign
of deep thought) and quiver like a balance ; hence they are said
'to poise their words upon the quivering balance of a thrust-out
lip'—a caricature of the simple figure *ponderare verba.*   Jahn
compares LUC., Hermot., 1, 1 : καὶ τὰ χείλη διεσάλενες ἠρέμα
ὑποτονθορύζων ; and Casaubon, ARISTAEN., 2, 3 : ἠρέμα τῶ χείλη
κινεῖ καὶ ἄττα δήπου πρὸς ἑαυτὸν ψιθυρίζει.

**83. aegroti veteris :** The *aegri somnia* of HOR., A. P., 7.   As
usual, PERSIUS exaggerates, and makes the sick man (*aegroti*) a
dotard to boot (*veteris*).   Jahn understands, 'a confirmed inva-
lid.'   Comp. JUV., 9, 16 : *aegri veteris quem tempore longo | torret
quarta dies,* etc.—**gigni | de nihilo nihilum :** The cardinal doc-
trine of Epicurus (LUCR., 1, 150), but not confined to him.

**85. hoc est quod palles :** G., 331, R. 2 ; A., 52, 1, *b.*   Comp. 1,
124.   The Cognate Accusative is susceptible of a great variety of
translations.   'Is this the stuff that you get pale on ?' (Pretor).
'Is this what makes you pale ?'—**prandeat :** The *prandium,* originally a military meal, was dear to the military stomach.   Comp.
*impransi correptus voce magistri,* HOR., Sat., 2, 3, 257.

**86. his :** Abl.   Conington makes it a Dative, and cites an evident Abl. to prove it, VERG., Aen., 4, 128.   Jahn comp. HOR.,

Sat., 2, 8, 83 : *ridetur fictis rerum.*—**multum :** with *torosa,* accord-ing to Jahn.

**87.** Conington notices the grandiloquence of the line. ' Cloth of frize ' is often ' matched ' with ' cloth of gold ' in PERSIUS.—**naso crispante :** ' curling nostrils.' The mob laughs, the soldiers snicker. The listening rabble is frankly amused. The crew to which the centurion belongs sneer too much to laugh out. Or perhaps the poet makes the distinction between the general *ri-dere* (γελᾶν) and the mocking laughter of *cachinnare* (καγχάζειν).

**88-106.** It is strange, as Pretor observes, that the sudden change introduced by this line should not have been noticed by the commentators. With a more mature artist there would be a suspicion of dislocation. As it is, the unity of the Satire would gain by omitting 66–87. PERSIUS composed slowly, and we find here as elsewhere traces of piecemeal work.

The preacher takes up his parable. A man feels sick, consults a physician, lies by ; is more comfortable, takes a fancy to a bath and a draught of wine. He meets a friend, perhaps his medical friend, on the way. ' My dear fellow, you are pale as a ghost.'— ' Pshaw !'—' Look out ! You are yellow as saffron, and bless me ! if you are not swelling.'—' Pale ? Why, you are paler than I am. Don't come the guardian over me. My guardian has been dead a year and a day.'—' Go ahead, I'm mum.'—He goes ahead, stuffs himself, takes his bath. While he is drinking a chill strikes him, and he is a dead man. No expense spared on the funeral. ' You can't mean that for me,' says a literalist. ' If I'm sick, you are another. I have no fever, no ague.' Nay, but you are subject to the worst of diseases—to the fever of covetousness, the fever of lust, to daintiness with its sore mouth, to fear with its cold chill, and, worse than all, to the raging delirium of anger.

**88. inspice :** ἐπίσκεψαι, a medical term. Comp. PLAUT., Pers., 2, 5, 15.—**nescio quid :** G., 469, R. 2 ; A., 67, 2, *e. Quid* is the Accusative of the Inner Object ' I have a strange fluttering at my heart.'—**aegris :** ' out of order.' As *aegris* is emphatic, co-ordinate in English. There is ' something wrong about my throat *and*—'

**89. exsuperat :** Neuter. Comp. *exsuperant flammae,* VERG., Aen., 2, 759.—**gravis :** ' foul.' So Ov., A. A., 3, 277 : *gravis oris* *odor.*—**sodes:** The original form is commonly supposed to be *si audes* (*saudes*), PLAUT., Trin., 2, 1, 18; from *audeo* (comp. *avidus*), ' if you have the heart,' ' an thou wilt,' A., 35, 2, *a*. Others put *sodes* under SA (pron.), as akin to *sodalis*, and comp. ἡϑεῖος, 'own dear friend,' '*mon cher.*' See Vaniček, *Lat. Etym. Wb.*, S. 165. *Sodes* = *socius* is an old tradition.

**90. requiescere:** ' keep quiet.'—**postquam vidit:** with a causal shade. See 5, 88; 6, 10, and G., 567; A., 62, 2, *e*.

**91. tertia nox:** The patient thinks that he has the more common semitertian, whereas he has the quartan. When the third night comes without a chill, he fancies that he is safe.

**92. de maiore domo:** The 'great house' is clearly that of a rich friend, rather than that of a large dealer. Casaubon compares JUV., 5, 32 : *cardiaco numquam cyathum missurus amico.*— **modice sitiente lagoena:** Thirst and capacity are near akin; a flagon of moderate thirst is a flagon ' of moderate swallow,' as Conington renders it. The personification of the flagon is old and not uncommon. See the humorous epigram, ANTHOL. PAL., 5, 135.

**93. lenia Surrentina:** *Lenia* is either ' mild ' or ' mellow.' The Surrentine was a light wine often recommended to invalids, PLIN., H. N., 14, 6, 8; 23, 1, 20.—**loturo:** He asks *before* bathing; he drinks *after* bathing. For the custom Jahn compares SEN., Ep., 122, 6.—**rogabit:** So Jahn (1868) and Hermann. Jahn (1843) reads *rogavit*, like the Greek Aorist in descriptions. The Future makes it more distinctly a supposed case.

**94. videas:** rather optative than imperative in its tone.

**95. surgit:** ' is swelling,' ' getting bloated.'—**tacite:** ' insensibly ' (Conington).—**pellis:** ' hide.' Comp. JUV., 10, 192 : *deformem pro cute pellem.*

**96. At tu deterius:** *Le trait est comique. Ce serait de la gaieté, si Perse savait rire*, Nisard.—**ne sis mihi tutor,** etc.: Proverbial. So HOR., Sat., 2, 3, 88 : *ne sis patruus mihi.*

**97. iam pridem sepeli:** Comp. *Omnes composui. Felices! Nunc ego resto*, HOR., Sat., 1, 9, 28. *Sepeli* for *sepelii* (*sepelivi*), a rare contraction. — **turgidus hic epulis:** HOR., Ep., 1, 6, 61 : *crudi tumidique lavemur*, and comp. JUV., 1, 142 seqq : *paena tamen praesens, cum tu deponis amictus* | *turgidus et crudum pavonem in*

*bulnea portas* | *hinc subitae mortes atque intestata senectus.*—**hic:**
'our man.'—**albo ventre:** *Turgidus epulis* is one feature, *albo
ventre* another. *Ventre* does not depend on *turgidus.* The color
(λευκός) is a sign of weakness and sickness. The swollen belly
makes a ghastly show.—**lavatur:** 'takes his bath.' Comp. G.,
209; A., 39, *c*, N.

**99. sulpureas mefites:** *Mefitis* is originally the vapor from sul-
phur-water; hence the propriety of the epithet *sulpureas.*

**100. calidum triental:** The wine was heated to bring out the
sweat. *Bibere et sudare vita cardiaci est*, SEN., Ep.,15,3.—**triental:**
restored by Jahn (1843) for *trientem*, to which he returned in
1868. *Triens* is the measure, ⅓ sextarius, *triental* would be the
vessel. Comp. with this passage LUCIL., 28, 39–40 (L. M.): *ad
cui? quem febris una atque una ἀπεψία* | *vini inquam cyathus unus
potuit tollere.*

**101. crepuere:** Vivid Aorist, not a simple return to the narra-
tive form. Comp. 5, 187. For the Greek, which PERSIUS imitates, see Kühner, *Ausf. Gramm.* (*2te Ausg.*), 2, 138.—**retecti:** He
shows his teeth when he chatters.

**102. uncta:** Remember the large use of oil in Italian cookery.
—**cadunt** = *vomuntur*, but there is a certain helplessness in *cadunt.*
—**pulmentaria:** originally ὄψον, 'relish,' afterward 'dainties.'
See the Dictionaries.

**103. hinc:** 'hereupon.' **tuba:** Trumpets announced the death,
and trumpets were sounded at the funeral. See HOR., Sat., 1, 6,
42.—**candelae** = *cerei*, 'wax lights,' supposed by Jahn and others
to have been used chiefly when the death was sudden, on the
basis of SEN., Tranq., 11, 7.—**tandem:** 'After all the preliminary
performances' (Macleane). — **beatulus:** μακαρίτης. Jahn cites
AMM. MARCELL., 25, 3: *quem cum beatum fuisse Sallustius respon-
disset praefectus, intellexit occisum.* 'The dear departed' (Conington). 'Our sainted friend.'—**alto:** A mark of a first-class funeral.

**104. conpositus:** 'laid out.' 'By foreign hands thy decent
limbs *composed*,' POPE. — **crassis lutatus amomis:** Every word
is contemptuous: 'bedaubed with lots of coarse ointments.' The
Plural *amoma* indicates the cheap display. With *crassis*, comp.
HOR., A. P., 375: *crassum unguentum;* with *amomis*, JUV., 4,
108: *amomo* | *quantum vix redolent duo funera.*

**105. in portam:** A custom at least as old as Homer, Il., 19, 212. *Porta* here = *ianua, fores,* but 'nowhere else' (Macleane). —**rigidas:** The gender of *calx* is unsteady. See Neue, *Formenlehre,* 1, 694.

**106. hesterni Quirites:** 'Citizens of twenty-four hours' standing' (Conington); slaves left free by him. Hence *capite induto,* with the *pilleus* 'cap of liberty' on. The winding up of the man reminds one of Petron., 42 : *bene elatus est, planctus est optime, manumisit aliquot.*

**107.** Persius hauls out his man-of-straw, his *souffre-douleur,* and makes him talk.—**Tange venas:** 'Feel my pulse,' the regular expression, as in Sen., Ep., 22, 1 : *vena tangenda est.*—**miser:** Comp. v. 15. 'You're another!' 'Poor creature yourself' (Conington).—**pone in pectore dextram:** If you are not satisfied with my pulse, put your hand on my heart.

**108. nil calet hic:** After some hesitation, I have given the whole passage from *Tange miser* to *non frigent* to one person, who anticipates the verdict of the monitor by *nil calet hic* and *non frigent.* 'You must admit that my heart is not hot nor my feet cold.' At the same time the very clearness is an objection.

**109. Visa est si forte:** On the form of the conditional, see G., 569; A., 59, 2, *b.* On the obvious thought, see 2, 52 foll.; 4, 47.

**111. rite:** 'regularly.'—**positum est:** 'served up.'

**112. durum holus:** 'tough cabbage,' 'half boiled' (Pretor). —**populi** (= *plebis*) **cribro:** 'A coarse, common sieve.' Hence *p. c. decussa farina,* 'coarse-bolted flour,' the *panis secundus* of Horace, Ep., 2, 1, 123, the 'seconds' of the modern miller. The ancients were very dainty in this article. The parasite in Alciphron (1, 21, 2) expresses his disgust at the ἄρτος ὁ ἐξ ἀγορᾶς.

**114. putre quod haud deceat:** The Relative with the Subjunctive is parallel with the Adjective. G., 439, R. Comp. 1, 14. *Haud deceat,* 'it won't do,' 'it won't answer.'—**plebeia beta:** The beet is a vulgar vegetable, Mart., 13, 13 (Jahn). The irony is evident, as the beet is proverbially tender. See Dictionaries, s. v. *betizare.*

**115. excussit:** *Excutere aristas* seems to be a vulgar expression, like the English 'raise a goose-skin, goose-flesh, duck-flesh.'

—**aristas** = *pilos.* Jahn refers to VARRO, L. L., 6, 49.—**timor albus :** See note on Prol., 4.

**116. face supposita :** The heart is the caldron and passion the fire-brand.

**118. Orestes :** the typical madman.

---

## ' FOURTH SATIRE.

THE theme of this Satire is contained in the closing verses. It is the Apollinic γνῶ̂3ι σαυτ̀ν. Want of self-knowledge is the fault which is scourged. The basis is furnished by the Platonic dialogue, known as the First Alcibiades, and the characters are the same. The person lectured under the mask of Alcibiades is a young Roman noble, in whom commentators of a certain school have recognized the familiar features of Nero.

ARGUMENT.—Socrates is supposed to be addressing Alcibiades. You undertake to engage in politics? You rely on your genius, do you? What do you know of the norms of right and wrong, you callow youngster? What do you know of the subtle distinctions of casuistry, that you undertake to say what is just and what is unjust? You have a goodly outside, but that is all, and you are fitter for a course of hellebore than for a career of statesmanship. What is your end and aim in life? Dainty dishes and basking in the sunshine? The first old crone you meet has the same exalted ideal. Or do you boast of your descent? You praise your lineage, you trumpet forth your beauty, just as yon market-woman cries up her greens (1–22).

You do not know yourself. Who knows himself? Every one sees his neighbor's faults, no one his own. You sneer at the curmudgeon who groans out a health over the sour stuff he gives his laborers on a holiday (23–32). And while you make mock at him, some fellow, who is standing at your side, nudges you with his elbow, and tells you that you are as bad as he, though in another way (33–41). And so we give and take punishment. This is our plan of life. We hide our faults from ourselves. We get testimonials from our neighbors to impose on our own consciences. Awake to righteousness! Put your goodness to the test! If you yield to the temptation of covetousness, of lust, in vain will you drink in the praises of the rabble. Reject what you are not. Let Rag, Tag, and Bobtail take away their tributes. Live with yourself, and you will find out how scanty is your moral furniture (42–52).

---

Jahn regards this Satire as the earliest of the six, and it certainly shows even greater immaturity than the others. The well-known individuality of Socrates is coarsely handled, the irony lacks the subtle play, the mischievous good-nature of the great Athenian; and though the glaring anachronisms may be defended by such exemplars as HORACE (notably in Sat., 2, 5), there is all the difference in the world between the sly humor of the older poet, who peeps from behind the Greek mask and winks at the Roman audience, and the grim contortions of the beardless representative of the bearded master.

The indecency of a part of the Satire is considered by Teuffel a valid objection to the view taken by Jahn, but the imagination of early youth and the experience of corrupt old age often meet in disgusting detail, and the obscenities of bookish men are among the worst in literature. Add to this the peculiar views of the Stoic school as to the corruption of the flesh (2, 63), and the consequent Stoic tendency to degrade the body by the most contemptuous representations of physical functions, and we can the more readily understand how MARCUS ANTONINUS, the purest character of his time, should have besmirched his Meditations with passages which lack a parallel for their crudity; and why PERSIUS, the poet of virginal life, should have outdone the *praegrandis senex* of Attic comedy in the coarseness of his expressions.

**1-22.** Socrates exposes the incompetence of Alcibiades for affairs of state, his lack of ethical training, his need of a just balance, his grovelling views of life, his puerile pride in his ancient family and in his handsome face. Socrates and Alcibiades were contrasts so tempting that dialogues between them were favorite philosophical exercises.

**1. rem populi** = *rem publicam.*—**tractas?** On the form of the question, see G., 455; A., 71, 1, R. Comp. PLATO, Alc. I., p. 106 C: διανοεῖ γὰρ παριέναι συμβουλεύσων Ἀθηναίοις ἐντὸς οὐ πολλοῦ χρόνου, and further, p. 118 B, and Conv., p. 216 A.—**barbatum:** The beard was the conventional mark of the philosopher in the time of PERSIUS; it is an anachronism in the case of Socrates, who lived before shaving was the rule and the beard a badge. However, the custom was old in PERSIUS's day, and the slip is slight. So Plato's long beard is noticed by EPHIPPUS ap. ATHEN., 11, p. 509 C (3, 332 Mein.). Comp. JUV., 14, 12: *barbatos—magistros.*—**crede:** advertises a want of art.

**2. sorbitio:** 'draught,' 'dose.' So SEN., E. M., 78, 25.—**tollit** = *sustulit.* A solitary Historical Present with a relative is harsh to us for all the examples and all the commentators.

**3. quo fretus?** See 3, 67. Comp. PLATO, Alc. I., p. 123 E: τί

οὖν ποτ᾽ ἔστιν ὅτῳ πιστεύει τὸ μειράκιον.—**magni pupille Pericli :**
Because Alcibiades owed his start in life to his guardian and
kinsman Pericles. See PLAT., l. c. p. 104 B. For the form *Peri-*
*cli*, see G., 72 ; A., 11, I., 4.

**4. scilicet :** Ironical, 1, 15 ; 2, 19. ' Of course.' Comp. the
old ' God wot.'—**ingenium et rerum prudentia :** ' wit and wisdom.' *Prudentia* may be translated ' knowledge,' and *rerum*
' world,' ' life,' but not necessarily. See 1, 1.—**velox :** Predicative (Schol.), ' have been quick in coming ' (Conington).

**5. ante pilos :** ' before your beard.' ' A contrast with *barba-*
*tum magistrum* ' (Conington), but *b.* can hardly be used in the same
breath as the mark of mature years and as the ensign of a philosopher.—**venit :** On the number, see G., 281, Exc. 2 ; A., 49, 1, *b.*—
**dicenda tacendaque :** Comp. HOR., Ep., 1, 7, 72—*dicenda tacenda*
*locutus*—for the expression. For the sense, Conington comp.
AESCHYLUS, Cho., 582 : σιγᾶν ὅπου δεῖ καὶ λέγειν τὰ καίρια. In
HORACE it means ' all sorts of things ;' here, ' what you must say,
what leave unsaid.'

**6. commota fervet bile :** Comp. HOR., Od., 1, 13, 4 : *fervens*
*difficili bile tumet iecur.*

**7. fert animus :** Well-known phrase of Ov., Met., 1, 1. So in
Greek, φέρει ὁ νοῦς, ἡ γνώμη, ἡ φρήν. The verse has a stately irony,
and should have a stately translation. ' The spirit moves you '
(Pretor) is degraded to slang. ' Your bosom's lord biddeth you
wave a hush profound.'—**fecisse :** Comp. 1, 91.—**sllentia :** Comp.
3, 81.

**8. maiestate manus :** ' with majestic hand ' (G., 357, R. 2), ' by
the imposing action of your hand ' (Conington).—**quid deinde loquere ?** The orator has not considered his speech. ' Now
that you have got your silence, what have you got to say.'—
**Quirites :** PERSIUS drops his Greek. Alcibiades is a mere quin-
tain.

**9. puta :** ' put case,' ' say,' ' for instance,' is an iambic Imperative, with the ultimate shortened, like *cavĕ*, *vidĕ*, etc., 1, 108.
Hermann gives it to Socrates, which is favored by the sense ;
Jahn and others to Alcibiades, as caricatured by Socrates, which
is favored by the position. Heinrich reads *puto*.

**10. scis etenim,** etc. : *and* (well you may) *for you know how,*

G

etc. On *scis*, see 1, 53; on *etenim*, 3, 48. Comp. PLATO, l. c. 110 C: ᾤου ἄρα ἐπίστασθαι καὶ παῖς ὤν, ὡς ἔοικε, τὰ δίκαια καὶ τὰ ἄδικα. It may be necessary to observe that all this is sarcasm. Coning-ton takes it literally, and considers these statements as so many concessions. — **gemina lance** =*geminis lancibus*. Comp. Ov., A. A., 2, 644: *geminus pes.*

**11. ancipitis:** 'wavering.'—**rectum discernis:** 'You can dis-tinguish the straight line when it runs among crooked lines on either hand — ay, even when your square with twisted leg is but a faulty guide.' The straight line is virtue, the crooked lines are vices. The difficulty of picking out the right course is much enhanced when the rule by which we go is itself warped—that is, 'as Casaubon explains it, when justice has to be correct-ed by equity.' The *regula* here is not the *regula* of 5, 38, but the *norma*, or carpenter's square.

**13. potis es:** See 1, 56.—**theta:** θ, the initial of θάνατος, was the mark of condemnation used in the time of PERSIUS, instead of the older C (*condemno*). It was also employed in epitaphs, in army lists, and the like, for 'deceased.' Translate 'black mark.'

**14. quin desinis:** See 2, 71.—**tu:** The elision of the monosyl-lable is harsh (Jahn). See 1, 51. 66. 131.—**igitur:** 'If all this is so, why then—.' Comp. the indignant *igitur* (εἶτα) of 1, 98.— **summa pelle decorus:** HOR., Ep., 1, 16, 45: *Introrsus turpem, speciosum pelle decora.*—**nequiquam:** 'because you can not im-pose on me.' Comp. 3, 30 (Conington).

**15. ante diem:** 'before your time.'—**blando caudam iactare popello:** Casaubon thinks that a peacock is meant, Jahn suggests a horse. The Scholiast says that the image is that of a (pet) dog. *Pelle decorus* would not apply to the peacock, nor very well to the horse. It does apply to Alcibiades as the lion's whelp of ARISTOPH., Ran., 1431. Comp. the famous description in AE-SCHYL., Agam., 725 (Dindorf). The comparison of politicians with lions is found also in PLATO, Gorg., 483 E. The only difficulty lies in *blando popello*, but petting implies *blanditiae* on both sides. 'The dog fawns on those who caress him' (Conington).—**popello:** contemptuously, 6, 50; HOR., Ep., 1, 7, 65.

**16. Anticyras:** There were two towns of that name, one on the Maliac Gulf, the other in Phocis; both famous for their hellebore, but especially the latter. The town for its product, after the pattern of Hor., Sat., 2, 3, 83; A. P., 300 (Jahn). The Plural is the familiar poetic exaggerative. — **meracas :** 'undiluted,' 'without a drop of water.' Hor., Ep., 2, 2, 137 : *expulit helleboro morbum bilemque meraco.* On the use of hellebore as a prepara- tive for philosophy, comp. the well-known experience of Chrysip- pus : οὐ ϑέμις γενέσϑαι σοφόν, ἢν μὴ τρὶς ἐφεξῆς τοῦ ἐλλεβόρου πίῃς, Lu- cian, Vit. Auct., 23 (1, 564 R.).—**melior sorbere**＝*qui melius sor- beres* (comp. *quo graves Persae melius perirent,* Hor., Od., 1, 2, 22).

**17. summa boni**＝*summum bonum.*—**uncta patella :** 'rich dish- es.' Comp. 3, 102. The reference to a sacrificial dish (3, 26) is less likely. As the character of Alcibiades is not kept up with any care by Persius, it is hardly worth while to note that he was a most sensitive *gourmet,* as is shown by the curious anecdote, Teles ap. Stob., Flor., 5, 67.—**vixisse :** The Perfect with inten- tion. G., 275, 1; A., 58, 11, *e.* 'To have the satisfaction of *hav- ing lived* on the daintiest fare,' so that you may say when you come to die, *vixi dum vixi bene.* Comp. Sen., Ep., 23, 10 : *Id agendum est ut satis vixerimus.*

**18. curata cuticula sole :** with reference to the *apricatio* or *in- solatio.* Comp. Juv., 11, 203 : *nostra bibat vernum contracta cuti- cula solem.* What was a matter of hygiene became a matter of luxury. The sun-cure has been revived of late years. *Curare cuticulam, cutem, pelliculam* is commonly used of 'good living' generally, 'taking very good care of one's dear little self.' See Hor., Ep., 1, 2, 29. 4, 15; Sat., 2, 5, 38; Juv., 2, 105.— **haec :** δεικτικῶς.—**i nunc :** '*Irridentis vel exprobrantis formula,*' Jahn, who gives an overwhelming list of examples (comp. Hor., Ep., 1, 6, 17; 2, 2, 76). The usage requires it to be connected with *suffla.* 'Go on, then, and blow as you have been blowing.' *Suffla* in this sense is quite as 'low' as our Americanism. Persius has the aristocrat's contempt for superfine language, and by a natu- ral reaction falls, not unfrequently, into slang. Jahn compares 5, 13 and 3, 27, and the Greek proverbial expression φυσᾷ γὰρ οὐ σμικροῖσιν αὐλίσκοις ἔπι. Add Menand., fr. 296 (4, 157 Mein.) : οἷοι λαλοῦμεν ὄντες οἱ τρισάϑλιοι | ἅπαντες οἱ φυσῶντες ἐφ᾽ ἑαυτοῖς μέγα. 'Mouth it out' (Conington), 'spout it out' (Macleane).

**20. Dinomaches :** The mother of Alcibiades came of the great house of the Alcmaeonidae, and it was to her that he owed his connection with Pericles. The Gen. without *filius* (G., 360, R. 3; A., 50, 1, *b*) is rare in the predicate.—**candidus** = *pulcher.* Comp. 3, 110. The beauty of Alcibiades is well known, PLAT., l. c. p. 104 A.—**esto:** εἶεν; an ironical concession.

**21. dum ne:** Comp. G., 575; A., 61, 3. Final sentences are often elliptical (comp. note on 1, 4). ' Only you must admit that,' etc.; ' *dum ne neges deterius sapere.*'—**pannucia:** Here not ' ragged,' but 'shrivelled.' Comp. MART., 11, 46, 3.—**Baucis:** The name is copied from the Baucis of OVID, Met., 8, 640, the wife of Philemon, the Joan of the antique Darby; a poor woman, who had a patch of vegetables. The *anicula quae agreste holus vendebat,* in PETRON., 6, is a similar figure.

**22. bene:** with *discincto,* according to Jahn, who compares *bene mirae,* 1, 111. Mr. Pretor says that if thus combined, ' *bene* is weak and adds nothing to the picture.' He forgets that there is such a thing as being *male discinctus.* Comp. HOR., Sat., 1, 2, 132: *discincta tunica fugiendum est ac pede nudo.* If *bene* is combined with *cantaverit,* it must be used in its mercantile sense with *vendere, cantare* being equivalent to *cantando vendere.* 'When she has cried off her herbs at a good figure.'—**discincto vernae:** *Verna,* of itself a synonym for all that is saucy and pert, is heightened by *discinctus,* for which see 3, 31.—**ocima:** 'basil,' 'watercress,' or what not, stands for ' greens' generally. Jahn thinks that it was an aphrodisiac, referring to EUBUL., fr. 53 (3, 229 Mein.). PERSIUS, as we have seen, delights in picturesque detail, and his comparisons must not be pressed. Alcibiades cries his wares, just as the herb-seller cries hers. So the ' applewoman ' or ' orange-girl ' in modern times might be selected as the standard of a rising politician, hawking his wares from hustings to hustings, from stump to stump. The far-fetched interpretation that *ocima cantare* = *convicia ingerere,* because, as PLINY tells us (19, 7), ' basil is to be sown with curses,' may be mentioned as a specimen of the way in which the text of our author has been smothered by learning.

**23-41.** The satire becomes more general. No one tries to know his own faults; each has his eyes fixed on his neighbor's short-comings. Take some rich skinflint, and, as soon as he is mentioned, the details of his meanness will be spread before us. And yet you are as great a sinner in a different direction. Comp. M. ANTON., 7, 71 : γελοῖόν ἐστι τὴν μὲν ἰδίαν κακίαν μὴ φεύγειν ὃ καὶ δυνατόν ἐστι, τὴν δὲ τῶν ἄλλων φεύγειν ὅπερ ἀδύνατον.

**23. Ut:** *how.*—in sese descendere : ' go down into his own heart.' The thought is simply *noscere se ipsum.* The heart is a depth, a well, a cellar, a sea. This is not the *recede in te ipsum quantum potes* of SEN., Ep., 7, 8. Comp. M. ANTON., 4, 3. Still less is it Mr. Pretor's ' enter the lists against yourself,' which would make ' self' at once the arena and the antagonist.

**24. spectatur :** The positive (*quisque*) must be supplied from the preceding negative. Comp. G., 446, R. ; M., 462 b.—**mantica :** According to the familiar fable of Aesop (PHAEDR., 4, 10), each man carries two wallets. The one which holds his own faults is carried on his back ; the other, which contains his neighbor's, hangs down over his breast. Comp. CATULL., 22, 21 : *sed non videmus manticae quod in tergo est.* PERSIUS reduces the two wallets to one. Each man's knapsack of faults is open to the inspection of all save himself.

**25. quaesieris :** G., 250 ; A., 60, 2, *b ; ἔροιτ' ἄν τις.* PERSIUS gets away from Socrates and Alcibiades into a land of shadowy second persons. One of these is supposed to ask another whether he knows a certain estate. The casual question leads to a caustic characteristic of the owner, which is interrupted by another indefinite character, who quotes an *ignotus aliquis,* and the general impression at the close is that every body is violently preached at except the son of Dinomache, with whom we started. —**Vettidi :** With the characteristic of Vettidius, comp. HORACE's Avidienus (*cui canis cognomen,* Sat., 2, 2, 55), and the ἀνελεύθερος and the μικρολόγος of THEOPHRASTUS.

**26. Curibus :** in the land of the Sabines, the land of frugal habits. Comp. 6, 1.—**miluus errat :** So Jahn (1868). *Miluus* is trisyllabic, as in HOR., Epod., 16, 31. Hermann, *oberrat ;* Jahn (1843), *oberret.* The expression is proverbial : *quantum milvi volant,* PETRON., 37. Comp. JUV., 9, 55.

**27. dis iratis genioque sinistro :** Comp. HOR., Sat., 2, 3, 8 : *iratis natus paries dis atque poetis.* A substantive expression of quality without a common noun is rare in Latin as in English (M.,

287, Obs. 3), but not limited in time.  See Dräger, *Histor. Syntax*, § 226.  'The aversion of the gods and at war with his
genius,' his 'second self,' who 'delights in good living,' *quia
genius laute vivendo gaudere putabatur* (Jahn).

**28. quandoque** = *quandocumque*, as HOR., Od., 4, 1, 17. 2, 34.—
**pertusa** = *pervia*, according to Jahn ; 'roads and thoroughfares'
(Conington) ;  = *calcata, trita*, Heinr., which seems more natural.
—**compita :** 'The *compitalia* is meant.  Comp. CATO, R. R., 5, 4 :
*Rem divinam nisi compitalibus in compito [vilicus] ne faciat.*  It
was one of the *feriae conceptivae*, held in honor of the *Lares
compitales* on or about the 2d of January.  It is said to have
been instituted by Servius Tullius, and restored by Augustus
(SUET., Aug., 31), and was observed with feasting.  Comp. CATO,
R. R., 5, 7, and *uncta compitalia.*  ANTHOL. LAT., 2, 246, 27 B. n.
105, 27 M.'  So Pretor, after Jahn.  With *com-pit-a* comp. Greek
$\pi\acute{\alpha}\tau$-ος, *path.*—**figit :** The suspension of the yoke symbolizes the
suspension of labor.  The yoke stands for the plough as well,
TIBULL., 2, 1, 5.

**29. metuens deradere :** See 1, 47.  Comp. HOR., Sat., 2, 4, 80 :
*metuentis reddere soldum.*—**limum :** 'the dirt' on the jar.
Comp. *sive gravis veteri craterae limus adhaesit*, HOR., Sat., 2, 4,
80.  The Scholiast understands 'the seal.'

**30. hoc bene sit :** The formula in drinking a health.  Comp.
PLAUT., Pers., 5, 1, 20.  Here used also as a kind of grace.—
**tunicatum | caepe :** πολύλοπον κρόμμυον (Casaubon).  *Tunicatum
caepe*, 'bulbous or coated onion,' as opposed to the *sectile porrum*,
or 'chives' (Pretor).  It may be going too far to exclude *epitheta
ornantia* from PERSIUS, but he certainly uses them sparingly.
*Tunicatum* is commonly understood to mean 'skin and all,' as we
say of a potato, 'jacket and all.'  Comp. JUV., 14, 153 : *tunicam
mihi malo lupini.*  But as the skin of an onion is not very 'filling,'
and as *tunica* may be used in the sense of 'coat' or 'layer,' the
slight change to *tunicatim*—'layer by layer'—has suggested itself to me.  It is not a whit more exaggerated than JUVENAL's
*filaque sectivi numerata includere porri* (14, 133).

**31. farrata olla :** 'porridge-pot of spelt,' an every-day meal
with others, holiday fare with these unfortunates, hence *plaudentibus.*  The Abl. of Cause.  *Farratam ollam* (Jahn [1843] and

Hermann) may be defended by Stat., Silv., 5, 3, 140 (cited by Jahn): *fratrem plausere Therapnae*, but there is danger of the miser's eating it.

**32. pannosam:** 'mothery.' Every word tells. It is not wine, but vinegar; it is not even good vinegar, but vinegar that is getting flat; it is not even clear vinegar, but the lees of vinegar; and not even honest lees, but mothery lees.—**morientis:** 'Dying vinegar' is not so familiar to us as 'dead wines.' Comp. Mart., 1, 18, 8.—**aceti:** Comp. *faece rubentis aceti*, Mart., 11, 56, 7.

**33.** Picture of a sensualist.—**figas in cute solem:** εἰληθερεῖν, 'fix the sun in your skin,' 'let the sun's rays pierce your skin,' instead of *bibere, combibere solem*, Juv., 11, 203 (quoted above, v. 18), and Mart., 10, 12, 7; or the more prosaic *sole uti*, Mart., 1, 77, 4.

**34. cubito tangat:** an immemorial familiarity. Examples range from Homer, Od., 14, 485 to Aristaen., 1, 19, 27. Persius has in mind Hor., Sat., 2, 5, 42: *nonne vides (aliquis cubito stantem prope tangens) inquiet*, etc.

**35. acre | despuat:** 'empty acrid spittle,' sc. on you. Others read *in mores* with Jahn (1843). Jahn (1868) reads with Hermann, *Hi mores*. Of course it is impossible to analyze this spittle, which flows to the end of v. 41. See the Introduction to the Satire. '*Persium*,' as Quintilian says of Horace, *in quibusdam nolim interpretari* (1, 8, 6). This is one of the passages that called down on our author the rebuke of that verecund gentle man Pierre Bayle: *Les Satires de Perse sont dévergondées*.

**42-52.** Such is life. We hit and are hit in turn. We disguise our faults—our *vulnera vitae*—even from ourselves, and appeal to that common jade, common fame, for a certificate of health. But temptation reveals the corruption within. You are guilty of avarice, lust, swindling, and the praises of the mob are of no moment. Be yourself. Examine yourself, and know how scantily furnished you are.

**42. caedimus,** etc.: Hor., Ep., 2, 2, 97: *caedimur et totidem plagis consumimus hostem* (Casaubon). The resemblance here, as often elsewhere, is merely verbal, as in Horace 'the passage of arms is a passage of compliments' (Conington).—**praebemus:** 'expose,' 'present.'

**43. vivitur hoc pacto :** Negatively expressed *non aliter vivitur*. In other words : *haec est condicio vivendi*, HOR , Sat., 2, 8, 65, which Casaubon compares. ' These are the terms, this the rule of life.'— **sic novimus** = *notum est* (Jahn). ' So we have learned it.' ' This is its lesson.'—**ilia subter** G., 414, R. 3. The danger of the wound is well known.

**44. caecum :** ' hidden.'—**lato balteus auro :** The baldric covered the groin, and was often ornamented with bosses of gold. Comp. VERG., Aen., 5, 312 : *lato quam circumplectitur auro | balteus.* This broad gold belt is the symbol of wealth and rank.

**45. ut mavis :** Ironical. HOR., Sat., 1, 4, 21.—**da verba :** Comp. 3, 19.—**decipe nervos :** ' cheat your muscle,' ' cheat yourself into the belief that you are sound ;' and certainly self-deception seems to be required by the context. Otherwise *decipe nervos* might be considered as equivalent to *mentire robur, pro sano te iacta, sanum te finge.*

**47. non credam ?** G., 455 ; A., 71, 1, R.—**inprobe :** The *inprobus* is hard-headed as well as hard-hearted. Comp. *plorantesque inproba natos—reliquit*, JUV., 6, 86.

**48. amarum :** Jahn reads *amorum* in his ed. of 1843, but was sorry for it. In 1868 he reads *amarum*, and punctuates so as to throw it into the grave of the next line.

**49. si puteal :** A *versus conclamatus* (Jahn). The old explanation makes this passage refer to exorbitant usury. The *puteal* here meant is supposed to be the one mentioned by HOR., Sat., 2, 6, 13—the *puteal Libonis*, situated near the praetor's tribunal, and on that account a favorite haunt of usurers, who would naturally have frequent occasion to appear in court. Comp. the poplar-tree, which was the rendezvous of a certain ' ring ' of contractors in Athens, ANDOC., 1, 133. Local allusions of this kind are the despair of commentators ; the *puteal* is, after all, as mysterious as a ' corner ' to the uninitiated, and we can only gather that *puteal flagellare* is slang for some recondite swindling process, which required a certain amount of knowingness (hence *cautus*). Conington renders, ' flog the exchange with many a stripe.' We may Americanize by ' clean out, thrash out Wall Street.' The Neronians, Casaubon at their head, understand the passage as referring to Nero's habit of going out at night in disguise and maltreating people in the street—see TAC., Ann., 13, 25; SUET., Nero, 26—and *cautus* is supposed to allude to the measures which he took for his personal safety.

**50. bibulas donaveris aures:** The student is by this time familiar with PERSIUS's way of hammering a familiar figure into odd shapes. If ears drink in, then ears are thirsty; if they are thirsty, then they tipple; and if you can give ear, you can bestow ears. 'In vain would you have given up your thirsty ears to be drenched by the praises of the mob.' *Donaveris*, Perf. Subj., μά-την παρεσχηκὼς ἂν εἴης τὰ ὦτα. Future ascertainment of a completed action. G., 271, 2.

**51. cerdo:** Κέρδων, a plebeian proper name. Conington translates by the 'Hob and Dick' of SHAKSPEARE's Coriolanus. The common rendering, 'cobbler,' is a false inference from MART., 3, 59, 1; 99, 1.

**52. tecum habita:** Comp. 1, 7.—**noris:** The punctuation of all the editors makes *noris* an Imperative Subjunctive. Still a kind of condition is involved = *si habites, noris.* G., 594, 4; A., 60, 1, *b.* One of the most threadbare quotations from Latin poetry.

---

## FIFTH SATIRE.

THE theme of the Fifth Satire is the Stoic doctrine of True Liberty All men are slaves except the philosopher, and PERSIUS has learned to be a philosopher—thanks to Cornutus, to whom the Satire is addressed. Compare and contrast HORACE's handling of a like subject in Sat., 2, 3. In Teuffel's commentary on his translation of this Satire, the matter is briefly summed up in these words: HORACE is an artist, PERSIUS a preacher. See Introd., xxvi. Comp. also HOR., Sat., 2, 7, 46 seqq.

ARGUMENT.—PERSIUS speaks: Poets have a way of asking for a hundred mouths, a hundred tongues, whether the theme be tragedy or epic. —CORNUTUS: A hundred mouths, a hundred tongues! What do you want with them? Or, for that matter, with a hundred gullets either, to worry down the tragic diet which other poets affect. You do not pant like a bellows, nor croak like a jackdaw, nor strain your cheeks to bursting in the high epic fashion. Your language is to be the language of every-day life, to which you are to give an edge by skilful combination. Your utterance is modest, and your art is shown in rasping the unhealthy body of the age, and in impaling its faults with high-bred raillery. Be such your theme. Let others sup full with tragic horrors, if they will. Do you know nothing beyond the frugal luncheon of our daily food (1–18).

PERSIUS: It is not my aim to have my pages swollen with 'Bubbles from the Brunnen of Poesy.' We are alone, far from the madding crowd, and I may throw open my heart to you, for I would have you know how great a part of my soul you are. Knock at the walls of my heart, for you are skilful to distinguish the solid from the hollow, to tell the painted stucco of the tongue from the strong masonry of the soul. To this end I fain would ask—and ask until I get—a hundred voices, to show how deeply I have planted you in my heart of hearts ; to tell you all that is past telling in my inmost being (19–29). When first the purple garb of boyhood withdrew its guardianship, and the amulet—no longer potent—was hung up, an offering to the old-fashioned household gods, when all about me humored me, and when the dress of manhood permitted my eyes to rove at will through the Subura with all its wares and wiles, what time the youth's path is doubtful, and bewilderment, ignorant of life, brings the excited mind to the spot where the great choice of roads is to be made—in that decisive hour I made myself son to you, and you took me, Cornutus, to your Socratic heart. Where my character was warped, the quiet application of the rule of right straightened what in me was crooked. My mind was constrained by reason, wrestled with its conqueror, and took on new features under your forming hand. How I remember the long days I spent with you, the firstfruits of the festal nights I plucked with you. Our work, our rest we ordered both alike, and the strain of study was eased by the pleasures of a modest table (30–44). Nay, never doubt that there is a harmony between our stars. Our constellation is the Balance or the Twins. The same aspect rules our nativities. Some star, be that star what it may, blends my fate with yours (45–51).

We are attuned each to other; but look abroad, and see how different men are from us and from each other. Each has his own aims in life. One is bent on active merchandise, one is given up to sluggish sleep, another is fond of athletic sports. One is drained dry by dicing, another by chambering and wantonness ; but when the chalk-stones of gout rattle among their fingers and toes, they awake to the choke-damp and the foggy light in which they have spent their days, and mourn too late their wasted life (52–61).

But you delight to wax pale over nightly studies. A tiller of the human soul, you prepare the soil, and sow the field of the ear with the pure grain of Stoic wisdom. Hence seek, young and old, an aim for your higher being, provision for your hoary head (62–65).

'Hoary head, you say ?' interposes an objector. 'That can be provided for as well to-morrow.' To-morrow ! 'Next day the fatal precedent will plead.' Another to-morrow comes, and we have used up yesterday's to-morrow, and so our days are emptied one by one. To-morrow! It is always ahead of us, as the hind wheel can never overtake the front wheel, though both be in the self-same chariot (66–72).

The remedy for this and all the other ills of life is True Liberty—not such as gives a dole of musty meal, a soup-house ticket to the new-made citizen; not such as makes a tipsy slave free in the twinkling of an eye. Now Dama is a worthless groom, and would sell himself for a handful of provender. Anon he is set free, as you call it—becomes Marcus Dama. Excellent surety! Most excellent judge! If Marcus says it is so, it is so. Your sign and seal here, good Marcus. Pah! This is the liberty that manumission gives. Up speaks Marcus: 'Well! Who is free except the man that can do as he pleases? I can do as I please. *Argal* I am free as air.'—'Not so,' says your learned Stoic. 'Your logic is at fault. I grant the rest, but I demur to the clause "as you please." ' —'The praetor's wand made me my own man. May I not do what I please, if I offend not against the statute-book?' (73–90).

'Do what you please!' cries PERSIUS, who identifies himself with the Stoic philosopher. 'Stop just there and learn of me; but first cease to be scornful, and let me get these old wives' notions out of your head. The praetor could not teach you any thing about the conduct of life with all its perplexities. As well expect a man to teach an elephant to dance the tight-rope. Reason bars the way, and whispers, "You must not do what you will spoil in the doing." This is nature's law, the law of common-sense. You mix medicine, and know nothing of scales and weights? You, a clodhopper, and undertake to pilot a ship? Absurd, you say; and yet what do you know of life? How can you walk upright without philosophy? How can you tell the ring of the genuine metal, and detect the faulty sound of the base alloy? Do you know what to seek, what to avoid, what to mark with white, what with black? Can you control your wishes, moderate your expences, be indulgent to your friends? Do you know how to save and how to spend? Can you keep your mouth from watering at the sight of money, from burning at the taste of ginger? When you can say in truth, "All this is mine," then you are truly free. But if you retain the old man under the new title, I take back all that I have granted. You can do nothing that is right. Every action is a fault. Put forth your finger—you sin. There is not a half-ounce of virtue in your silly carcass. You must be all right or all wrong. Man is one. You can not be virtuous by halves. You can not be at once a ditcher and a dancer. You are a slave still, though the praetor's wand may have waved away your bonds. You do not tremble at a master's voice, 'tis true, but there are other masters than those whom the law recognizes. The wires that move you do not jerk you from without, but masters grow up within your bosom' (91–131).

Here the dialogue is dropped. We leave Dama, whose personality has been getting fainter all the time, and are treated to a series of more or less dramatic scenes in illustration of the Ruling Passions.

So Avarice and Luxury dispute about the body and soul of an un-Stoic slave (132–160).

A Lover tries to break the chain that binds him to an unworthy mistress (161–175).

Another is led captive by Ambition at her will (176–179).

Yet another is under the dominion of Superstition (180–188).

But why discourse thus? Imagine what the military would say to such a screed of doctrine. I hear the horse-laugh of Pulfennius, as he bids a clipped dollar for a hundred Greek philosophers—a cent apiece (189–191).

———

This Satire is justly considered by many critics the best of all the productions of PERSIUS, as it is the least obscure. The warm tribute to his master Cornutus may have had its share in commending the poem to teachers, who, of all men, are most grateful for gratitude. But apart from this revelation of a pure and loving heart, the peculiar talent of PERSIUS, which consists in vivid portraiture of character and situation, appears to great advantage in this composition. True, the introduction is not wrought into the poem, and the poet's discourse is too distinctly a Stoic school exercise, and reminiscence crowds on reminiscence, but there is a certain movement in the Satire, or Epistle, as it were better called, which carries us on over the occasional rough places, without the perpetual jolt which we feel every where else on the 'corduroy road' of PERSIUS's *Gradus ad Parnassum*.

**1-4.** PERSIUS: Oh for a hundred voices, a hundred mouths, a hundred tongues!

**1. Vatibus hic mos est:** Comp. HOR., Sat., 1, 2, 86 : *regibus hic mos est. Vatibus*, with a sneer. See Prol., 7.—**centum sibi poscere voces:** Examples might be multiplied indefinitely from HOMER to Charles Wesley. Comp. Il., 2, 489 : οὐδ᾽ εἴ μοι δέκα μὲν γλῶσσαι, δέκα δὲ στόματ᾽ εἶεν; and VERG., Aen., 6, 625 : *non mihi si linguae centum sint oraque centum;* also Georg., 2, 43; Ov., Met., 8, 532. Conington burlesques the passage by translating *poscere* 'put in a requisition for,' and *optare* 'bespeak.' By such devices humor of a certain kind might be extracted from elegies, and VERGIL be made 'to put in a requisition for Quintilius at the Bureau of the Gods,' HOR., Od., 1, 24, 12.

**3. seu ponatur:** The mood after *seu—seu* is determined on general principles (A., 61, 4, *c*). In practice, however, the Indicative is more common (G., 597, R. 4). The Subjunctive is to be explained by G., 666 (see last example), and A., 66, 2.—**ponatur**=*proponatur* (CIC., Tusc. Dis., 1, 4, 7). Comp. Ɵεῖναι, Ɵέσις. Jahn understands it as *ponere lucum*, 1, 70, *posuisse figuras*, 1, 86. Perhaps there is a play on the different senses of *ponere*. 'Serve up' would not be bad in view of vv. 9, 10.—**hianda :** 'To be spouted by some doleful actor.' '*Hianda* has reference to the tragic mask, in which a wide aperture was cut for the mouth, to facilitate a distinct enunciation. From the appearance presented by the speaker, it soon came to be used of a bombastic style of utterance. Comp. *carmen hiare*, PROP., 2, 31, 6, and *grande Sophocleo carmen bacchamur hiatu*, JUV., 6, 636.' Pretor, after Jahn.

**4. vulnera Parthi :** Is *Parthi* object or subject ? The passage is a reminiscence of HOR., Sat., 2, 1, 15 : *aut labentis equo describat vulnera Parthi*. If *Parthi* is the object, an interpretation which is favored by the Horatian passage and by the propriety of the epic theme—for why should a Roman enlarge upon the wounds that the Parthian deals ?—*ducentis ab inguine ferrum* must be rendered ' drawing the dart from his groin.' Still *ab* is not a suitable preposition, nor can it be defended by such expressions as *ducere suspiria ab imo pectore*, Ov., Met., 10, 402. Others think of ' trailing the shaft from his groin,' in which it had been imbedded. Comp. v. 160 : *a collo trahitur pars longa catenae.* If *Parthi* is the subject, translate, ' The Parthian who draws the arrow from [the quiver] near his groin.' The Eastern nations wore the quiver low, the Greeks upon the shoulder. This line refers to epic poetry as the preceding to tragedy.

**5-18.** CORNUTUS : What need have you of a hundred mouths ? You have no foolish tragedy to cram, no big epics to mouth. Your simple satire demands a simple style, the talk of every day, only better put. Your business is to scourge and pierce, and yet remember that you are a gentleman. Let these themes suffice you, and leave to others the stage-horrors of cannibalic feasts; yourself content with the pot-luck of the Roman cit.

**5. Quorsum haec :** Comp. HOR., Sat., 2, 7, 21.—**aut :** G., 460, R.; A., 71, 2.—**robusti carminis offas :** ' dumplings of substantial poetry,' ' lumps of solid poetry ' (Conington). *Offa* is a

dumpling of meal or flesh. Comp. APUL., Met., 1, 3, on the choki-
ness of a certain *polentae caseatae offula grandior*.

**6. ingeris :** ' cram.' The whole passage is intended to be
coarse. ' What great gobbets of stuffing song are you cramming
yourself with, that you require a hundred throats to strain them
down ?' Others understand : *ingeris* sc. *populo*. See v. 177.—
**centeno gutture** =*centum gutturibus*. So *centena arbore*, VERG.,
Aen., 10, 207 (Conington).

**7. grande :** See 1, 14.—**locuturi :** See 1, 100.—**nebulas :** Jahn
is reminded of HOR., A. P., 230 : *nubes et inania captet*. Observe
that *legunto* suggests the culinary figure below. The mists represent the vegetables, Procne and Thyestes furnish the meat.—**Helicone :** See Prologue. PERSIUS is as intensely Roman in poetic
practice as he is Greek in philosophic theory.—**legunto :** The
Imperative, instead of the Subjunctive, gives the tone of an edict
or of a cookery-book.

**8. Prognes—Thyestae :** See Classical Dictionaries for the familiar myths. Observe the balance. Procne served up her son,
Thyestes made a dinner off his. Both are common tragic themes.
See HOR., A. P., 91. 186–187.—**olla fervebit :** ' Who are going to
set Thyestes's pot a-boiling ' (Conington).

**9. Glyconi :** Glyco was a stupid actor of the day, who could
not understand a joke. The Neronians have made the most of
the fact, as reported by the Scholiast, that G. was manumitted
by Nero, who paid his half-owner Vergilius 300,000 sesterces for
his share. So, for instance, Lehmann (*De A. Persii Satira Quinta*,
p. 17), who has nosed out all manner of subtle Neronian flavors
in this innocent satire.—**cenanda :** Comp. 3, 46.

**10. coquitur dum :** When the action with *dum*, ' while,' is co-
extensive with the action in the leading clause, the limit may be
expressed by *until*, ' while it is smelting ' = ' until it is smelted '—
**massa :** See note on 2, 67.

**11. folle :** The wind is squeezed ' with ' or ' in ' the bellows
rather than ' from ' the bellows. The Scholiast notices the Horatian reminiscence, Sat., 1, 4, 19 : *at tu conclusas hircinis follibus
auras | usque laborantes, dum ferrum molliat ignis | ut mavis, imi-
tare*. Comp. also JUV., 7, 111 : *tunc immensa cavi spirant menda-
cia folles*.—**nec clauso murmure,** etc. : ' Nor with pent-up mur-

mur croak to yourself until you are hoarse some solemn nonsense.'

**13. scloppo:** So Jahn (1868), instead of *stloppo* (1843). This is supposed to be a word coined to express the sound (comp. *bombis*, 1, 99). Conington renders 'plop.' Vaniček records it under SKAR, S. 183, and it may well be the 'slap' with which the distended cheeks are reduced, and hence the 'plop' which is heard. The childish trick may be witnessed wherever there are children. PERSIUS multiplies absurd and meaningless noises without any sharp distinction.

**14. verba togae:** 'the language of every-day life.' The *fabula togata* is Roman comedy, as opposed to the *fabula praetexta*, or Roman tragedy, and to the *f. palliata*, the subjects of which were Greek. PERSIUS insists on the connection of the national satire with the national comedy, and the scanty remains of the *fabula togata* deserve close comparison.—**sequeris**=*sectaris*. Prol., 11. —**acri iunctura:** 'nice grouping,' 'telling combination.' The words are familiar, but the setting is new. Comp. HOR., A. P., 47: *notum si callida verbum | reddiderit iunctura novum;* and 242: *tantum series iuncturaque pollet | tantum de medio sumptis accedit honoris.* An important passage, as showing the intense self-consciousness of the poet's art.

**15. ore teres modico:** Jahn comp. *ore rotundo*, HOR., A. P., 323. The mouth stands for the style, and the position of the mouth symbolized the utterance (*ore magis quam labris loquendum est*, QUINT., 11, 3, 81). *Teres* as in CIC., De Orat., 3, 52, 199: *est [oratio] et plena quaedam sed tamen teres et tenuis, non sine nervis et viribus.* 'A moderate rounding of the cheek' (Conington); but although in view of v. 13 it would be desirable to retain the figure, it is hardly possible. 'With smooth and compassed tone.' As *teres ore*=*ore modico*, Hermann (*L. P.*, II., 46) comp. Ov., Fast., 6, 425: *lucoque obscurus opaco.*—**pallentis mores:** The 'spirit of the age' is also the 'body of the age.' Hence the figure. 'Pale' with disease and vice (comp. 4, 47), 'guilty.'—**radere:** Comp. 1, 107.

**16. ingenuo ludo:** 'with high-bred raillery,' 'with raillery that a gentleman may speak and hear.' PERSIUS has in mind εὐτραπελία, the πεπαιδευμένη ὕβρις of ARISTOTLE, Rhet., 2, 12, as

Conington suggests.—**defigere :** Variously explained. So 'post up,' 'placard' (Casaubon) ; 'pin to the ground' (Conington) ; 'pierce,' like an arrow (Jahn) ; 'sting,' like a hornet, as in Ov., Fast., 3, 753 : *milia crabronum coeunt et vertice nudo,* | *spicula de-figunt oraque summa notant.* Comp. the use of *figere,* 3, 80.

**17. hinc :** From every-day life. König compares HOR., A. P., 318 : *vivas hinc ducere voces.*—**quae dicis :** So Jahn (1868), after the best MSS. In 1843 we find *dicas,* which is more natural, but not necessary.—**Mycenis :** Dative, far more forcible than the lo-cative Ablative. Jahn comp. Prol., 5 : *illis relinquo,* a reading which he afterward abandoned. See G., 344, R. 3.

**18. cum capite et pedibus :** served up to Thyestes after he had finished his dinner. Comp. AESCHYL., Ag., 1594 ; SEN., Thyest., 764.—**plebeia prandia :** Your theme is 'human nature's daily food,' not the heroic suppers of 'raw-head and bloody-bones' that teach us nothing. *Mensa* is contrasted with *prandia* (comp. SENECA'S *sine mensa prandium,* cited 1, 67) as 'banquet' with 'meal,' '*Tafel*' with '*Tisch.*'

**19-29.** PERSIUS : You understand my aims. I do not care to swell my page with frothy nonsense. And now that we are alone, I desire you to examine my heart, that you may see how you are enshrined in it—a theme for which I might well desire a hundred voices.

**19. equidem :** Here in accordance with common usage. See 1, 110.—**bullatis nugis :** 'air-blown trifles' (Gifford). *Bullatis :* so Jahn (1868) with Hermann. The reading of the oldest MSS., *pullatis,* 'sad colored,' explained now as 'tragic stuff' (because mourners were *pullati*) ; now as stuff for the groundlings (be-cause the common people were *pullati*), is scarcely tenable. *Ampullatis,* Jahn's conjecture, though defended by Lachmann (LUCRET., 6, 1067), is metrically bad ; but the sense is excellent, and the reference would be to a passage which PERSIUS must have had in his mind. HOR., A. P., 97 : *proicit ampullas et ses-quipedalia verba.* Even Thyestes is mentioned in the context, l. c. 91. *Bullatis,* 'bubbly.' Hermann (*L. P.,* I., 32) comp. *alata avis,* and makes *bullatis* refer to *tumorem et inanem verborum stre-pitum.*

**20. dare pondus fumo :** Casaubon comp. HOR., Ep., 1, 19, 42 :

*nugis addere pondus.* HORACE uses the expression in the sense of ' attaching importance.' PERSIUS means that these trifles are fitted to lend importance, to give seeming substance to mere vapors. *Fumus* is a synonym for ' humbug.' On *dare idonea = idonea quae det*, see G., 424, R. 4 ; A., 57, 8, *f*.

**22. excutienda :** See 1, 49. But the figure changes below, or there is a figure within a figure, the heart being compared to a wall, the wall to a dress. On the construction, see G., 431 ; A., 72, 5, *c*.

**23. pars animae :** Comp. *te meae partem animae*, HOR., Od., 2, 17, 5 ; *animae dimidium meae*, Od., 1, 3, 8.—**Cornute:** See Introduction, ix.

**24. ostendisse :** once for all. See G., 275, 1 ; A., 58, 11, *d*.—**pulsa :** κροῦε. See 3, 21. — **dinoscere cautus :** HOR., Sat., 1, 6, 51 : *cautum adsumere dignos*. Comp. Prol., 11.

**25. solidum crepet :** like *sonat vitium*, 3, 21. G., 331, R. 2 ; A., 52, 3, *a*.—**pictae tectoria linguae :** The comparison is taken from a stuccoed party-wall painted to look solid. Comp. AFRAN. ap. NON., 152, 28, v. 14 (Ribbeck): *fallaci aspectu paries pictus putidus (= puter)*. The notion in *pictae* belongs rather to *tectoria* than to *linguae*—'painted tongue-stucco.' The figure will not bear close examination any more than the stucco.

**26. his, ut = *ad haec ut*. Comp. *hoc ut*, v. 19. Others read *hic*.—**centenas = *centum*. G., 310, R. ; A., 18, 2, *d*.—**deposcere :** Notice the determination that lies in *deposcere*.

**27. quantum fixi :** This is not conceived as a dependent interrogative, as is shown by v. 29, where the antecedent of the parallel clause is expressed. G., 469, R. 3.—**sinuoso :** Comp. PLIN., H. N., 2, 37 : *cor prima domicilia intra se animo et sanguini praebet sinuoso specu. Sinuoso pectore = in recessu mentis*, 2, 73.

**28. voce :** carelessly repeated after *voces*.—**pura :** ' honest.'

**29. non enarrabile :** i. e., save by the hundred voices. There is no contradiction, and even if there were—this is supposed to be poetry.—**fibra :** 1, 47.

**30-51.** When first I put away the things of boyhood and encountered the temptations of youth, and stood bewildered at the cross-roads of life, I threw myself into your sheltering arms, and put myself under your guiding hand. Happy the memory of those days and nights, as they brought common work and common rest. Surely a common star controls our destinies and makes us one.

**30. pavido:** variously interpreted of the fear—1. Which an entrance on life breeds; 2. Which requires the protection of the *praetexta;* 3. Which the rule of tutors and governors inspires. The third view is favored by *blandi comites,* as Conington remarks. Comp. MART., 11, 39, 2: *et pueri custos assiduusque comes* with v. 6: *te dispensator, te domus ipsa pavet.*—**custos purpura:** 'the guardian purple.' *Purpura=praetexta,* the dress of boyhood, which was of itself a protection. This was exchanged for the *toga* when the nonage was over. *Per hoc inane purpurae decus precor,* HOR., Epod., 5, 7.—**mihi:** If *cessit* is taken absolutely, *mihi* may depend on the predicative notion in *custos=quae mihi custos fuerat.* Casaubon explains, *mihi cessit, ut iam annis maiori vel etiam ut hosti.* It seems best to combine the two: 'When the purple resigned its dreaded guardianship over me.'

**31. bulla:** the well-known 'boss,' which contained amulets and the like. Comp. 2, 70.—**succinctis:** 'Like *cinctutis* (HOR., A. P., 50), *incinctos* (Ov., Fast., 2, 632), in allusion to the *cinctus Gabinus,* in which primitive dress they (the Lares) were always represented. It was worn over the left shoulder, leaving the right arm free' (Pretor). Conington renders *succinctis,* 'quaint.'

**32. blandi:** (*fuerunt*).—**comites:** Jahn considers these *comites* the same as those mentioned in 3, 7. See note. The epigram of MART., cited above, v. 30, makes for this view: the harsh tutors have become *blandi comites.* But most commentators prefer to take *comites* in its general sense.—**tota Subura:** On the construction, see G., 386; A., 55, 3, *f.* The Subura, as the focus of business life, was the haunt of persons who are sufficiently characterized as *Suburanae magistrae,* MART., 11, 78, 11.

**33. permisit sparsisse:** On the Inf., see G., 532, R. 1; A., 70, 3, *a.* On the tense, note on 1, 41. With the phraseology, Jahn comp. VAL. FLACC., 5, 247: *tua nunc terris, tua lumina toto | sparge mari. Spargere* is a happy word for a rapid, roving glance.—**iam:** ἤδη. The English idiom often refuses to give the exact force of *iam.* The youngster has got a 'sure enough' *candidus umbo.* The contrast in time is the former *praetexta.*—**can-**

**didus umbo:** '*Umbo* was the knot into which the folds of the toga were gathered after passing the left shoulder' (Pretor). Of course the *umbo* was *candidus*, as the *toga* was.

**34. iter ambiguum:** See 3, 56.—**vitae nescius error:** is bewilderment from ignorance of life.

**35. deducit:** So Jahn (1843), a reading which he has strangely forsaken (1868) for *diducit*. Schlüter puts it neatly thus: *homines in compita ubi viae diducuntur, deduci dicuntur*. *Compita* does not mean the roads, but the place where the roads meet—the crossing (Schol.). *De* adds the notion of decision to *ducit*. Comp. *in discrimen deducere*, Cic., Fam., 10, 24, 4. The youth is brought to a point where he must choose.—**trepidas:** See 1, 74.

**36. supposui:** Almost 'I made you adopt me.' *Supponere* is used of supposititious children. As Persius's own father died while the poet was young, there is a tone of orphanage about the expression that appeals to our sympathy. 'I threw myself as a son into your arms.'—**suscipis:** is the correlative of *supposui*.

**37. Socratico sinu:** The loving care of Socrates is meant, as well as his wisdom, as Jahn has observed.—**fallere sollers:** On the construction, see G., 424, R. 4; A., 57, 8, *f*, 3; Prol., 11. 'Skilful to deceive,' in the sense of the gradual Socratic approach. The rule is not rudely applied, but cheats the warped nature into rectitude. Jahn's note amounts to this, that a ruler that understands deception, understands detection, and hence is a true ruler.

**38. regula:** 'ruler.' See note on 4, 12.

**39. premitur ratione:** Comp. Verg., Aen., 6, 80: *fera corda domans fingitque premendo.*—**vinci laborat** = *dum vincitur laborat, cum labore vincitur*. '*Laborat* shows that the pupil's mind cooperated with his teacher' (Conington).

**40. artificem:** Passive, *arte factum*, 'artistic,' 'finished.' The figure is of course taken from moulding in wax or clay.—**ducit vultum:** Comp. *exigite ut teneros mores ceu pollice ducat | ut si quis cera vultum facit*, Juv., 7, 237; only there the workman moulds, here the material. Transl. 'take on,' 'assume,' as in Ov., Met., 1, 402: *saxa ducere formam* (Jahn).—**pollice:** The thumb is largely used in moulding. See Juv., l. c., and Ov., Met., 10, 285; Stat., Achill., 1, 332, quoted by Jahn.

**41. etenim:** καὶ γάρ. See 3, 48.—**memini consumere:** See

Prol., 2.—**soles** = *dies*. The antithesis runs throughout. *Soles —opus—seria* are opposed to *noctes—requiem—mensa*.

**42. primas noctes:** 'the early hours of the night.'—**epulis:** 'for feasting.' Others, 'from feasting,' i. e., for study, 3, 54; 5, 62.—**decerpere:** The expression is a cross between *carpe diem* (HOR., Od., 1, 11, 8) and *partem solido demere de die* (HOR., Od., 1, 1, 20). *Decerpere* is to pluck with resolute, eager hand.

**43. unum opus et requiem** = *unum opus et (unam) requiem* (Jahn). Casaubon comp. VERG., Georg., 4, 184.

**44. laxamus seria:** Jahn comp. VERG., Aen., 9, 223: *laxabant curas*.

**45. non equidem hoc dubites:** On *equidem*, see note on 1, 110. With *non dubites* comp. *non accedas*, 1, 5.—**foedere certo:** Jahn comp. MANIL., 2, 475: *iunxit amicitias horum sub foedere certo. Foedus certum*, 'fixed law,' 'fixed principle.'

**46. consentire dies:** On the Inf., instead of the normal *quin* with Subj., see G., 551, R. 4; M., 375 c., Obs. 2. For the thought, comp. HOR., Od., 2, 17, 21: *utrumque nostrum incredibili modo | consentit astrum.*—**ab uno sidere duci:** Astrology was very popular in PERSIUS's time, having been brought into vogue by Tiberius. It was the aristocratic mode of divination, and is compared by Friedländer (*Sittengesch.*, 1, 347) with the spiritualism and table-turning of the present day. Philosophy was not proof against it; indeed, the later Stoics always had a leaning to it, and Panaetius was the only one that rejected it (Knickenberg, l. c. p. 79). All people of 'culture' talked about 'horoscope,' 'nativity,' and 'malign aspect,' just as the same class in our time speak of 'the spectroscope,' 'heat a mode of motion,' and 'the survival of the fittest.' HORACE and PERSIUS, who imitates HORACE, have caught up some of the current terms, and travel along the Zodiac in blissful ignorance of their own stars.

**47. aequali Libra:** So HOR., Od., 2, 17, 17: *seu Libra seu me Scorpios adspicit.* Comp. the whole passage.

**48. Parca tenax veri:** Comp. *Parca non mendax*, HOR., Od., 2, 16, 39. 'Fate is represented with scales in her hands, also as marking the horoscope on the celestial globe' (Jahn). The *Parca* of mythology is identified with the *Fatum* of the Stoics.—**seu:** Observe the irregularity of *vel—seu* instead of *seu—seu.*—**nata**

**fidelibus:** 'ordained for faithful friends.' 'The hour of birth is said to be born itself, as in AESCHYL., Ag., 107, ξύμφυτος αἰών; SOPH., O. R., 1082, συγγενεῖς μῆνες' (Conington).

**49. Geminos:** Casaubon quotes MANIL., 2, 628: *magnus erit Geminis amor et concordia duplex.*

**50. Saturnumque gravem,** etc. : 'We together cross malignant Saturn by propitious Jove.' 'Saturnine' and 'jovial' are remnants of astrological belief. *Nostro* is not only 'our,' but 'on our side,' 'propitious.'

**51. nescio quod:** almost $= aliquod.$ See v. 12.—**est quod temperat:** On the Mood, see G., 634, R. 1; M., 365, Obs. 2. With the expression, comp. HOR., Ep., 2, 2, 187: *scit genius, natale comes qui temperat astrum,* where the parts are reversed.—**me tibi temperat:** The Dative is used after the analogy of *miscere.* 'Blends my being with thine.'

**52-61.** Our aims, our lives are one. But 'many men, many minds.' Each has his passion—the merchant, the man of ease, the lover of sport, the gamester, the rake—but they have to reckon with disease at last, and groan over the failure of their lives.

**52. Mille hominum species:** The Schol. quotes HOR., Sat., 2, 1, 27: *quot capitum vivunt, totidem studiorum | milia.* Proverbial is TER., Phorm., 2, 3, 14 : *quot homines, tot sententiae: suos cuique mos.*—**usus rerum:** 'practice of life,' 'practice.' See 1, 1, note. —**discolor:** 'of various hue.'

**53. velle suum cuique est:** Comp. VIRG., Ecl., 2, 65 : *trahit sua quemque voluptas.* On *velle suum,* see 1, 9.—**nec uno vivitur voto:** Comp. 2, 7 : *aperto vivere voto.* The negative form of a proposition following the positive strengthens it. *Nec uno,* 'far different.' With the examples that follow, Jahn comp. HOR., Ep., 1, 18, 21 seqq.

**54. mercibus mutat piper:** On the Abl., see G., 404, R.; A., 54, 8. The normal construction is *merces mutat pipere;* the other does not occur in archaic Latin nor in model prose. HORACE is the first to use it, e. g., Od., 3, 1, 47; Epod., 9, 27. LIVY introduces it into prose, but employs it only once (5, 30, 3). So Dräger, *Histor. Syntax,* § 235.—**sub sole recenti:** The Schol. comp. HOR., Sat., 1, 4, 29 : *hic mutat merces surgente a sole ad eum quo | vespertina tepet regio.*

**55. rugosum piper:** 'wrinkled pepper,' 'shrivelled pepper,' the shrivelling being the effect of the hot Eastern sun. None of your Italian pepper, but the genuine Eastern article. See note on 3, 75.—**pallentis cumini:** like *pallidam Pirenen*, Prol., 4, attribute for effect, an imitation and, strange to say, without attempt at enhancement, of the *exsangue cuminum* of HOR., Ep., 1, 19, 18. *Cuminum pallorem bibentibus gignit*, PLIN., H. N., 20, 14, 57. Cumin was considered an indispensable condiment. The large use of it is shown by the compounds in Greek (κυμινοδόχη—θήκη, κτέ)—see Seiler ad ALCIPHRON., 3, 58—and it ranks with pepper in PETRON., 49; with salt in ALEXIS, fr. 169 (3, 465 Mein.). Add PLUTARCH, Quaest. Conv., 5, 10.

**56. inriguo somno:** *Inriguo* is active. Sleep waters him, as it were, and increases his fat. Comp. VERG., Aen., 3, 511 : *fessos sopor inrigat artus*. 'Dewy sleep' is almost too sweet for the passage. König, a prosaic soul, thinks of the 'sweaty sleep' of a man who is gorged with meat and drink.

**57. campo:** The gymnastic exercises of the *campus*, and especially of the *campus Martius* in Rome, are familiar. See HOR., Od., 1, 8, 4 ; Ep., 1, 7, 59 ; A. P., 162, referred to by Jahn.—**decoquit =** *coquendo vires absumit*. The word is employed of a man who has used up, run through, his means. So CIC., Phil., 2, 18, 44 : *tenesne memoria praetextatum te decoxisse?* Here it is the man who is used up, who is made to go to pot.

**58. putris:** Gr. τακερός. 'In wanton dalliance melts away' (Gifford).—**lapidosa cheragra:** Comp. HOR., Ep., 1, 1, 31 : *nodosa cheragra*. The chalk-stones of gout are compared with hailstones.

**59. fregerit:** Perf. Subj. in a generic sense. G., 569, R. 2 (end). Comp. *postquam illi iusta cheragra | contudit articulos*, HOR., Sat., 2, 7, 15 seqq.—**veteris ramalia fagi:** The comparison is between the fingers and the knotty boughs. Comp. HESIOD'S πέντοζος, O. et D., 744.—**fagi:** *Fagus*, φηγός, and 'beech' (BHAG) are etymologically, but not botanically, the same. See Curtius, *Grundzüge*, No. 160.

**60.** A forcible passage, on which Conington says : 'The conception here is of life passed in a Boeotian atmosphere of thick fogs and pestilential vapors, which the sun never penetrates—

probably with especial reference to the pleasures of sense, of which PERSIUS has just been speaking. So the "vapor, heavy, hueless, formless, cold," in Tennyson's "Vision of Sin." '—**crassos dies:** *sub crasso aere* (Jahn).—**transisse:** Heinr. comp. TIB., 1, 4, 33: *vidi iam iuvenem, premeret cum serior aetas, | maerentem stultos praeteriisse dies.*—**lucem palustrem:** 'boggy' = 'foggy light' is 'light choked by fog.' *Crassos dies lucemque palustrem* must be connected closely—'gross days in foggy light'—so as to get rid of an awkward Zeugma with *transisse*.

**61. sibi:** with *ingemuere* (Conington).—**iam seri:** 'too, too late.' On *iam*, see v. 33. On *seri*, G., 324, R. 6 ; A., 47, 6.—**ingemuere:** like the Gr. Aorist. Comp. v. 187 and 3, 101. G., 228, R. 2 ; A., 58, 5, *c.* 'Heave a sigh' (Conington).—**relictam:** *anteactam* (Casaubon). *Iam post terga reliquit | sexaginta annos,* JUV., 13, 16.

**62-65.** Contrast of Cornutus's noble mission. His creed the only creed for life.

**62. at:** in lively contrast.—**nocturnis:** Comp. 1, 90.—**inpallescere:** Comp. 1, 26.

**63. purgatas:** *Purgare* is an agricultural term like our 'clean,' and the metaphor is kept up. The field is the ear.—**inseris:** where we should expect *seris.*—**fruge Cleanthea:** Cleanthes is selected here on account of his strict life and virtuous poverty, in opposition to the luxury and wealth of the *Romulidae,* as Knickenberg remarks, l. c. p. 9.—**petite:** Mr. Pretor supposes that this is Cornutus's invitation to the world. But if Cornutus speaks here, where does PERSIUS come in again?—unless he takes up the cudgels for his master in v. 66.—**finem** = τέλος.—**viatica:** Jahn quotes DIOG. LAERT., 1, 5, 80 : ἐφόδιον ἀπὸ νεότητος εἰς γῆρας ἀναλάμβανε σοφίαν; and 5, 11, 21 : κάλλιστον ἐφόδιον τῷ γήρᾳ ἡ παιδεία.—**miseris:** 'wretched else.'—**canis:** G., 195, R. 1.

**66-72.** 'There is time enough for that,' says an impersonal sinner. 'To-morrow will do as well.' ' "To-morrow, and to-morrow, and to-morrow." To-morrow never becomes to-day.'

**66. Cras hoc fiet,** etc. : 'I will do this that you ask of me to-morrow.' 'You will do to-morrow just what you are doing to-day.' Jahn comp. Ov., R. A., 104 : *Cras quoque fiet idem.* Hermann arranges : *Cras hoc fiet idem. Cras fiet ?* 'This will, can be

done to-morrow as well as to-day.' 'To-morrow, you say?'
Comp. PETRON., 82 : *quod hodie non est, cras erit.*

**67. nempe diem donas :** 'Well, what of it? Suppose I go on
the same way to-morrow ; it will only be a day—a great present,
forsooth, to be haggling about !' On *nempe*, see G., 500, R. 2.—
**cum venit—consumpsimus :** more lively than *cum venerit—con-
sumpserimus* (G., 229). One clause is involved in the other. G.,
236, R. 4. This seems to be better than making *venit* iterative,
and *consumpsimus* an Aoristic Perf.

**69. egerit :** 'unloads,' 'carts off.' *Egerere* is the opposite of
*ingerere* (v. 6). Comp. SEN., Ep., 47, 2 : *venter maiore opera omnia egerit quam ingessit.* Jahn makes *egerit = impulerit*, in order to save the figure. Compare *truditur dies die*, HOR., Od., 2,
18, 15, and PETRON., 45 : *dies diem trudit;* and 82 : *vita truditur.*
But even this does not save the figure, and the sudden change
of metaphor is in PERSIUS's vein.—**paulum erit ultra :** 'To-morrow will always be a little further on,' is the common rendering,
the figure changing at this point.

**70. quamvis—vertentem :** A later construction. G., 611, R. ;
M., 443, Obs.—**cantum :** 'tire.'

**72. cum curras :** 'seeing that you are running.' Here *cum*
is nearly equivalent to *si*, as it is thrown by *sectabere* into the
future, and is thus made hypothetical. Comp. G., 591, R. 3, and
584.

**73-90.** What men need is Liberty—not the freedom of the
city, which insures a quota of damaged corn ; not the freedom
of the freedman, which gives a slave a name to be free, while he
is yet a slave ; but the liberty wherewith Philosophy sets men
free. The freedman demurs to this hard doctrine, but a Stoic
adept silences him by his 'Short Method.'

**73. hac, ut, quisque :** *Hac* is the adverb, *ut = qua, quisque =
quicunque* (comp. *quandoque = quandocumque*, 4, 28), a sad complex
of harshnesses, which may be rendered thus : 'Liberty is what is
wanted ; not after the prevalent (G., 290, 7) fashion, by which
each man that has worked his way up to a Publius in the Veline
tribe is owner of a ticket for a ration of musty spelt.' Other read-
ings, such as *hac quam ut quisque* (Passow), *hac qua quisque* (Meis-
ter), are mere devices to relieve the grammatical situation, which

is doubtless unnatural in the extreme, as *hac* seems to belong to *libertate*, and *ut quisque* is a familiar combination. Conington makes *non hac* the beginning of an independent sentence, and translates: 'It is not by *this* freedom that every fire-new citizen, who gets his name enrolled in a tribe, is privileged to get a pauper's. allowance for his ticket.'—**Velina :** Comp. HOR., Ep., 1, 6, 52: *hic multum in Fabia valet, ille Velina.* The Veline was one of the last two tribes instituted (Becker, *Röm. Alt.*, 2, 1, 170), and is supposed by some to be one of the four city tribes to which the *libertini* were restricted. The name of the tribe to which a man belongs is put in the Abl. (as a whence case). So *M. Larcius L. f. Pomptina Pudens* (Becker, l. c. 198).

**74. Publius :** Only freemen were entitled to the *praenomen.* Comp. HOR., Sat., 2, 5, 32: *Quinte, puta, aut Publi (gaudent praenomine molles | auriculae).*—**emeruit :** literally 'has served his time' (of a soldier), 'has worked his way up to be a Publius' (supplying *esse*).—**tesserula :** the well-known *tessera frumentaria*, SUET., Aug., 41.

**75. Quiritem :** Rare in the Singular (Schol.).

**76. vertigo :** the 'twirl' of the familiar process of *manumissio per vindictam.* 'The lictor touched the slave with the *vindicta*, the master turning him round and "dismissing him from his hand" with the words *Hunc hominem liberum esse volo*' (Conington).—**facit :** is causal as well as *faciat.* G., 627, R. ; A., 63.—**Dama :** Δημᾶς = Δημήτριος ; according to others for Δημέας (Mehlhorn, *Gr. Gr.*, 183), a common slave's name. — **non tressis :** Jahn comp. *non semissis homo*, VATIN. ap. CIC., Fam., 5, 10, 1.

**77. vappa :** 'dead wine,' hence 'mean liquor.'—**lippus :** the effect of drinking.—**in farragine tenui :** 'in the matter of,' and hence 'for a poor feed of corn.'

**78. verterit — exit** = *si verterit — exit.* G., 257 ; A., 57, 5. Comp. v. 189. The Perf. is aoristic, 'give him a whirl.'—**momento :** literally by the 'motion,' 'by virtue,' 'by the act of twirling.' 'By dint' would give an ironical turn.

**79. Marcus :** as *Publius*, v. 74. Jahn cites an inscription: M · FVFIVS · M · L · DAMA. — **papae :** Ironical admiration.

H

'Wondrous change! Every body will trust this thief, this liar now!' *Papae* (Gr. παπαῖ, βαβαί). 'Whew!' 'Prodigious!'— **recusas?** Fie on you, if you do! See note on 4, 1.

**80. adsigna tabellas:** 'your hand and seal to this document,' 'witness this document.'

**82. mera:** 'pure and simple' (ironical).—**pillea:** See 3, 106.

**83. An quisquam — Bruto:** These words are generally assigned to Dama, and it is certainly more humorous to make the promoted stable-boy argue in mood and figure than to rake up one of PERSIUS's dead-alive spectators, as König does, and after him Pretor. *Quisquam*, because of the negative answer expected. See 1, 112, and G., 304 ; A., 21, 2, *h*.

**84. ut voluit:** The Stoic formula did not differ from the popular definition. Certainly it does not sound recondite to say: *libertas est potestas vivendi ut velis*, CIC., Parad., 5, 1, 34; or with ARRIAN, Diss., 4, 1, 1 : ἐλεύθερός ἐστιν ὁ ζῶν ὡς βούλεται, but the words must be understood in their Stoic sense.

**85. Mendose colligis:** φαύλως συλλογίζει. 'Your syllogism is faulty.' 'Marcus, thou reasonest ill.'

**86. stoicus hic:** 'our Stoic friend' (Conington). PERSIUS himself.—**aurem—lotus:** Comp. v. 63 and 1, 126. *Lotus* may be reflexive. G., 332, R. 2; A., 53, 3, *c*, R.—**aceto:** Vinegar was used in cases of deafness, CELS., 6, 7, 2, 3 (König).

**87. accipio — tolle:** 'PERSIUS admits the major, but denies the minor; denies both that the man has a will (*volo*), and that he is free (*licet*) to follow it' (Conington). Mr. Pretor limits the concession to *vivere* (τὸ ζῆν), and explains: 'The mere fact that you are a living creature, I admit; the inference contained in *licet* and *ut volo*, I altogether deny.' 'This dissection of the argument word by word' may be 'more in keeping with the character of the Stoic'—the Stoics were great choppers of logic—but it is not in keeping with the style of PERSIUS, who is subtle every where except in his arguments.

**88. Vindicta:** the *festuca*, or 'wand,' with which the lictor struck the manumittend. See v. 76.—**postquam recessi:** with a causal tone. See note on 3, 90.—**meus:** 'my own man,' hence 'my own master' (G., 299, R.) ; *mei iuris* (Schol.).

**90. Masuri rubrica:** 'The canon of Masurius.' 'Masurius Sabinus, an eminent lawyer, lived in the reigns of Tiberius and Nero, and wrote a work in three books, entitled *Ius Civilę.' Rubrica,* ' because the titles and first few words of the laws were commonly picked out with vermilion. Comp. *perlege rubras | maiorum leges,* Juv., 14, 192' (Pretor, after Jahn). A low creature like Dama has a soul that is not above the statute-book; lofty spirits, like our Stoic, and believers in the higher law sneer at the canon and its maker. So MARC. ANTONIN., ap. FRONT., Ep., 2, 7 (p. 32 Naber), speaks of *deliramenta Masuriana.* Comp. QUINT., 12, 3, 11.—**vetavit :** for *vetuit,* reminds us of the slip of another youthful genius, Kirke White, and his ' rudely blow'd.' There is no sufficient warrant for the form.

**91-131.** A Stoic sermon. Text: Do nothing that you will spoil in the doing. You know nothing as you ought to know it, and you can do nothing as you ought to do it. You are ignorant of the first principles of morals; you have no control over your desires, your appetites. You may call yourself free, but you are a slave for all that. For one master without, you have a legion of masters within.

**91. Disce:** Comp. 3, 66.—**naso:** the simple Abl. as a whence case. Comp. 1, 83. The nose is the familiar seat of anger. THEOCR., 1, 18: καί οἱ ἀεὶ δριμεῖα χολὰ ποτὶ ῥινὶ κάθηται. For Biblical parallels, see Gesenius or Fürst, s. v. אַף. The anger is shown by snorting, or, as here, by snarling.—**rugosa :** Comp. *corruget nares,* HOR., Ep., 1, 5, 23.—**sanna :** 1, 62.

**92. dum revello :** '*while* I *am* plucking ' = ' *until* I *have* plucked.' See note on v. 10.—**veteres avias :** ' old grandmothers,' for ' inveterate, rooted, grandmotherish notions.' Comp. *patruos sapere,* 1, 11, and ὁ λεγόμενος γραῶν ὕθλος, PLAT., Theaet., 176 B.—**de pulmone:** The lung is the seat of pride in 3, 27 (comp. *suffla,* 4, 20). Jahn regards it here as the seat of wrath.

**93. erat:** ' as you thought.' G., 224, R. 3 ; A., 58, 3, *d.*—**tenuia rerum officia :** ' mastery of the subtle distinctions of duty.' *Tenuia,* a trisyllable, as often. G., 717. *Rerum,* parallel with *vitae.* See 1, 1.

**94. usum rapidae vitae :** ' the right management of the rapid course of life.' The metaphor is taken either from a river (*rapidus amnis, rapidi fluminum lapsus, rapidum flumen, rapidus*

*Tigris*, Hor.), which sweeps away the man who does not understand its current, or from a race-course in which there is no stop-
ping, as Conington thinks (3, 67). Others understand *rapidae*
simply as 'fleeting.'

**95. sambucam:** The ordinary translation, 'dulcimer,' is not
strictly correct, though 'dulcimer' suggests the exotic refinement
of the *sambuca*, a four-stringed instrument of Eastern origin, synonymous with cultivated luxury.—**citius aptaveris:** θᾶττον ἂν
ἁρμόσειας; written out = *citius aptaveris quam praetor det*, but it
is better not written out. Notice the Perf. Subj. 'You would
sooner *succeed in making* a dulcimer fit, sooner *get* a dulcimer
*to fit* [the hand of] a gawky camp-porter.'—**caloni:** used in its
original sense of a soldier's hewer of wood and drawer of water.
Persius, who has no admiration for soldiers themselves, would
naturally select a soldier's drudge as a type of awkwardness and
stupidity. So, in effect, Conington.—**alto:** We combine 'tall
and gawky;' 'hulking' (Conington). Comp. the sneer at the
*ingentis Titos*, 1, 20, and *Pulfennius ingens*, 5, 190, and the ἀνὴρ
τρισκαιδεκάπηχυς of Theocr., 15, 17.

**96. stat contra:** 'confronts,' 'stops the way.' Jahn comp.
Mart., 1, 53, 12: *stat contra, dicitque tibi tua pagina: Fur es*, a
parallel which no conscientious commentator can quote without
qualms. Juv., 3, 290: *stat contra starique iubet.*—**ratio:** 'Right
reason' here is equivalent to *natura* below, which is itself equivalent to *publica lex hominum.* See Knickenberg, l. c. p. 20 seqq.
—**secretam:** 'private.'—**garrit:** It is hard choosing between
*gannit* and *garrit.* Martial has *garrire in aurem, in auricu-
lam*, 1, 89, 1; 3, 28, 2, and *aurem dum tibi praesto garrienti*, 11,
24, 2; Afran., ap. Non., 452, 11 (283 Ribb.): *gannire ad aurem
numquam didici dominicam.*

**97. liceat:** with reference to v. 84.

**98. publica lex hominum naturaque:** 'The universal law of
human nature.' Of course in the peculiar Stoic sense. See note
on 3, 67. 'The doctrine of a supreme law of Nature, the actual
source and ideal standard of all particular laws, was characteristic of the Stoics, and lay at the bottom of the Roman juristical
notion of a *ratio naturalis* or *ius gentium*' (Conington).

**99. teneat actus:** As *tenere cursum* is sometimes used in the sense of ' check a course,' ' refrain from a course,' so *tenere vetitos actus* means to refrain from, or, as Pretor translates, ' hold in abeyance forbidden actions.'   To this effect König.  But as *tenere cursum* is also used in the sense of ' hold a course, keep on a course,' Jahn's version, which makes it a law of nature for weak ignorance to pursue forbidden actions, is not without justification.   In that case *fas est* = ' it is to be expected,' as in *operi longo fas est obrepere somnum*.   For the thought of the necessity of sin for the ignorant, see v. 119.   But the immediate context favors the former interpretation.   Casaubon's *tenere vetitos* = *habere pro vetitis* is without warrant in usage.

**100-104.** Popular illustrations of the doctrine drawn from medicine and navigation, and from Hor., Ep., 2, 1, 114 : *navem agere ignarus navis timet : abrotonum aegro | non audet, nisi qui didicit dare.*

**100. certo conpescere puncto,** etc. : ' although you do not know how to check [that is, to bring to the perpendicular and keep there] the tongue or index [of the steelyard by putting the equipoise or pea] at a certain point.'  ' Although you do not know how to use the steelyard ' (*statera*).   On the *examen*, see 1, 6 ; *punctum* is one of the points or notches (*notae*) on the graduated arm.   With *nescius conpescere* comp. *callidus suspendere*, 1, 118, and Prol., 11.—**natura** = *lex*, as above.

**102. peronatus :** The *pero* was a thick boot of raw-hide, *crudus pero*, Verg., Aen., 7, 690, and Juv., 14, 186 : *quem non pudet alto | per glaciem perone tegi, qui summovet Euros | pellibus inversis* (Jahn).   The *peronatus arator* is a clodhopper, a country bumpkin.

**103. luciferi rudis :** Not a good stroke.  Some knowledge of the stars was necessary for the ploughman himself, as Casaubon remarks.  See Verg., Georg., 1, 204 seqq.  So notably of the Pleiades, Hesiod, O. et D., 383. 615.—**Melicerta :** Portunus, patron of sailors, Verg., Georg., 1, 437.—**perisse :** Comp. Hor., Ep., 2, 1, 80 : *clament periisse pudorem | cuncti paene patres.*

**104. frontem :** the seat of modesty for modesty itself.   In English, ' face,' ' front,' and ' forehead ' are used for the absence of modesty ; but ' frontless ' and ' effrontery ' accord with the usage here and in Juv., 13, 242 : *quando recepit | eiectum simul attrita*

*de fronte pudorem?*—**de rebus :** 'from the world,' or omitted.
See 1, 1.—**recto talo :** Comp. Hor., Ep., 2, 1, 176 : *cadat an recto
stet fabula talo.* Jahn comp. further Pind., Isthm., 6, 12 : ὀρθῷ
ἕστασας ἐπὶ σφυρῷ, and Eur., Hel., 1449 : ὀρθῷ βῆναι ποδί. Transl.
' uprightly.'

**105. ars :** Philosophy. [*Philosophus*] *artem vitae professus,*
Cic., Tusc. Dis., 2, 4, 12 ; *sapientia ars est,* Sen., Ep., 29, 3.—**speciem :** Jahn gave up in 1868 the hopeless *specimen* of 1843, which left
*qua* in the next line utterly unprovided for. That this aberra-
tion of a distinguished scholar should have been followed at all
is a sad instance of *Nachbeterei*—a German word, not exclusively
a German vice.

**106. ne qua :** sc. *species.* *Ne* because of the general notion of
apprehension in the sentence, as after *videre.* G., 548, R. 2 ; A.,
70, 3, *e.*—**subaerato auro :** *Subaeratus* is a translation of ὑπόχαλκος. Ὑπόχαλκον νόμισμα is literally a coin (of gold or silver) with
copper underneath. Of course we should say gilt or silvered
copper coin. *Subaerato auro,* Abl. Abs. — **mendosum tinniat :**
With *mendosum* comp. *sonat vitium,* 3, 21 ; *solidum crepet,* v. 25 ;
with *tinniat,* Quint., 11, 3, 31 : *sonis homines, ut aera tinnitu,
dinoscimus.* Translate the line : ' that no [seeming truth] give a
faulty ring, due to the copper underneath the gold.'

**107. forent :** On the sequence, see G., 511, R. 2 ; A., 58, 10, *a.*

**108. illa prius creta,** etc. : Comp. Hor., Sat., 2, 3, 246 : *sanin
creta an carbone notandi.*

**109. modicus voti :** On the Gen., see G., 374, R. 2 ; A., 50, 3, *c.*
—**presso lare :** ' Your establishment within your means ?' *Pres-
sus* opposed to *diffusus.* — **dulcis :** ' indulgent.' Observe the
' sweet reasonableness' of the ancient religionist. He, too, was an
apostle of ' sweetness and light.'

**110. iam nunc—iam nunc :** ' At the very moment,' ' just at the
right time,' hence ' at one instant, at another.'—**astringas—laxes :**
' shut tight—open wide.'—**granaria :** 6, 25, Plural of abundance.
Comp. 2, 33.

**111. inque luto :** It was a favorite trick of the Roman boys to
solder a piece of money to a stone in the pavement, in order to
have a laugh at any one who might stoop to pick it up (Scholiast). Similar pranks are common enough now. Comp. Hor.,

Ep., 1, 16, 63 : *qui liberior sit avarus | in triviis fixum cum se de-mittit ob assem | non video.*

**112. glutto :** On the formation, see *cachinno*, 1, 12. 'Licker-ish-mouthed that you are' would give the coarse tone.—**sali-vam :** Doth not our mouth water?—**Mercurialem :** Excited by gain and not by food. See 2, 12. 'Water of treasure-trove' (Conington).

**113. haec mea sunt, teneo :** The commentators notice the legal tone.—**cum dixeris :** G., 584.

**114. -que ac :** a rare combination.—**praetoribus ac Iove dex-tro :** a kind of Zeugma = *praetoribus* [*auctoribus*] *et Iove dextro*, 'by the grace of the praetors and Jove.' The Jupiter here meant is the *Iuppiter Liberator* (Ζεὺς ἐλευθέριος), so famous in connection with the death of PERSIUS's friend, Thrasea Paetus, TAC., Ann., 16, 35. See Introd., xiii.

**115. sin :** '(if not) but if,' G., 593 ; A., 59, 1, *a ;* Ribbeck, l. c. 14.—**cum :** 'whereas,' 'after,' adversative.—**nostrae farinae :** 'one of our grain, batch, set,' 'one of our kidney'—doubtless a proverbial expression. The metaphor is taken from the mill or from the bakery. The batch referred to is the Stoic school. Of course the statement is ironical. 'Whereas (to judge by your bold pretensions to liberty) you were a little while ago in our set.'

**116-118.** The drift of the passage is plain enough. 'A change of fortune does not bring with it a change of character. If you possess all that you say you possess, then you are free and wise. But if you are, after all, the same old man, I take back all that I have granted. You are a fool, a slave.' This familiar Stoic thesis is covered over with a mass of confused metaphors, at least according to the commentators and translators.—**pellicu-lam veterem retines :** is supposed to be : 1. An ass in a lion's skin, after HOR., Sat., 1, 6, 22 ; or, 2. A snake that has not cast its slough (Jahn).—**astutam servas vulpem :** is the fox dressed up like a lion, HOR., Sat., 2, 3, 186.—**vapido pectore :** contains an allusion to 'dead wine,' *vappa*, v. 77, and is opposed to *incoc-tum generoso pectus honesto*, 2, 74.—**funem reduco :** 1. Of a beast that has had rope allowed it and is pulled in ; 2. Of a cock-chaf-er that is played at the end of a string (AR., Nub., 763).—**fronte**

**politus :** words that do not fit in very satisfactorily with ass, fox, flat wine, restiff beast, or buzzing cock-chafer. My admiration of PERSIUS is not unqualified, but this medley is almost too wild even for his turbid genius; and here, as elsewhere, commentators have been misled by looking at mere verbal coincidences with HORACE. There is an Aesopic fable (149 Halm), the moral of which gives the substance of this passage : ὁ λόγος δηλοῖ ὅτι οἱ φαῦλοι τῶν ἀνϑρώπων, κἂν τὰ προσχήματα λαμπρότερα ἀναλάβωσι, τὴν γοῦν φύσιν οὐ μετατίϑενται. In this fable, which bears a family likeness to Ϝαλῆ ποτ᾽ ἀνδρός (BABR. 32), *La Chatte Metamorphosée en Femme* (LA FONTAINE, 2, 18), Zeus, charmed with the cleverness of Reynard, had made him king of the beasts; but wishing to try whether fortune had changed his character, he caused a beetle to fly before His Majesty's eyes as he was borne by in state. The fox could not withstand the temptation, leaped from the litter, and tried to catch the game in such unseemly guise that Zeus deposed him. The fox is Dama, made Marcus; nay, become a philosopher (*nostrae farinae*), and the philosopher is king : *sapiens—dives | liber, honoratus, pulcher, rex denique regum*, as HORACE puts the Stoic doctrine (Ep., 1, 1, 107). But if despite his fair seeming, his smooth regal brow (*fronte politus*), he retains his old nature (*pelliculam veterem*), and the old Reynard—the old rascal that swindled his master for a feed of corn—is still in his heart (*astutam servas sub pectore vulpem*), our *deus ex machina* takes back all that he has granted; he is a slave still.

**117. relego :** So Jahn. Inferior MSS. have *repeto*. *Relego* evidently suggested the new figure, *funem reduco.*

**119. digitum exsere, peccas :** a favorite expression with the Stoics to show that the wise man alone understands the conduct of life. EPICTET., fr. 53 : ἡ φιλοσοφία φησὶν ὅτι οὐδὲ τὸν δάκτυλον ἐκτείνειν εἰκῆ προσήκει (Casaubon).

**120. nullo ture litabis :** Comp. 2, 75. Here *litabis = litando impetrabis.*

**122. fossor :** 'a ditcher, a clown, a clodhopper.' *Fossor = incultus.* Comp. 'navvy.' JUVENAL (11, 80) speaks of the *squalidus fossor;* CATULLUS (22, 10) combines *fossor* and *caprimulgus ;* EUR. (El., 252), σκαφεύς and βουφορβός.

**123. tris tantum ad numeros moveare :** ' dance three steps in time.' *Ad*, as often, of the standard; *numerus* = ῥυϑμός; *moveri* of the dance, as in Hor., Ep., 2, 2, 125, and as *motus* in Od., 3, 6, 21 : *motus doceri gaudet Ionicos | matura virgo.*—**satyrum :** a kind of Cognate Accusative, as in Hor., l. c. : *qui | nunc satyrum, nunc agrestem Cyclopa movetur.* Persius selects the *satyrus* in distinct opposition to the *agrestis Cyclops*, a more congenial dance for the *agrestis fossor.* See the commentators on Horace.—**Bathylli :** Bathyllus was a famous dancer in the time of Augustus. More bookishness. See Phaedr., 5, 7, 5; Juv., 6, 63.

**124. Liber ego :** The language of Dama. Only Dama is fading out. 'Persius meets this reassertion of freedom with a new answer. Before he had contended that fools had no *rights;* now he shows that they have no independent *power*' (Conington).— **Unde datum hoc sentis :** So Hor., Sat., 2, 2, 31 : *Unde datum hoc sentis,* only *sentis* here is equivalent to *censes* (Jahn). On the interrogative with the Participle, see 3, 67. *Unde datum,* 'Who allowed you?' *unde* being = *a quo.* Comp. *inde,* 1, 126, and G., 613, R. 1; A., 48, 5.—**tot subdite rebus :** Comp. Hor., Sat., 2, 7, 75 : *tune mihi dominus rerum imperiis hominumque | tot tantisque minor* = ἥσσων = *subditus.*

**125. an :** 'or' (do you mean to say?) 'what?' See 1, 41.— **relaxat :** in a general sense. Exit Dama. Enter Impersonal *Tu.*

**126. I puer :** sample order of a sample master.—**strigiles :** A man might go to a common bath, but he would not like to use a common scraper (στριγίλις, ξύστρα). On the *strigilis,* see, if needful, the commentators on Juv., 3, 263.—**Crispini :** Perhaps the bath-keeper. The name is Horatian, Sat., 1, 2, 120, and elsewhere.

**127. si increpuit :** The slave loiters, the master scolds.— '**cessas nugator :**' Much more effective in the mouth of the master than as an apodosis to *si increpuit,* as Hermann has it, and Jahn (1868); though Schlüter's remark, *verba 'cessas nugator?' dominum, non philosophum decent,* does not amount to much, when we consider that the philosopher is Persius himself. *Nugator* is used here of wasting time; but the use of *nugari* and its forms, which were often addressed to slaves, is wider, like the English 'fool.' So in Petron., 52, a boy lets a cup fall, and Trimalchio cries, *ne sis nugax.* With *cessas* comp. Hor., Ep., 2, 2, 14 : *semel*

H 2

*hic cessavit.* 'What do you mean by this loitering, you dawd-ler, you?'—**servitium acre:** 'the goad of bondage,' as Conington suggests. *Acre,* from the same radical as *aculeus.*

**128. nihil nec quicquam:** G., 482, R. 3.

**129. nervos:** 'wires.' The figure of the puppet (*sigillarium,* ἄγαλμα νευρόσπαστον) was a favorite one with the Stoics, to judge by M. ANTONINUS, who uses it very often, e. g., σιγιλλάρια νευρο-σπαστούμενα, 7, 3; νευροσπαστία, 6, 28. Comp. HOR., Sat., 2, 7, 80: *tu mihi qui imperitas alii servis miser atque | duceris ut nervis ali-enis mobile lignum.*—**agitet:** 'There is nothing from without to set your wires going.' Your masters are within.—**iecore:** See 1, 25.

**130. domini:** An immemorial figure. So SOPHOCLES of Love. *Di meliora, inquit, libenter vero istinc sicut a domino agresti ac fu-rioso profugi,* CIC., Cat. Mai., 14, 47.—**qui:** 'how?'—**exis** = *evadis.* See 1, 46; 6, 60.

**131. atque** = *quam.* G., 311, R. 6.—**hic** = *de quo loquimur.* G., 290, 3.—**metus erilis** = *metus eri.* G., 360, R. 1; 363, R.; A., 50, 1, *a.* 'If I be a master, where is *my fear?*' Mal., 1, 6. The as-sumption of Hendiadys, 'fear of the master's whip,' is unneces-sary, and makes the passage less forcible.

**132-191.** The remainder of the Satire is taken up with de-scriptions of the ruling passions: Avarice (132–142), Luxury (143–160), Love (161–175), Ambition (176–179), Superstition (180–189). The language is lively and mimetic, and forcibly recalls the connection between comedy and satire.

**132-160.** Avarice finds you snoring, makes you get up, thrusts a bill of lading in your hand, cuts out work for you—not very honest work either—and chides you till she gets you to the ship. As you are about to embark, Luxury takes you aside, remon-strates with you, reminds you of the annoyances of a sea voyage. And all for what? The difference between five and eleven per cent. Why so greedy? 'Life let us cherish.' Enjoy it while you may. And so you are in a strait betwixt two. First you submit to one, then to the other master; and when you have once rebelled, you must not say, 'I have broken my bonds.' So a struggling hound may wrench away the staple, but drags the chain after it.

**132. Mane stertis:** a reminiscence of himself, 3, 3.

**134. saperdam :** Sing. for the Plur.  Comp. *mena*, 3, 76.  The *saperda* (σαπέρδης, κορακῖνος) was a cheap fish for salting.  The best came from the Palus Maeotis (Sea of Azow, Balik-Denghis, or Fish-sea), where they were caught in vast quantities.  'Salt herring.'—**Ponto :** a whence case.

**135. castoreum, stuppas, hebenum, tus :** A mere hodge-podge. Comp. MENAND., fr. 720 (4, 279 Mein.) : στυππεῖον, ἐλέφαντ', οἶνον, αὐλαίαν, μύρον.  The wares are mainly Eastern.  Musk came from Pontus, ebony and frankincense from the Far East.—**lubrica Coa :** 'slippery Coans' may be understood of 'oily (or laxative) Coan wines,' HOR., Sat., 2, 4, 29, or of 'soft Coan vestments,' which were little more than woven air, HOR., Od., 4, 13, 13.  The use of *Coa* for 'Coan robes' is sustained by Ov., A. A., 2, 298 : *Coa decere puta*, even if HOR., Sat., 1, 2, 101, be cavilled at, and the effect is droller.

**136. recens primus piper :** *Recens*, 'fresh,' 'just in ;' *primus*, 'forestall the market.'—**ex sitiente camelo :** The thirsty camel brings the scene before our eyes—comp. *ante boves*, 1, 74—and shows that the genuine Indian pepper is meant, the *rugosum piper* of v. 55.  The camel must have come a long way to be thirsty (*sitim quadriduo tolerat*, PLIN., H. N., 8, 18), but Madam Avarice will not let her slave wait until the camel has been unloaded and has had its drink.

**137. verte aliquid ; iura :** *Verte aliquid* is said with impatience, and *aliquid* is to be urged  Comp. *frange aliquid*, 6, 32 ; *dest aliquid*, 6, 64 ; *fodere aut arare aut aliquid ferre*, TER., Heaut., 1, 1, 17.  'Do something or other in the way of trade.'  This obviates Jahn's objection, who finds the expression tame after the preceding list, and prefers to make *vertere* = *versuram facere*, 'borrow money' (to pay debts), and to interpret *iura* of swearing out of the obligation.  But the connection in which *iura* stands shows that it is professional, and hence dishonorable ; and though *verte aliquid* is not necessarily immoral, observe that in English we add 'honest' to the phrase 'turn a penny,' if we wish to prevent a sinister interpretation, which is the interpretation here, as König remarks.  As for the 'tameness,' *mercare* is 'tame' after *vende animam lucro*, 6, 75.

**138. varo :** or *baro*, 'lout.'  This obscure word is entered by

Vaniček (*Etym. Wörterb.*, S. 36) under KAR (KVAR)—comp. *varus*, 'crooked'—so that *varo* would be 'a wrong-headed creature,' 'a perverse blockhead.' The verb *obvaro* occurs in ENNIUS (Trag., 2 Vahl.), and *varo* (Subst.) would be a formation like *cachinno* (1, 12) and *palpo* (5, 176).—**regustatum digito terebrare salinum:** After the Greek proverb: ἀλίαν τρυπᾶν (of extreme poverty). Casaubon quotes, and every body after him, APOLL. TYAN., Ep., 7: ἐμοὶ δ' εἴη τὴν ἀλίαν τρυπᾶν ἐν Θέμιδος οἴκῳ. 'To taste and taste until you bore a hole with your finger in the salt-cellar.' 'To lick the platter clean.'—**salinum:** Only the most advanced philosophers professed to consider salt, which even the miser could not well dispense with (4, 30), as a luxury. So Thrasycles, in LUC., Tim., 56: ὄψον δὲ ἥδιστον θύμον ἢ κάρδαμον ἢ εἴ ποτε τρυφῴην ὀλίγον τῶν ἀλῶν.

**139. perages:** according to Casaubon, an imitation of the Gr. διάγειν. Warrant for the ellipsis of *vitam* or *aetatem* seems to be lacking. Some wish to read *perges* here, and combine it with *terebrarē*. If so, the word *perges* must not be translated 'continue' (τρυπῶν διατελεῖς), but 'proceed.' See the Dictionaries. There is no authority for making *perages* = *perges*.—**vivere cum Iove:** Madam Avarice is blasphemously familiar in her expressions. 'To live on good terms with Jupiter.'

**140. pellem:** simply 'a skin,' which might serve as many purposes as a modern traveller's shawl. Jahn interprets it as meaning a sort of packing cloth (*segestre*), and compares PETRON., 102. This is much more likely than the *pastoria pellis* of Ov., Met., 2, 680, the βαίτη of THEOCR., 3, 25, elsewhere called νάκος, 5, 2, 'a peasant's coat of raw hide.'—**succinctus:** 'high girt,' hence 'equipped.'—**oenophorum:** 'a wine case.' Comp. HOR., Sat., 1, 6, 109: *pueri lasanum portantes oenophorumque.*

**141. Ocius ad navem:** It matters not who says this: 'Off to the ship this instant.' We are on the wharf, where such cries are in the air; but if we must assign them to somebody, they are best assigned to the master, who hurries the slaves on board. —**quin:** G., 551, 1; A., 70, 4, *g.*—**trabe vasta:** 'mammoth ship.' The man's greed is indicated by the size of the ship, as contrasted with the slenderness of his personal equipment. *Vastum Aegae-*

*um*, another reading, would be an epithet wasted, a rare extravagance in PERSIUS.

**142. rapias :** ' scour.' Casaubon comp. STAT., Theb., 5, 3 : *rapere campum.* So VERG., Georg., 3, 103 : *campum | corripuere.* The notion is that of devouring.—**sollers :** ' artful ' (literally, all-art).

**143. seductum :** Comp. 2, 4 ; 6, 42.—**quo deinde ruis ?** So VERG., Aen., 5, 741. *Deinde,* ' next.'

**144. quid tibi vis ?** Comp. HOR., Sat., 1, 2, 69. G., 351, R. ; A., 51, 7, *d.*—**calido :** is proleptic. ' Your breast is heated by a rising of potent bile.'—**mascula** $=robusta$ (Jahn). *Mascula bilis* means *bilis nigra,* μελαγχολία. Conington compares the Greek use of ἄρσην as κτύπος ἄρσην, SOPH., Phil., 1455. See 6, 4.

**145. intumuit :** Comp. 2, 14 ; 3, 8.—**non exstinxerit :** οὐκ ἂν σβέσειε. G., 629 (250) ; A., 60, 2, *b.*—**urna :** nearly three gallons, half an amphora.—**cicutae :** the remedy for madness from this cause, HOR., Ep., 2, 2, 53.

**146. mare transilias :** G., 251 ; A., 57, 6. Conington's ' skip across ' would hardly answer for HORACE'S *non tangenda rates | transiliunt vada,* Od., 1, 3, 24. Tr. ' vault over.'—**torta cannabe :** ' Twisted hemp ' is ' rope,' but PERSIUS probably means a ' coil of rope.'—**fulto :** with *tibi.* Jahn quotes JUV., 3, 82 : *fultusque toro meliore recumbet.* A coil of rope will be your cushion and a bench your table.

**147. Veientanumque rubellum :** The *Veientana uva* (MART., 2, 53, 4) yielded a coarse red wine. *Et Veientani bibitur faex crassa rubelli,* MART., 1, 103, 9. Not a happy stroke, as Teuffel has observed. A sea voyage does not involve bad wine.

**148. vapida pice :** ' fusty pitch.' Jars were pitched to preserve the wine.—**laesum :** ' damaged.'—**sessilis obba :** ' broad-bottomed˙jorum,' ' squab jug ' (Gifford). *Obba* is an obsolete word for a large drinking-cup. Conington's ' noggin ' does not hold enough.

**149. quincunce :** As an *as* a month is twelve per cent. per annum, so $\frac{5}{12}$ *as* (*quincunx*) is five per cent., and *deunx* eleven.

**150. nutrieras :** We use ' nursing ' in similar connections, but rather in the sense of ' husbanding.' The figure is an extension of the Greek τόκος. See SHAKSP., M. of V., 1, 3, where the ' breed

for barren metal' embodies an ancient prejudice. Comp. further
HOR., Ep., 1, 18, 35: *nummos alienos pascet.*—**nummi—pergant
avidos sudare deunces:** So Jahn (1843). 'May go on to sweat
out a greedy eleven per cent.' Hermann edits: *nummos—peragant avido sudore deunces*, and so Jahn (1868). H. (*L. P.*, II., 57)
refers to *bona peragere* (6, 22), and says that the merchant, dissatisfied with his modest five per cent. which had increased his
capital, goes in for eleven per cent., which gobbles it up, and has
his sweat for his pains. On *pergant*, see note on v. 139; with
*sudare deunces* comp. VERG., Ecl., 4, 30: *sudabunt roscida mella.*

**151. indulge genio:** See note on 2, 3.—**nostrum est quod
vivis:** Variously interpreted. 'Your real life is mine,' i. e., 'only
that part of life which you bestow on me is life' (Casaubon, and
so, in effect, Jahn). 'Your life belongs to me and you (*nostrum*
answering to *carpamus dulcia*), not to any one else, such as Avarice, and it is all that we have' (Conington). 'It is all in our
favor that you are alive' (Pretor)—clearly wrong. There is an
evident reminiscence of the Horatian *quod spiro et placeo, si placeo, tuum est* (Od., 4, 3, 24), which sustains Casaubon's view.

**152. cinis et manes et fabula fies:** See note on 1, 36. There
are clearly three stages, as Conington suggests: 'first ashes, then
a shade, then a name.' With *fabula fies* comp. HOR., Ep., 1, 13,
9: *fabula fias*, and Od., 1, 4, 16: *iam te premet nox fabulaeque
manes.*

**153. vive memor leti:** So HOR., Sat., 2, 6, 97.—**hoc quod loquor inde est:** 'What I am saying—this speech of mine—is so
much off, so much time lost.' Comp. *dum loquimur fugerit in-
vida | aetas*, HOR., Od., 1, 11, 7.

**154. en quid agis?** See 3, 5.—**duplici hamo:** 'a couple of
hooks.' If *hamo* is a fish-hook, *scinderis* is a metaphor within a
metaphor. 'You are like a fish distracted by two hooks,' not
knowing which to bite at. Comp. HOR., Ep., 1, 7, 74: *occultum
visus decurrere piscis ad hamum*, and for *scinderis*, VERG., Aen., 2,
39: *scinditur incertum studia in contraria vulgus.* The execu-
tioner's hook, which others understand, is generally *uncus;* JUV.,
10, 66: *Seianus ducitur unco.*

**155. sequeris:** See note on 3, 5.—**subeas oportet:** G., 535, R.
1; A., 70, 3, *f*, R.

**155. oberres:** Gr. δραπετεύειν, 'go at large' (Pretor).

**156. nec—dicas** = *neu dicas.* See note on 1, 5.

**159. nam et:** (Don't say so) 'for.' ' Why, there's the dog that, like you (*et*), breaks its fastening.'—**luctata:** 'by a wrench.'—**nodum:** ' is the knot by which the chain is fastened to the bar of the door, (*sera*). Comp. PROP., 4, 11, 25–6: *Cerberus et nullas hodie petat improbus umbras,* | *sed iaceat tacita lapsa catena s e r a*' (Pretor).—**et tamen:** So Jahn (1868). *At tamen,* the reading of most MSS., can not stand, if Madvig is right in maintaining that *at tamen* always means ' at least.' Hermann's *ast tamen* is well supported by MSS., and is more vigorous than *et.*

**160. a collo:** G., 388, R. 2 ; A., 42, 2.—**pars longa catenae:** The long chain hampers its flight, and makes it easier to catch. The comparison clearly suggests the next picture.

**161-175.** PERSIUS, knowing little of love or liaison, goes to his Greek books for an example, and finds it, where it was not far to seek, in MENANDER'S Eunuch. HORACE (Sat., 2, 3, 259 seqq.) follows TERENCE'S adaptation, PERSIUS seems to have stuck to the original. Hence the dialogue is between Chaerestratus (Χαιρέστρατος), the young master, and Davus (Δᾶος), the confidential servant, and not between Phaedria and Parmeno, as in the Latin dramatist.

CH. Davus, I'm going to put a stop to this sort of thing.—D. Thank Heaven for that!—Ch. But—I should not like to hurt her feelings. Do you think she'll cry ?—D. Well, if you talk that way, you had better not kick over the traces at all. She will give it to you soundly when she gets hold of you again, and she will get hold of you again as soon as she calls you. Don't be making suppositions. Go back to her in no case.

A man who can make such a resolution and keep it—here is your free man, not the lictor's whirligig.

**161. Dave, cito:** Observe how he jerks out the words between the gnawings.—**credas iubeo:** G., 546, R. 3.—**finire dolores,** etc.: From HOR., l. c. 263 : *an potius mediter finire dolores.*

**162. praeteritos:** logically superfluous with *finire,* and yet not bad dramatically ; ' that I have been having, undergoing.'—**crudum:** predicative, ' to the raw,' to the quick.' Comp. 1, 106 : *demorsos unguis.*

**163. a d rodens:** more natural than *abrodens.* 'He is in meditation, not in despair' (Hermann). — **siccis:** opp. to *madidis, ebriis.* 'What! shall I be a standing disgrace in the way of my sober relations?'

**164. rumore sinistro:** 'What? make myself the talk of all the scandal-mongers by squandering my estate?'

**165. limen ad obscenum:** 'at a bawdy-house.' See note on 1, 109. He puts the case strongly. Remember that he is shut out. — **frangam:** colloquial, 'smash up,' 'make flinders of.' — **Chrysidis:** In TERENCE the lady's name is Thais, not Chrysis. — **udas:** 'dripping.' With what? With perfumes (LUCR., 4, 1179), with wine (HOR., Od., 1, 7, 22), with tears (Ov., Am., 1, 6, 18), with rain (HOR., Od., 3, 10, 19), with the sweat of the commentators of PERSIUS.

**166.** Comp. HOR., Sat., 1, 4, 51: *ebrius et, magnum quod dedecus, ambulet ante | noctem cum facibus.* — **ante fores canto:** Antique erotic literature is full of the caterwaulings of excluded lovers (παρακλαυσίθυρα).

**167. puer:** 'Davus encourages his master, hence *puer* instead of TERENCE and HORACE'S *ere*' (Conington). 'My young master' gives the tone here, 'my boy' below. — **sapias:** 'I do hope you are going to show your sense.' Rather optative than imperative. — **dis depellentibus:** *depulsoribus = dis averruncis.* The Gr. is ἀποτρόπαιος, ἀπωσίκακος, ἀλεξίκακος. Comp. ἀποτρόποισι δαίμοσι, AESCH., Pers., 203 (quoted by Pretor).

**169. Nugaris:** 'at your old nonsense, I see.' See v. 127. — **solea:** The slipper was and is a matronly instrument of torture (LUC., D. D., 11, 1), and hence the fun of its application to grown-up men, as in the familiar story of Hercules and Omphalé, LUC., D. D., 13, 2. 'To slipper' would be understood as well in a modern nursery as βλαυτοῦν was in à Greek gynaikonitis. *Philtra quibus valeat mentem vexare mariti | et solea pulsare natis,* JUV., 6, 611–12. — **obiurgabere:** a *terminus technicus.* PETRON., 34: *colaphis objurgare puerum iussit.* — **rubra:** A dramatic touch. This 'No Goody Two Shoes' wore the fashionable red slippers. Comp. the *talon rouge* of the last century.

**170. ne trepidare velis** = *noli trepidare.* 'Pray don't undertake to be restiff, to be plunging about.' Chaerestratus is a wild beast in the toils. This suggests *ferus*, and then the metaphor is dropped, unless *exieras*, v. 174, be a remnant of it.

**171.** The distribution of what follows is not clear. Jahn and Hermann make Davus's speech end with *dicas*, so that *haud mora* is the reply which the slave puts into the mouth of his master. 'If she should call you, you would say : " Anon, anon, mistress."' Chaerestratus speaks the words from *Quidnam* to *accedam*, and Davus concludes with *si totus—nec nunc*. If Jahn's view be adopted, I do not see how we are to reject the old conjecture *ne tunc* or *nec tunc* for the reading *ne nunc, nec nunc*, v. 174. According to Heinrich, followed by Macleane and Conington, *haud mora* is adverbial, and the words *quidnam—accedam* are attributed by Davus to Chaerestratus. 'In TERENCE,' says Conington, 'the lover has received a summons before the scene begins, and he deliberates whether to obey it. In PERSIUS he is trying to resolve under the pressure of disappointment, and even then can not make up his mind; so that his servant tells him that if he *should* be summoned back, he is pretty sure to entertain the question.' · I have followed Heinrich's arrangement. Speech within speech is as characteristic of PERSIUS as metaphor within metaphor.

**172. nec nunc :** So Jahn in his ed. of 1868. *Ne nunc,* his former reading, for *ne nunc quidem*, condemned by Madvig, has a doubtful support in HOR., Sat., 2, 3, 262, a clear support in PETRON., 9. 47.—**arcessat :** So Jahn for *arcessor*, which is excessively harsh, by reason of the double change, person and mood, in *supplicet*.

**174. si exieras :** εἰ γ' ἐξέβης. 'If (as you pretend you did) you got away heart-whole and fancy-free, don't go to her even now.' *Si* with Pluperf. Ind. (not iterative) is not common, CIC., N. D., 2, 35, 90. Others read *exieris*.—**nec nunc :** sc. *accedas*.—**hic, hic :** The Adverb, as appears from *in festuca.* Comp. HOR., Ep., 1, 17, 39 : *hic est aut nusquam quod quaerimus.*

**175. festuca :** is generally explained as a synonyme for *vindicta*. Others refer it to the practice of throwing stubble on the manumitted slave, PLUT., De Sera Num. Vind., p. 550 (Conington).— **ineptus :** 'as if a lictor could make a man truly free !' (Jahn).

**176-179.** Ambition's Slave.

**176. palpo :** literally 'patter, stroker,' 'softsawder-man,' i. e., electioneerer. Another of the *verba togae.* See note on 1, 12.

*Palpo* is explained by Io. Sarisberiensis (ap. Jahn) as ' one who feels his way with the people;' but this is not so simple nor so much in accordance with the use of *palpare*.—**ducit hiantem:** Comp. Hor., Sat., 1, 2, 88: *emptorem inducat hiantem*, where Bentley reads *ducat* on account of this passage. Also Verg., Georg., 2, 508: *hunc plausus hiantem— | corripuit*, and Solon, 13, 36 (Bergk), χάσκοντες κούφαις ἐλπίσι τερπόμεθα.

**177. cretata** = *candidata.* Togas were chalked then, as belts are pipe-clayed now. The candidate naturally put on his best. ' My Lady Canvass in holiday attire, in spotless white.'—**vigila:** ' Be up early,' in the same sense as our phrase, ' You must get up early to do this or that.' There is no special reference to the morning *salutatio.*—**cicer:** Comp. Hor., Sat., 2, 3, 182: *in cicere atque faba bona tu perdasque lupinis, | latus ut in circo spatiere et aeneus ut stes.* The vetch was a vulgar vegetable.

**178. nostra:** *nobis aedilibus celebrata* (Jahn). On the ironical First Person, see 3, 3.—**Floralia:** See the Dictionaries.

**179. aprici** = *apricantes.* See 4, 18. 19. To ' love to live i' th' sun ' (Shaksp.) is common to the feebleness of age and the luxury of youth, 4, 33.—**quid pulchrius:** Snatch of the old men's chat (Hermann). Ironical comment of Persius (Jahn). The former is more in Persius's manner.

**at:** An abrupt transition to the Thraldom of Superstition (180–188). Whether the slave of superstition is identical with the slave of ambition or not is not certain—probably not.

**180. Herodis—dies:** Probably Herod's birthday, celebrated by the sect of the Herodians. Persius takes Herod as the most familiar Jewish personage to indicate Jewish superstition. On the spread of Judaism in the Roman Empire, see Friedländer, *Sittengesch.*, 3, 489.—**uncta fenestra:** The ' window ' is ' greasy ' from the oil-lamps.

**181. lucernae:** Those who wish illustrations for what they can see with their own eyes, may consult Friedländer, l. c. 1, 292. The lights remind one of the Feast of Tabernacles.

**182. violas:** Comp. Juv., 12, 90: *omnis violae iactabo colores.* The violet may be our violet or the pansy *(viola bicolor).*—**rubrumque amplexa catinum:** The tunny is so large that it embraces the dish, and is not embraced by it. Comp. Hor., Sat., 2,

4, 77 : *angustoque vagos piscis urgere c a t i n o.* *Rubrum*, the common color of pottery.

**183. cauda thynni :** The tunny has a large tail, hence some such adjective as 'taily' is desiderated. Comp. note on 6, 10.— **natat :** Makes fun of the fish's swimming in the circumstances. —**tumet :** 'bulges.' The big belly of the jar looks as if it were 'swollen' with wine.

**184. labra movet tacitus :** Comp. Hor., Ep., 1, 16, 60 : *labra movet, metuens audiri* (of a prayer to Laverna). A recondite allusion to the secret prayer of the Jews is unlikely.—**recutita sabbata** = *recutitorum sabbata.* Comp. Ov., Rem. Am., 219, 220 : *nec te peregrina morentur | sabbata.*—**palles** = *pallidus times.* G., 329, R. 1 ; A., 52, 1, *a.* Comp. our English 'blanch' or 'blench.'

**185. tum :** As soon as the man has got over his Jewish fright he is assailed by other superstitions.—**lemures :** 'hobgoblins.' See note on 2, 3. Comp. Hor., Ep., 2, 2, 208 : *somnia, terrores magicos, miracula, sagas,| nocturnos lemures, portentaque Thessala rides ?*—**ovoque pericula rupto :** The Schol. refers these words to the Gr. ᾠοσκοπική (Jahn). 'The priests used to put eggs on the fire, and observe whether the moisture came out from the side or the top, the bursting of the egg being considered a very dangerous sign.' So Conington, after the Scholiast. *Lemures* and *pericula* have no strict grammatical connection. Some supply *timentur* out of *palles*, others connect with *incussere* by Zeugma.

**186. grandes galli :** Juvenal's *ingens | semivir* (6, 512). The peculiar worship of Cybelé had long been familiar to the Romans.—**sistro :** The σεῖστρον, or 'timbrel,' was peculiar to the service of Isis, which had been imported more recently. On its significance, see Plut., De Isid. et Osir., p. 376. The vibratory theory of life, with its perpetual sensuous unrest, is no novelty, as some of its eloquent advocates seem to think.—**lusca :** Why *lusca ?* The priestess is supposed to have been struck blind by Isis, who visited offenders in that way. Comp. Ov., Ep. ex P., 1, 1, 53, and Juv., 13, 93 : *Isis et irato feriat mea lumina sistro.* One homely explanation is that the priestess, being one-eyed, had betaken herself to religion in despair of a husband ! (Schol.)

**187. incussere :** Gr. Aorist. Comp. 3, 101. The expression, 'strike the gods into you,' after the analogy of *incutere metum*, *terrorem*, is the other side of VERGIL's famous *magnum si pectore possit | excussisse deum* (Aen., 6, 78).—**inflantis :** 'who have a way of swelling.' Compare the use of *depellentibus* for *depulsoribus*, v. 167. See G., 439.

**188. praedictum :** 'prescribed.'—**alli :** The superstitious usage here referred to has not yet been paralleled.

**189-91.** Last scene of all. Horse-laughter of the muscular military.

**189. Dixeris—ridet** = *si dixeris—ridet.* Comp. v. 78.—**varicosos :** Comp. JUV., 6, 397: *varicosus fiet haruspex* (from long-standing). Varicose veins would naturally be common with men who were as much on their legs as the soldiers of that day. But as *varicare* means to stand or walk, as if one had *varices*, 'to straddle' (QUINT., 11, 3, 125), and as *vāricus* means 'straddling' (Ov., A. A., 3, 304), it seems better to translate *varicosos* 'straddling' here, always remembering the origin. With the change of quantity, comp. *văcillo* and *vācillo* (*vaccillo*), Lachm., *Lucret.*, p. 37.—**centurionum :** See note on 3, 77.

**190. crassum ridet :** Comp. *subrisit molle*, 3, 110.—**Pulfennius :** Jahn's last. The name is variously written. Notice a similar trouble about a *hircosus centurio* in CAES., B. G., 5, 44, once Pulfio, now Pulio. Heinrich recognizes a fellow-countryman in *Vulfennius* (Wulfen).—**ingens :** Comp. *torosa inventus*, 3, 86; *caloni alto*, 5, 95.

**191. Graecos :** Comp. *doctores Graios*, 6, 38.—**curto :** 'clipped.' —**licetur :** A similar notion is worked out with admirable humor in LUCIAN's Vitarum Auctio.

---

## SIXTH SATIRE.

THE Sixth Satire is addressed to Caesius Bassus, a friend of PERSIUS. The theme of it is the Proper Use of the Goods of this Life, which takes the personal form of a vindication of the poet's course in preferring moderate enjoyment to mean parsimony or grasping avarice.

ARGUMENT.—Are you by this time snugly ensconced by your Sabine fire? And *do* the chords of your lyre wake to life at your vigorous touch? O cunning craftsman! in whose song the noble tongue of our sires is set to manly music, while young and old alike feel the play of your sportive wit, which in all its sport never forgets the gentleman (1-6).

While you are yonder, I am in my dear Liguria, where the coast is warm, the sea is wintry but kindly, the rocks bar out the storm, and the shore retreats far inland.

'Luna's port—'tis well worth while, good people, to know it.'

This was a saying of Ennius, as he woke up in his senses from his Pythagorean dreams and became plain Quintus, instead of the 'blind old man of Scio's rocky isle,' and a wise saying of that hearty old cock it was (7-11).

Well, here I am, caring nothing for the rabble rout, caring nothing what an ill wind may be getting up for my flock. My neighbor may have a better patch of ground, men of lower birth may be growing rich over me. I will not fret myself into a crooked old man for that, nor dine without a bit of something nice, nor nose out a swindle in the imperfect seal of a flagon of flat wine (12-17).

How men differ in such matters! The very same horoscope may bring forth rights and lefts. Here is one that even on his birthday allows himself only the scantiest and meanest fare. Here is another that eats up, like a spirited lad as he is, a vast estate. For my part, 'Enjoyment, enjoyment,' is my motto, although I do not intend to treat my freedmen to turbots, and do not understand the difference between cock-ortolan and hen-ortolan after they are cooked (18-24).

Now this is the way to live, I take it. Up to your harvest, up to the last grain of your garners. What are you afraid of? It is a mere matter of harrowing, and lo! another crop is there (25, 26).

But you say, Mr. Critic, 'There are claims on one. A friend is shipwrecked, the poor fellow is utterly ruined. One must do something for him.'

Well and good! Sell a piece of land, give the proceeds to the needy friend, and keep him from begging up and down with a pictorial appeal to the benevolent (27-33).

Ay, but what of the heir? He will dock the funeral meats, if you dock the estate. One, sure, would not be stenchful when one's dead, and your bones will not be perfumed, or the perfumes will be stale or adulterated. One can not expect to diminish one's property without paying for it. Why, I heard Bestius say of your Greek teachers, from whom you learned this precious wisdom of yours, that ever since this new doctrine came to town the very haymakers have been spoiling their good, wholesome fare by rancid grease.

Well, what of all this—the heir's neglect and Bestius's fault-finding—would you fear them beyond the grave? (34-41).

But come, my heir, let us dismiss the critic, and have a quiet chat to-

gether.  Consider the claims on me.  Here comes a glorious piece of
news from the Emperor.  The Germans have been defeated with great
slaughter.  A grand triumph is preparing.  This is no time to hold back.
I am going to bring out a hundred pairs of gladiators in honor of the occasion.  Forbid it, if you dare.  If you don't like that, I am going to
give largess to the people—none of your vile vetches, but oil and pasties.
Do you object?  Out with it (42–51).

What do you say?  'My farm is hardly worth having after that.'
Well, if you don't want it, I can get some of the women to take it; and
if there is none of them left, I can go to the next village, and Hodge will
accept.  'A son of earth?' you say; 'a nobody?'  Pshaw!  If you come
to that, I can just remember who my great-great-grandfather was.  Two
generations further back and I come to a son of earth, a nobody, and
Hodge is a relation—a distant relation, but still a relation—a kind of
great-great-uncle.  Believe me, the Lord No Zoo is father of us all (52–
60).

You are an impatient heir, I must say.  Why can't you wait for my
shoes until I take them off?  I am the God of Fortune to you, just as he
is painted in the pictures, with a purse in his hand.  Will you take what
I leave, and be glad to get it?  It falls short; I know it does.  But if I
have lessened it, it is for myself that I have lessened it, and what is left
is all yours.  Don't stop to ask about that old legacy, and serve up a
stale dish of fatherly advice.  I know how fathers talk.  'Credit yourself by the interest.  Debit yourself by the expenses.  What is the remainder?'  Remainder?  Fudge!  Souse the cabbage, boy.  Don't spare
the oil.  Am I to dine off cow-heel and turnips on a holiday, that your
graceless grandson may stuff himself with *pâté de foie gras*, and indulge
himself in aristocratic connections?  Am I to go through the eye of a
cambric needle that he may have a priestly paunch? (61–74).

Furthermore, if you are not content with the little that I can leave
you, sell your life for gain.  Try every trade.  Try every nook and corner of the earth.  Go to Cappadocia, for instance, where you can make
something by dealing in slaves, and become an adept in that dainty business.  Double your capital.  'I have done so.  Nay, I have trebled it,
quadrupled it, decupled it.  Tell me where to draw the line.'  Tell you
where to draw the line?  Why, Chrysippus himself could not find the
limit between wealth and poverty.  A dollar more does not make a man
rich, a dollar less does not make him poor.  Where is the turning-point?
And yet this man talks as if the turning-point had been found! (75–80.)

---

The Sixth Satire is the most obscure and unsatisfactory of the poems
of PERSIUS, and baffled interpreters have taken refuge in the hypothesis
that the Satire is incomplete.  The roughness of the metre and the
harshness of the transitions favor this view; but parts are wrought

out with all the minuteness of detail that is characteristic of our author's style, and some of the highest authorities, such as Jahn, consider the Satire complete. The close, as Mr. Pretor remarks, is exactly in PERSIUS'S manner, and we must look elsewhere in the Satire for the breaks—if breaks there be.

**1-11.** Are you spending the winter on your Sabine farm, Bassus, and have you resumed your poetry ?   I am in my Ligurian resort, so praised by Ennius.

**1. iam :** in the question implies uncertainty, ' actually ?' ' so ?' **—bruma** = *brevuma* = *brevissuma* (*dies*), ' the shortest day,' ' wintersolstice,' ' midwinter.'—**foco :** contrast between the *fireside* of the land of the Sabines and the open-air *warmth* of Liguria.—**Basse :** ' Caesius Bassus, one of the intimate friends of PERSIUS, was deputed by Cornutus to edit his Satires after his death.   He is classed with HORACE, as a lyric poet, by QUINTILIAN (10, 1, 96), who, however, thinks him inferior to some of his own contemporaries, and he is probably the same with the author of a treatise on Metres, which is referred to by various grammarians, and still exists in an interpolated epitome, but different from Gabius or Gavius Bassus, who wrote works on the origin and signification of words and on the gods.   Bassus was killed, according to the Scholiast, in the famous eruption of Vesuvius' (Conington, after Jahn).   See also v. 5.—**Sabino :** The simplicity of the Sabines has already been noted (see 1, 20), and Jahn thinks that the life about the fireside (VERG., Georg., 2, 532) is an indication of the primitive tastes of Bassus and his family.   *Sabino* also prepares the way for *tetrico* (below).   Comp. *tetrica ac tristis disciplina Sabinorum*, LIV., 1, 18 (quoted by Jahn).

**2. tetrico :** ' austere.'—**vivunt :** PERSIUS was thinking of HORACE'S *vivuntque commissi calores* | *Aeoliae fidibus puellae*, Od., 4, 9, 11. 12.   *Iam vivunt*, ' wake to life ' (Pretor), where ' wake ' represents *iam*.   See note on 5, 33.

**3. mire :** is an Adjective or an Adverb, according as *opifex* is a Substantive or an Adjective.—**opifex :** Commentators supply *es*, but the Nom. can be used in characteristic exclamation.   See G., 340, R. 1, and comp. 1, 5.   With *opifex intendisse* comp. Prol., 11, and *egregius lusispe* below.   For the Perf., see 1, 41, note.—**veterum primordia vocum :** Perhaps ' the racy richness of our early

tongue.' LUCR. (4, 531) uses *primordia vocum* of the beginnings
of articulate sound, as QUINT., 1, 9, 1, uses *dicendi primordia* of instruction in the rudimentary preparation for rhetoric.   Bassus,
as the whole context shows, affected to belong to the *antiquiores
homines*, and imitated the diction of an earlier time.   PERSIUS
belongs to a different school of art, and his friendship makes
him guarded.   Jahn understands a grammatical poem, of which
LUCILIUS furnishes a familiar example in his Ninth Book (see L.
Müller's *Lucilius*, p. 221), but, as Pretor remarks, *numeris—marem
strepitum fidis intendisse Latinae* indicates lyric poetry.

**4. marem strepitum :** like ἄρρην φθόγγος.   Comp. HOR., A. P.,
402 : *mares animos.*—**fidis Latinae :** Stress is to be laid on *Latinae*.   PERSIUS himself is intensely Latin in his vocabulary.—**intendisse :** ' VERG., Aen., 9, 774, speaks of stringing the numbers
on the chords; PERSIUS goes further [and fares worse], and talks
of stringing sounds on the numbers ' (Conington).

**5. mox :** points to another side of Bassus's poetry, the non-
lyrical, probably satires, for one *Bassus in satyris,* mentioned by
FULGENTIUS (ap. Jahn), is most likely our man, despite Jahn's
objections.—**iocis :** Heinrich, *ex coni.*   The passage is a very
difficult one.   The interpretation turns on the two words, *iocos*
(or *iocis*), *senes* (or *senex*), as the reading *egregios* for *egregius* may
be discarded.

> (1.) Jahn reads in both editions (1843 and 1868) *iocos* and
> *senes.*
> (2.) Hermann's *senex*, the reading of Montepess., was enthusi-
> astically advocated by Hermann himself.
> (3.) Heinrich's *iocis* has the merit of making a perfectly clear
> sense, and is accepted by Mr. Pretor.
> (1.) If we read *iocos* with the MSS., *iuvenes* must be consid-
> ered an Adjective, and *iuvenes iocos = iuvenilis iocos.*   This
> almost compels us to make *senes* an Adjective also, and the
> following translation may be given : ' Rare genius for car-
> rying on the frolics of youth [in song], and for giving play
> with virtuous skill to the jests of the aged.'
> (2.) Hermann's reading labors under the difficulty of requir-
> ing us to understand *senex* of Bassus, who was not an old
> man at the time ; but compare the note on *praegrandi sene,*

1, 124. Notice also the want of balance in the absolute *lusisse.* 'Then showing yourself excellent in your old age at wakening young loves and frolicking over the chords with a virtuous touch' (Conington). *Iocus* is often used of love. Comp. CATULL., 8, 6 : *ibi illa multa tum iocosa fiebant.*

(3.) Heinrich's *iocis* gives us, 'Rarely skilled to rally the young with jibe and jest and have a fling at old sinners, but all in high-bred style.' *Pollice honesto* is the *ingenuo ludo* of 5, 16. Comp. also 2, 74 : *generoso honesto;* and the *honesta oratio* of TER., Andr., 1, 1, 114 : *quae opponitur plebeiae,* as Gesner says, s. v. It is hardly necessary to say that the English language has no synonyme for *honestus,* which embraces the goodly outside as well as the pure heart.

Mr. Conington translates Hermann's text and comments on Jahn's. *Lusisse senes* he understands as *amavisse senili more,* the poet being said to do the deed he writes about, VERG., Ecl., 9, 19. It would be far more simple to make *iocos senes = amores senilis,* harsh as that would be. Old men's philanderings are fair game for the satirist or comic poet to have his fling at (*lusisse*). *Turpe senilis amor,* as the master says, Ov., Am., 1, 9, 4. Compare the Casina of PLAUTUS.—**pollice :** the cithern being played chiefly with the thumb.

**6. lusisse :** Comp. *scit risisse,* 1, 132 —**mihi :** The step-father of PERSIUS probably had a seat there.

**7. intepet :** The warmth of the coast made it a favorite resort for invalids. It is not unlikely that PERSIUS was a man of delicate constitution.—**hibernat :** According to some, 'my sea winters,' that is, 'rests for the winter,' is not vexed by the keels of ships (Schol.). According to others, 'is wintry,' like *hiemat* (the more common word in this sense). A stormy sea was supposed to lash itself warm. Jahn quotes, among other passages, CIC., N. D., 2, 10, 26 : *maria agitata ventis tepescunt.*—**meum :** 'my sea,' 'my favorite haunt.' Some have inferred falsely from this passage that Luna was the birthplace of PERSIUS.

**8. latus dant :** 'present their giant side,' 'interpose a mighty barrier' against the winds. Jahn comp. VERG., Aen., 1, 105 : *un-*

I

*dis dat latus.*—**valle** = *sinu.* The Abl. of manner may be translated locally; 'into a deep bay' (Conington).—**se receptat:** 'retreats,' 'retires' from the storms. So HORACE (Od., 1, 17, 17;
Epod., 2, 11) speaks of a *reducta vallis.* Jahn refers the frequent-
ative to the windings of the bay. 'Keeps retreating,' 'retreats
further and further,' might very well be said from the traveller's
point of view. The description of the harbor, now the Gulf of
Spezia, is said to be very accurate.

9. **Lunai portum,** etc.: ENNIUS, Ann., v. 16 (Vahl.). Luna,
from which the harbor took its name, was not on the gulf, but
on the eastern side of the Macra (Magra), near the modern Sar-
zana.—**est operae:** Commonly explained by the ellipsis of *pre-
tium.* But the Gen. is very elastic.—**cognoscite:** is easier in
tone, *cognoscere* is easier for translation. **cives:** 'good people
all.' Ger. *Leutlein.* Jahn notices the *antiqua gravitas* of *cives.*

10. **cor Enni:** Comp. *re-cor-dor* and *cor-datus,* and our 'get
*by heart.*' So *credidit meum cor,* ENN., Ann., 374 (Vahl.). See
MART., 3, 26, 4; 11, 84, 17. The expression is little more than
*cordatus Ennius,* as in the familiar passage, *tergemini vis Gery-
onaï,* LUCR., 5, 28. So *corpore Turni,* VERG., Aen., 7, 650; Greek,
βία, ἴς, δέμας, στόμα ('Ανύτης στόμα, ANTHOL. P., 9, 26, 3). On the
same principle are based such combinations as *mens provida Re-
guli,* HOR., Od., 3, 5, 13, and *venit et Crispi iucunda senectus,* JUV.,
4, 81, and *Montani quoque venter adest,* l. c. 107. 'Ennius, in his
sober moments' (Gifford).—**destertuit:** On the Tense, see G.,
563; A., 62, 2, *a.* 'Snored off his being,' i. e., the dream that he
was Homer. Ennius's dreams are touched up in Prol., 2, where
it has been mentioned that Ennius dreamed that he had seen*
Homer. For the further visions, see the citations in Vahlen's
ed. of ENNIUS, Ann., v. 15.

11. **Maeonides:** poetic 'flash-name,' like the 'Bard of Avon.'
—**Quintus:** 'plain Quintus' (Gifford). The Scholiast fancies
that *quintus* is a numeral, and gives the following order of trans-
migrations: 1. Pythagoras; 2. A peacock; 3. Euphorbus; 4. Homer. TERTULLIAN gives: 1. Euphorbus; 2. Pythagoras; 3.
Homer; 4. A peacock. The pun would be a wretched one,
but that is no objection; more serious is the wrong use of the
Preposition *ex* for *ab.* Heinrich combines confidently *Maeo-*

*nides Quintus,* 'Homer with a Roman *praenomen.*' Conington
follows doubtingly. — **pavone:** *Memini me fiere pavum,* ENN.,
Ann., v. 15 (Vahl.).—**Pythagoreo:** 'Since *Pythagoras*' time that
I was an Irish rat,' SHAKSP.

**12-17.** Here I am in happy unconcern, caring naught for vulgar herd or threatened flock. I do not pine because my neighbor waxes fat. Let who will get up in the world; I won't let
my hair turn gray for that, nor stint myself, nor poke my nose
into the wax of every jar of wine I open to see whether somebody has not been tampering with the seal.

**12. securus:** with Gen., VERG., Aen., 1, 350 ; 10, 326. — **quid
praeparet auster:** Jahn comp. *quid cogitet umidus auster,*VERG.,
Georg., 1, 462 ; and 444 : *arboribusque satisque Notus pecorique
sinister.*

**13. infelix:** with Dat.  VERG., Georg., 2, 239 : *tellus—infelix
frugibus,* quoted by Conington. — **pecori:** as it were, doubly
dependent.—**securus et:** The trajection of *et* (1, 23) gives *securus*
a better position.—**angulus:** as in *O si angulus ille | proximus
accedat,* HOR., Sat., 2, 6, 8.

**14. pinguior:** Jahn quotes appositely for the thought, *ferti-
lior seges est alienis semper in agris,* OV., A. A., 1, 349. So JUV.,
14, 142 : *maiorque videtur | et melior vicina seges.*—**adeo omnes:**
The emphasis of *adeo* may be given by repetition, *all, ay, all.*
The supposition is an extreme one, hence the Subjunctive *ditescant.* Notice the harsh elision at this point, which is avoided
by smoother writers.  PERSIUS has it fourteen times in all—eight
times in this one Satire—which may be interpreted as an indication of its incompleteness.

**15. peioribus:** Comp. HOR., Ep., 1, 6, 22 : *peioribus ortus.*
The social sense is the more prominent.—**usque** = *ubi-s-que,* ' no
matter where or when,' hence ' every where,' and, as here, ' always.'

**16. curvus:** ' bent double.'—**minui:** ' lose flesh ' (Conington).
—**senio:** before my time.  Comp. 1, 26.—**uncto:** synonymous
with ' dainty.'  Jahn comp. HOR., A. P., 422, and 3, 102 ; 4, 17.

**17. signum tetigisse:** Only good wines were sealed.  The
miser not only seals up his vile stuff, but, in his anxious scrutiny
into the state of the seal, butts his nose against it—perhaps with

the additional idea of helping the sense of sight with the sense of smell. *Recusem tetigisse = nolim tetigisse.* Comp. note on 1, 91.

**18-24.** Others may not agree with me in these views. Even twins born under the same star may be widely different. One gives himself a treat only on his birthday, and a poor treat it is. Another devours his substance before he comes of age. I am for enjoyment, but not for waste; for enjoyment, but not for a subtle discernment of the pleasures of the table.

**18. his:** On the Dat., see G., 388, R. 1; A., 51, 2, *g.* *His* is Neuter. 'These views of mine.'—**geminos:** Comp. Hor., Ep., 2, 2, 183 seqq.—**horoscope:** 'natal star,' 'star of nativity.' Comp. note on 5, 46.—**varo genio:** 'of diverging temper.' *Varus* is often used of distorted, bowed legs, and *varo genio* is only Persius's way of saying that the dispositions of twins often go apart.

**19. producis:** 'bring forth,' 'give birth to,' 'beget,' Plaut., Rud., 4, 4, 129; Prop., 5, 1, 89 (Conington). Jahn renders it *in lucem edit et educat,* which is more in conformity with general usage and with the notion of control in the star of nativity.—**solis natalibus:** This picture has been much admired. Every word tells. This high-day comes but once a year (*solis*), the cabbage is dry (*sine uncto*), he does not souse it with oil, as Persius does (*ungue, puer, caules,* v. 69), but moistens it (*tingat*) with fish brine (*muria*), which he has bought—sly fox that he is (*vafer*) —in a cup (a cupful at a time, to prevent waste), while, with his own hand (*ipse*)—for he trusts no other—he dusts (*inrorans*) the platter with the dear, precious pepper, sacred in his eyes (*sacrum*).

**20. muria:** was a cheap sauce, 'made of the *thynnus,* and less delicate than *garum,* made of the *scomber*' (Macleane); hence the point of buying it only as he wanted it—a small quantity at a time.—**empta:** Both Conington and Pretor direct us to combine *empta* with *muria.* It can not be combined with any thing else, as *calice* is rigidly masculine, Neue, *Formenl.,* 1, 691.

**21. sacrum:** *Acerbe dictum quia avarus tamquam sacro parcit* (Jahn). Jahn compares ἅλς θεῖος, but has not overlooked the real point, as Mr. Pretor intimates.—**inrorans:** Comp. *instillat* in a similar description of a miser (Avidienus), in Hor., Sat., 2, 2, 62.—**dente peragit:** 'gobbles up' (Conington). *Peragere,* 'go through,' 'run through.'

**22. magnanimus:** Ironical, like Hor., Ep., 1, 15, 27 : *rebus maternis atque paternis | fortiter absumptis.* 'High-hearted hero.' **—puer:** while a mere lad. 'Gifford notices the rapidity of the metre, and contrasts it with the slowness of v. 20.' It would have been more to the purpose if he had noticed the mockery of the position, which suspends the sense. 'He—his property—with nothing but his teeth—his vast estate—heroic being—runs through—while nothing but a boy.'

**23. rhombos:** It suffices to refer to Juv., Sat., 4.—**ponere:** 1, 53. For the construction, see Prol., 11.

**24. tenuis—salivas:** 'delicate juices,' 'subtle flavors.' *Saliva = sapor,* as in Plin., H. N., 22, 1, 22 : *sua cuique vino saliva,* by a natural transfer from the consumer to the consumed; or, as Conington puts it, from effect to cause. See 5, 112.—**sollers nosse:** Prol., 11.—**turdarum:** 'thrushes,' 'fieldfares,' a well-known delicacy, Hor., Sat., 2, 5, 10 ; Ep., 1, 15, 41. The Scholiast tells us that the feminine is used for the ordinary masculine, because the Brillat-Savarins of the period undertook to tell the sex by the taste. The difference between *turdorum* and *turdarum* reminds one of 'calipash' and 'calipee.'

**25-33.** The true course is to live fully up to your income and trust to the next crop. 'But suppose an extraordinary demand is made on you. Suppose a friend is shipwrecked.' What easier than to sell a piece of land and relieve his wants ?

**25. tenus:** here 'fully up to.' John makes *tenus* an Adverb, compares Verg., Aen., 1, 737 : *summo tenus attigit ore,* and explains *messe propria vive* as = *consume fructus agrorum tuorum usque ad finem, quoad suppetunt.*—**propria:** 'Is it not lawful for me to do what I will with *mine own ?*'

**26. emole:** to the last grain.—**occa:** Comp. Hor., Ep., 2, 2, 161 : *cum segetes occat tibi mox frumenta daturas.*—**in herba:** 'in the blade.' Ov., Her., 17, 263 : *adhuc tua messis in herba est.* Have something of the farmer's hopeful spirit. Comp. the Gr. proverb: ἀεὶ γεωργὸς εἰς νέωτα πλούσιος.

**27. ast:** 2, 39. An impersonal objector speaks.—**officium** = τὸ καθῆκον, which embraces our charity. The Stoics insisted on χρηστότης, without prejudice to ἀπάθεια. They wanted *benevolentia* without *misericordia.* See Knickenberg, l. c. p. 90. The poet

gets the better of the philosopher in PERSIUS.—**trabe rupta:**
Comp. 1, 89.—**Bruttia saxa:** In the toe of the Italian boot.

**28. prendit:** Casaubon comp. *prensantemque uncis manibus
capita aspera montis*, VERG., Aen., 6, 360 (of Palinurus).—**surdaque vota:** *Surdus* is 'dull of hearing' and 'dull of sound,' 'deaf,'
and, as here, 'unheard.' Comp. κωφός. The radical is SVAR,
'heavy;' 'neither his ear *heavy* that it can not hear.'

**29. Ionio:** sc. *sinu*, if we may judge by JUV., 6, 92: *lateque
sonantem pertulit Ionium.* Gr. Ἰόνιος κόλπος. Comp. THUC.,
1, 24 with 6, 30. It is used here in a wide sense, as is shown
by *Bruttia saxa*, v. 27. Comp. SERV. ad Aen., 3, 211: *sciendum
Ionium sinum esse immensum ab Ionia usque ad Siciliam.*
On the translation and construction of *Ionio*, see note on Prol.,
1.—**ipse:** the master of the vessel. G., 297, R. 1.

**30. de puppe dii:** Paintings of the gods. Comp. VERG., Aen.,
10, 171: *aurato fulgebat Apolline puppis.* The gods may have
been Castor and Pollux, no unlikely 'sign,' Acts, 28, 11. *Ingentes*
implies the size of the ship and the magnitude of the loss (Jahn).
See note on *trabe vasta*, 5, 141.—**obvia mergis:** Jahn comp. HOR.,
Epod., 10, 21: *opima quod si praeda curvo litore | porrecta mergos
iuveris.* Any large sea-bird will answer, such as 'cormorant.'

**31. lacerae:** Conington comp. Ov., Her., 2, 45: *at laceras
etiam puppes furiosa refeci.*—**et:** καί, 'if need be.'—**caespite vivo:**
Comp. HOR., Od., 1, 19, 13; 3, 8, 4; 'live sod,' 'green turf.' Here
landed property is meant, in contrast to the income, represented
by the *messis*.

**32. pictus:** See note on 1, 89. 'With his picture' (Conington).—**oberret:** 'go up and down the country.'—**tabula caerulea:** 'a sea-green board,' as might be expected from the subject.

**33-41.** 'But,' resumes the interlocutor, 'your heir will object
to your curtailing your property, and not show you the proper
respect when you are dead. You can't expect to diminish your
property without scath. And, in fact, you philosophers are very
much spoken against on account of the bad example you set, the
bad influence you have exerted on the common people.'—Well,
what of it? Would you care any thing about what was done to
you or said of you after you are dead?
The connection is much disputed.

**33. cenam funeris:** the *epulum funebre*, the 'funeral baked meats' of Hamlet, not the *silicernium* proper, not the *exigua feralis cena patella* of Juv., 5, 85, the scanty meal left at the funeral pile for the *dis manibus*.

**34. curtaveris:** G., 542; A., 70, 5, *b.*—**urnae:** Do not efface the personal conception (G., 344, R. 3; A., 51, N.) by translating 'put into.' The urn receives; hence *dabit*='commit,' 'consign.'

**35. inodora:** Ov., Trist., 3, 3, 69: *atque ea (=ossa) cum foliis et amomi pulvere misce;* Tib., 3, 2, 23 (Jahn).—**seu spirent:** 5, 3. —**cinnama—casiae:** On the Plural, see G., 195, R. 6; A., 14, 1, *a.* —**surdum:** 'faint,' a transfer from hearing to smell. On the construction, see 5, 25.

**36. ceraso:** This passage is our only authority for the fraudulent admixture. Tr., 'whether the cinnamon have lost the fragrance of its breath, or cassia be taken in adulteration with cherry-bark.'—**nescire paratus:** here 'fully resolved,' rather than as in 1, 132.

**37. tunc bona incolumis minuas:** In his ed. of 1868 Jahn has followed Sinner's suggestion, and transposed parts of vv. 37 and 41, so as to read *Haec cinere ulterior metuas* here, and *Tunc bona incolumis minuas* below, as Hermann had done before him, only Hermann puts the words in the mouth, not of the objector, but of Persius. I am unable to see how either arrangement helps us out of the difficulties of the passage. In his ed. of 1843, Jahn makes *tunc bona incolumis minuas?* the language of the heir, who asks angrily, 'Do you expect to diminish your property without suffering for it?' It is rather the language of the objector, who had just told Persius that he would miss a good funeral by curtailing his estate, and who goes on to cite Bestius, as another opponent of this new-fangled philosophy. Persius dismisses this tirade by the single question : 'What would all this be to you or me after we are dead?' This gets rid of Bestius as a new speaker. He is quoted by the objector. Mr. Pretor translates: 'Do you mean to say, Persius, that *you* would thus break up your property, while hearty and strong, instead of waiting to bequeath it by will on your death-bed?'—**incolumis:** χαίρων, *impune.*—**et:** Others besides the heir are dissatisfied.—**Bestius:** the *corrector*

*Bestius* of HOR., Ep., 1, 15, 37, who is quoted here by the opponent of PERSIUS, as inveighing against doctrines that have taught the lower classes to waste their substance on condiments and spoil their wholesome fare, after the pattern of such gentlemen as PERSIUS. Comp. *usque recusem—cenare sine uncto*, v. 16, and *ungue, puer, caules*, v. 69.

**38. doctores Graios:** Comp. 5, 191.—**Ita fit:** 'That is the way of it.'—**sapere nostrum:** 1, 9.—**urbi:** with *venit*. *Venire* with the Dat., like the Greek ἐλθεῖν, on account of the personal interest involved, 'came' being ='was brought,' *allatum est*. See Kühner, *A. G.*, 2, 351, and Weissenborn on LIV., 32, 6, 4.

**39. cum pipere et palmis:** notoriously foreign productions. Comp. *advectus Romam quo pruna et cottona vento*, JUV., 3, 83. *Palmis* = 'dates.'—**nostrum hoc:** 'this new wisdom of our day.' —**maris expers:** HOR., Sat., 2, 8, 15: *Chium maris expers*. The explanations are by no means convincing. *Maris expers*. (1) Not mixed with salt water, which was supposed to be wholesome, as in HORACE, l. c. (2) = *insulsum*, Heinr., the most simple, 'foolish philosophy,' 'insipid sapience.' (3) Devoid of manliness (Casaubon). Comp. 1, 103, 104, in which case *maris* would be a pun, as there is an evident Horatian reminiscence. See Introd., xxiii. But the Horatian passage is itself variously interpreted. (4) The rendering, 'innocent of the sea,' i. e., 'home-grown,' is in manifest contradiction to the drift of the passage.

**40. fenisecae:** Type of the rustic laborer. Comp. *fossor*, 5, 122. *Fenisecae*, the plebeian spelling for *faenisecae*, seems more appropriate here. —**crasso unguine:** They can not get a good article, but they are determined to imitate their betters, and so they take a poor one. With *crasso unguine* comp. 3, 104: *crassis amomis*.— **vitiarunt pultes:** On *vitiarunt* comp. 2, 65; *puls* is the national porridge, the *farrata olla* of 4, 31.

**41. cinere ulterior:** 'when you are the other side of the grave' (comp. 5, 152); περαιτέρω κόνεως (Casaubon).

**41-60.** PERSIUS turns on his heir: 'Glorious news has come of a great victory. I wish to celebrate it by games—by largess. Will you forbid it? If you don't want what is left, let it alone. I can get somebody to take it—some beggar, perhaps, related to me through that son of earth, Adam.'

**42. quisquis eris:** does not so much show 'the indifference of PERSIUS himself' to his successor as the utter lack of real personality in the Satire. See note on 1, 44.—**seductior:** Comp. 2, 4. *Paulum* with *seductior*. Comp. PETRON., 13: *seduxit me paululum a turba;* and PLAUT., Asin., 5, 2, 75; TER., Eun., 4, 4, 39. The Accusative with the Comparative is rare but sure, Dräger, l. c. § 245, *b;* for examples with *paulum*, SIL., 15, 21; STAT., Theb., 10, 938 (Freund).

**43. o bone,** etc.: The only passage in PERSIUS that deals with the political life of his time, the only passage that has any historic force. A keen observer in his narrow sphere, PERSIUS has hit off very happily the features of this droll triumph of Caligula's. True, he was only seven years old when it took place; but he lost his father when he was six, and yet recalls him vividly, and this parade must have made an abiding impression, whether he saw it or only heard of it. Caligula's German expedition is recounted in SUET., Calig., 43 seqq.: 'He ordered a triumph, which was to be unprecedentedly splendid, and cheap in proportion, as he had a right to the property of his subjects—changed his mind, forbade any proposal on the subject under capital penalties, abused the senate for doing nothing, and finally entered the city in ovation on his birthday' (Conington). With *o bone* comp. *heus bone*, 3, 94.—**laurus** = *laureata epistola*, the letter bound with bays, in which victories were announced.

**44. Germanae pubis:** 'flower of the German army' (Pretor), *pubes* being = ἡλικία.

**45. aris | frigidus excutitur cinis:** Of course to make room for new sacrifices, but *frigidus* intimates that the ashes had had time to cool; such occasions were rare. Comp. APUL., Met., 4, 83: *arae viduae frigido cinere foedatae. Aris*, Dat. *Excutitur* denotes haste. 'The ashes are hustled off.'—**postibus:** 'for the door-posts' (of temples, palaces, the residence of the *triumphator*, and other buildings). With the Dative comp. JUV., 6, 51: *necte coronam | postibus*.

**46. lutea gausapa:** 'yellow wools.' The coarse fabric known as *gausapa* was used to make yellow wigs for the mock German captives. The light hair of the Germans is a familiar characteristic, and a similar device is recorded of Domitian by TACITUS, Agr.,

39 (Jahn). As the captives were actually Gauls, Casaubon understands *gausapa* of the common Gallic costume.

**47. Caesonia:** the mistress, and, after the birth of a daughter and the divorce of Lollia, the wife of Caligula, SUET., Cal., 25.—
**ingentis Rhenos:** Jahn understands statues or pictures of the Rhine, to be carried in procession, referring to the Jordan on the Arch of Titus, and citing Ov., A. A., 1, 223 seqq., for the Euphrates and Tigris. Conington adds VERG., Georg., 3, 28, for the Nile, and considers the Plural *Rhenos* sarcastic. The more common interpretation regards *Rhenos* as *Rhenanos*. SUET., l. c. 47, mentions expressly the fact that Caligula picked out the tallest men he could find (*procerissimum quemque*) for the procession.

**48. genioque ducis:** On *genio*, see 2, 3. The genius of the Emperor was publicly worshipped, Ov., Fast., 5, 145. Caligula punished those who did not swear by his genius, SUET., Cal., 27. *Ducis* is sarcastic. 'So JUV., 4, 145; 7, 21, cails Domitian *dux*, with reference to a similar exploit, a sham triumph with manufactured slaves' (Conington, after Jahn).—**centum paria :** Comp. HOR., Sat., 2, 3, 85 : *ni sic fecissent gladiatorum dare centum | damnati populo paria atque epulum.* The number is absurd for any ordinary fortune, and the extravagance of the threat destroys the dramatic effect on the heir.

**49. induco :** The familiar Present for the Future. *Induco, verbum harenae* (Casaubon).—**aude :** We should say, 'I dare you' (Conington).

**50. oleum :** Largesses of oil by Caesar and Nero are recorded by SUET., Caes., 38, Nero, 12 (Jahn). — **artocreas :** ἀρτόκρεας = *visceratio*, 'bread-meat' for 'bread-and-meat.' Outside of the numerals, such copulative compounds (*dvandva* in Sanskrit) are rare, and chiefly late. Comp. *suovetaurilia*, νυχϑήμερον, the famous word of seventy-nine syllables in AR., Eccl., 1169, and Mod. Gr. ἀνδρόγυννον, 'man-and-wife.' Some consider *artocreas* a kind of meat-pasty.—**popello :** 4, 15.

**51, 52. dic clare :** It were very much to be wished that he had. The context seems to require, on the one hand, a motive for the silence of the heir; on the other, a motive for declining the inheritance. The interpretation of *non adeo—iuxta est* depends on the meaning of *exossatus*, which is sometimes rendered ' exhaust-ed,' 'impoverished,' ' worn out,' as if ' boneless' and ' marrow-less' were the same thing here ; sometimes, and with far more probability, ' cleared of stones.' A poetic allusion to the ' bones of Mother Earth,' Ov., Met., 1, 393 seqq. (Schol.), would be out of place, and the common culinary sense of *exossatus*, ' boned,' is in keeping with the homely character of PERSIUS's tropes. *Adeo* is sometimes considered a Verb, in the sense of *adire hereditatem ;* sometimes an Adverb, and connected now with *prohibeo* (from *pro-hibes*), now with *exossatus ;* and, finally, some give *exossatus—est* to the heir, others to PERSIUS. I subjoin the chief distributions and interpretations :

(1.) *Non adeo*, inquis. Exossatus ager iuxta est. Jahn (1843). (Do you mean to hinder me ? Out with it.) ' Not exact-ly,' you say. Here is a worn-out field hard by. If you won't have it, another will.

(2.) ' Non adeo,' inquis ? Exossatus ager iuxta est (Co-nington). You won't accept the inheritance, you say ? Here is a field, now, cleared for ploughing.

(3.) ' Non adeo,' inquis, ' exossatus ager iuxta est,' Jahn (1868), which may be rendered, ' I am sure that your land here is not in such very good order' (that you can afford such extravagance). Good order or not, I can find some one to take it off my hands, etc.

(4.) Hermann bases his interpretation on the Schol., and un-derstands *non adeo exossatus ager* to be a field that is not wholly cleared of stones, to which the heir points as a co-gent argument against his making a difficulty. He is afraid of a stoning from the people, as above he was afraid of doing any thing to disoblige the Emperor (*Lect. Pers.*, II., 64).

(5.) Teuffel agrees with Hermann's interpretation of *exossa-tus*, but separates *non adeo*, ' Not exactly.' See (1.). ' There is a field hard by from which the stones have [just] been dug up,' where they are lying in convenient heaps.

(6.) Heinrich takes *adeo* to be the Verb, *exossatus* as ' impover-ished,' and *iuxta = paene*.

(7.) *Non adeo*, inquis. *Exossatus ager iuxta est* is rendered by

Mr. Pretor, 'I can't quite forbid it; but let me suggest to you that your land is impoverished.'

(8.) König understands the heir to say: 'I will not accept. I have a well-tilled piece of land of my own hard by.'

I am not ashamed to acknowledge that the only point about which I am convinced is the impossibility of making *exossatus* mean 'impoverished.'

**53. amitis:** *Amita* is the aunt by the father's side. See note on 2, 31. PERSIUS left his property to his mother and sister, and all this string of suppositions is in keeping with the impersonal character of his heir. Teuffel notices the utter jumble of legal relations.—**proneptis patrui:** 'female cousin twice removed.'

**54. sterilis vixit:** 'has lived barren' means 'has died childless, without issue.'

**55. nihilum:** 'neither chick nor child.'—**Bovillas:** Bovillae lay between Rome and Aricia, and was the first stage on the Appian road, hence called 'suburban' by Ov., Fast., 3, 667 (Jahn). PERSIUS had an estate in the neighborhood.

**56. clivum ad Virbi:** MARTIAL's *clivus Aricinus* (2, 19, 3; 12, 32, 10), a noted station for beggars. JUV., 4, 17: *dignus Aricinos qui mendicaret ad axes.* Virbius was identified with Hippolytus, and worshipped as the hero of Aricia.—**Manius:** a typical beggar's name. There was a proverb: *multi Mani Ariciae,* FEST., s. v., with the explanation, *multos claros viros ibi fuisse.* The 'Arician aristocracy' must have become a term of contempt by the time of PERSIUS (πάλαι ποτ' ἦσαν ἄλκιμοι Μιλήσιοι).

**57. progenies terrae:** is the indignant remonstrance of the heir, *progenies terrae* being = the more familiar *terrae filius,* CIC., Att., 1, 13, 4 al.; our 'groundling' can answer only as a play on the word.—**quartus pater** = *abavus,* 'great-great-grandfather.'

**58. haud prompte, dicam tamen:** μόλις μέν, ἐξερῶ δ' ὅμως (Conington); μόλις μέν, ἀλλ' οὖν ἐξερῶ. Comp. [DEM.] 58, 26.—**adde etiam unum** = *atavum,* 'one step further back.'

**59. unum etiam** = *tritavum.*

**60. ritu | generis:** 'by regular descent' (Conington). Jahn connects *generis* with *avunculus.*—**maior avunculus:** *avii aut aviae*

*avunculus est* (Jahn), 'great-great-uncle.' PERSIUS qualifies this
statement by *prope*, 'something like,' but he has not only got the
degree wrong, but has passed over to the mother's side. The
thought of this *frigidiuscula ratio*, as Jahn calls it, does not need
illustration. Still, comp. JUV., 4, 99 : *unde fit ut malim fratercu-
lus esse gigantum.—*exit=*evadit*, 1, 45 ; 5, 130.

**61-74.** PERSIUS : 'You are getting impatient. Why not wait
for your turn ? I am Fortune. Wait until I drop my purse into
your hand, and then be satisfied with what I have left in it. *Tadius bequeathed me some money.* I know he did. What is that to
you ? None of your fatherly advice about looking after my balance at the banker's. What do I care about " balance ?" I will
eat a good dinner, and not starve myself for your spoilt grandson's sake.'

**61. qui prior es :** In this form of the λαμπαδηφορία 'the course
was marked out in stations, at each of which a new set of run-
ners stood ready to take up the race, and so long as the torch re-
mained alight, and the conditions of the race were thus fulfilled,
it could not exchange hands except at particular stations' (Pretor, after Jahn). Here the man in advance is represented as trying to get the torch out of PERSIUS's hands before he has reached
the station, while PERSIUS is yet running (*in decursu*), which Jahn
properly emphasizes. The interpretation is much disputed.—
**poscis :** implies impatience.

**62. Mercurius :** See note on 2, 11.

**63. pingitur :** Ἑρμῆς κερδῷος, 'with money-bag in hand.'
Comp. AR., Ach., 991, 992 : πῶς ἂν ἐμὲ καὶ σέ τις Ἔρως ξυναγάγοι
λαβών, | ὥσπερ ὁ γεγραμμένος, ἔχων στέφανον ἀνθέμων.—**vin tu
gaudere relictis :** *Gaudere* here almost = ἀγαπᾶν, 'be thankful
for whatever I shall leave you.' According to the ordinary rules
of grammar, *vis* would be the rhetorical, *vin* the genuine form of
the question (G., 455), but *ne* can not be pinned down by strict
rules, as has been remarked. See note on 1, 22.

**64. dest aliquid summae :** may be an objection of the heir, or
an anticipated objection. PERSIUS often reminds us of Mrs. Cau-
dle.—**minui mihi :** It was mine, and I diminished it to suit myself. It was mine to lessen ; what is left will be all your own to
keep.

**65. fuge quaerere**=*noli quaerere*, as in HOR., Od., 1, 9, 13.

**66. neu:** 3, 51.—**repone:** 'dish up again;' the *paterna dicta* may be considered a *crambe repetita*. Comp. QUINT., 2, 4, 29: *cum eadem iudiciis pluribus dicunt, fastidium movent velut frigidi et repositi cibi.* PERSIUS is nothing if not culinary. Jahn (1868) reads *oppone*, which is clearer but tamer. *Paterna d.* is simply 'the talk one hears from fathers,' severe old gentlemen on the stage.

**67. faenoris—reliquum est:** clearly a specimen of fatherly counsel. Every Polonius has something to say to his Laertes on this subject (Hamlet, 1, 3). PERSIUS's Polonius advises his son to keep an account, enter (*accedat*=*apponatur*, see note on 2, 2) his interest on the credit side, charge his expenses to the debit side, and find the remainder—in other words, to live carefully within the income of his property. Before the old gentleman gets through, PERSIUS repeats his last word mockingly: 'Remainder? Hang the remainder.' This is also Conington's view, who compares the commercial arithmetic lesson in HOR., A. P., 327 seqq.—**merces:** HOR. uses *merces* alone in the same sense as *faenoris merces* here, Sat., 1, 2, 14. 3, 88.—**hinc:** from the capital, or from the interest, or from both. I am inclined to refer *hinc* to the side of the account.

**69. ungue caules—festa luce:** See note on v. 19.

**70. urtica:** Comp. HOR., Ep., 1, 12, 7: *abstemius herbis | vivis et urtica;* and Sat., 2, 2, 117: *holus fumosae cum pede pernae* (Jahn).—**sinciput:** 'pig's cheek.' The swine was the common sacrifice and the common dish.—**aure:** *Fissa aure* seems to be nothing more than a picturesque detail. The pig's head was hung up in the smoke by a slit in its ear.

**71. tuus iste nepos:** Mr. Pretor sees a trace of incompleteness in the mention of *tuus iste nepos,* 'whose existence has never before been hinted at.' The *nepos* is hauled up out of the inane like the *quisquis* heir himself.—**anseris extis:** Comp. JUV., 5, 114: *anseris ante ipsum magni iecur.*

**73. patriciae:** implies great expense. This coarse combination of sensual pleasures is an argument in favor of the old-fashioned interpretation of *Calliroen*, 1, 134.—**trama:** Fr. *trame*, 'woof.' Such terms are apt to stick. Others translate falsely 'warp.'

'*Trama figurae* is "a thread-paper figure," as *trama* is the thread of the woof, which crosses that of the upright *stamen* or warp, and when the nap is worn off the cloths, these threads are laid bare.' Stocker, quoted by Pretor.

**74. tremat:** 'quiver,' like jelly, 'wag.'—**omento:** 'fatty caul,' 'fat,' 2, 47.—**popa:** used as a Substantive. Comp. Prol., 13. 'Alderman-belly,' instead of an 'aldermanic belly.' 'They which waited at the altar'—for the *popae* were the priests' assistants—'were partakers with the altar' (1 Cor., 9, 13), and waxed fat on the *iunicum omenta.* Pretor quotes PROP., 4, 3, 62: *succinctique calent ad nova lucra popae.*

**75-80.** Commentators notice the abrupt transition. Jahn says that the dialogue is dropped, but who expects invariably close connection between two heads of a sermon? In my judgment PERSIUS is still hammering away at his impatient heir, and bids him earn money for himself, if he is not content to wait for PERSIUS's death, and does not like PERSIUS's mode of living. 'Sell your life, ransack the world, drive every trade. Double, treble, quadruple, decuple your property. But you will find that there is no point where you can stop, where you will be rich enough.'

**75. vende animam lucro:** Casaubon comp. the Greek proverb: ϑανάτου ὤνιον τὸ κέρδος, and LONGIN., Sublim., 44: τὸ ἐκ τοῦ παντὸς κερδαίνειν ὠνούμεϑα τῆς ψυχῆς.—**excute:** (for the last time of eight) 'ransack.'

**76. latus mundi:** HOR., Od., 1, 22, 19 (Conington).—**nec** = *neu*. See 1, 7.

**77. Cappadocas:** The slaves of Cappadocia were, as a rule, tall and well grown (PETRON., 63), and good litter-bearers (MART., 6, 77, 4) (Jahn), but in other respects extremely undesirable cattle. —**rigida:** 'fixed upright.' *Rigidae columnae,* Ov., Fast., 3, 529 (Jahn).—**plausisse:** So Jahn (1868). In 1843 he edited *pavisse,* and comp. *quot pascit servos?* JUV., 3, 141, and other passages. But *pāvisse* may have been intended as a Third Conjugation Perf. from *păvio,* and hence = *plausisse.* So Longfellow uses 'dove' for 'dived.' Slaves were slapped to try their condition. On the Inf. and the Perfect, see *opifex intendisse,* v. 3, note.—**catasta:** 'platform.' The sense of the passage, 'Make yourself an expert in slave flesh.'

**78. feci—sistam:** words of the avaricious man. The passage is imitated from Hor., Ep., 1, 6, 34 : *mille talenta rotundentur, totidem altera, porro | tertia succedant et quae pars quadret acervum.*—**quarto:** as if he had written *ter* before.

**79. redit:** the regular word for 'income,' 'revenue.' Comp. *reditus.*—**rugam:** *Ruga = sinus,* 'fold in a garment.' The *sinus* answers to our 'pocket,' hence 'purse.' The *ruga,* then, is the *rugosum marsupium* (Heinrich), or the 'yet unfilled bosom' of Juv., 14, 327. 'It comes into a purse that wrinkles still.' To bring this out more clearly Mr. Paley (ap. Pretor) puts a semicolon after *deciens.*—**depunge:** So Jahn (1868) for his previous *depinge.* 'Prick a hole.'—**ubi sistam:** G., 469, 623; A., 67, 2, *b.*

**80. inventus:** Ironical. 'So some one has been found, Chrysippus, to mark the limit of your heap.' If you can find a man to put a bound to greed, you can find a man to solve the *sorites* of Chrysippus. The fallacy called the σωρείτης, or σωρίτης, Lat. *acervus,* is often mentioned; so in Hor., Ep., 2, 1, 47, where it is illustrated by pulling hair after hair from the tail of a horse, and taking year after year from the age of a poet. See Hamilton's Lectures on Logic, p. 268 (Am. ed.).

# CRITICAL APPENDIX.

THE first reading is the reading of this edition, which, in the absence of any statement to the contrary, coincides with Jahn's edition of 1868. Variations in spelling have been noted where they have been deemed instructive.

> J$^a$. = Jahn, ed. of 1843.
> J$^\omega$. =  "  " 1868.
> J. =  " both editions.
> H. = Hermann (1854).

## PROLOGUS.

**2. Parnaso:** Parnasso, H.—**4. Heliconidas:** Heliconiadas, J$^a$., H.—**5. remitto:** relinquo, J$^a$.—**7. adfero:** affero, J$^a$., H.—**8. chaere:** χαῖρε, J$^a$., H.—**9. picam:** picas, J$^a$.—**nostra verba:** verba nostra, H.—**12. refulserit:** J$^a$.; refulgeat, J$^\omega$., H.

## SATURA I.

**6. examenque:** examenve, J$^a$., H.—**8. nam Romae quis non:** nam Romae est quis non, J$^a$.—**a:** ac, J$^a$.; ah, H.—**9. tum:** tunc, J$^a$., H.—**11. tunc, tunc, ignoscite—'Nolo:'** J$^a$.; tunc, tunc—ignoscite, nolo, J$^\omega$., H.—**12. splene cachinno:** splene—cachinno, H.—**14. quod:** J$^a$., H.; quo, J$^\omega$.—**17. leges:** legens, J$^a$., H.—**19. nec:** neque, J$^a$.—**32. circa:** circum, J$^a$.—**umeros:** humeros, J$^\omega$., H.—**hyacinthia:** hyacinthina, J$^a$., H.—**35. supplantat:** subplantat, J$^\omega$.—**36. adsensere:** assensere, J$^a$., H.—**57. protenso:** propenso, J$^a$.—**60. Apula:** Appula, H.—**tantae:** tantum, Heinrich, Conington.—**66. derigat:** dirigat, J$^a$., H.—**69. adferre:** afferre, J$^a$., H.—**74. cum:** J$^a$.; quem, J$^\omega$., H.—**dictatorem:** dictaturam, H.—**76. Acci:** Atti, J$^a$.—**78. fulta:** fulta? H.—**82. exsultat:** J$^a$., H.; exultat, J$^\omega$.—**88. men moveat? quippe et:**

men moveat quippe et, Jᵃ., H.—**89. protulerim:** protulerim? Jᵃ., H.—**91. querela:** Jᵃ., Brambach; querella, Jᵂ., H.—**93. cludere:** claudere, Jᵃ., H.—**95. Appennino:** Apennino, Jᵃ.—**97. vegrandi:** praegrandi, H.—**102. euhion:** evion, Jᵃ.—**111. omnes, omnes:** omnes etenim, Jᵃ.—**114. meite:** meiite, Jᵃ., H.— **119. nec cum scrobe? nusquam?** nec cum scrobe, nusquam? Jᵂ., H.; nec cum scrobe? 'nusquam.' Jᵃ.—**130. heminas:** Jᵃ., H.; eminas, Jᵂ.

## SATURA II.

**5. libabit:** libavit *al.*—**9. murmurat:** immurmurat, Jᵃ.—**10. ebulliat:** ebullit *Cod. Montepessulanus.*—**14. conditur:** ducitur, Jᵃ.—**pro:** proh, Jᵃ.—**16. purgas?** purgas. Jᵃ.—**25. sulpure:** sulfure, Jᵃ., H.—**37. optet:** optent *al.*—**42. grandes:** Jᵃ., H.; pingues, Jᵂ.—**tucceta:** tuceta, Jᵃ.—**43. adnuere:** annuere, Jᵃ.— **45. arcessis:** accersis, H.—**47. flammas:** flamma, Jᵃ.—**48. et tamen:** ac tamen, Jᵃ.; at tamen, H.—**52. creterras:** crateras, Jᵃ. —**54. excutiat:** excutias, Jᵃ., H.—**61. terris:** terras *al.*—**caelestium:** coelestium, Jᵃ., H.—**inanes:** Jᵃ., H.; inanis, Jᵂ. *At vid. Ritschel. Prolegg. Trinum.*, xc.; *Neue, Formenl.*, 1, 257.—**62. quid iuvat hoc:** quid iuvat, hos, H.—**66. bacam:** baccam, Jᵃ., H.— **73. animo:** animi, H.

## SATURA III.

**11. harundo:** arundo, Jᵃ., H.—**12. querimur:** queritur, Jᵃ.— **umor:** humor, Jᵃ., H.—**13. quod:** Jᵃ., H.; sed, Jᵂ.—**14. querimur:** queritur, Jᵃ.—**15. hucine:** huccine, Jᵃ., H.—**17. pappare:** papare, Jᵃ.—**29. censoremne:** Casaubon.; censoremque, Jᵂ.; censoremve, Jᵃ., H.—**31. Nattae?** Jᵃ., H.; Nattae. Jᵂ.—**32. vitio et:** *om.* et H.—**46. discere non sano:** dicere et insano, H.— **48. iure: (;):** Jᵃ., H.; iure etenim, Jᵂ.—**53. bracatis:** braccatis, H.—**56. diduxit:** deduxit, H.—**58. adhuc:** adhuc? Jᵃ.— **59. malis!:** malis? Jᵃ.—**60. in quod:** in quo, H.—**68. qua:** quam, H.—**73. nec:** neque, Jᵃ.—**76. mena:** maena, Jᵃ.—**78. quod sapio satis est mihi:** quod satis est sapio mihi, Jᵃ., H.—**89. alitus:** halitus, Jᵃ., H.—**92. lagoena:** lagena, Jᵃ., H.—**94. rogabit:** rogavit, Jᵃ.—**94. istuc:** istud, Jᵃ., H.—**99. sulpureas exalante:** sulfureas exhalante, Jᵃ., H.—**mefites:** mephites, Jᵃ.

—**100. triental:** J*ª*.; trientem, J*ω*., H.—**105. rigidas:** rigidos, J*ª*.—**112. holus:** olus, J*ª*., H.

## SATURA IV.

**3. hoc:** o, H.—**9. hoc puta:** *hoc*, puta, H.; puto, Heinr.—**13. theta:** theta? H.—**19. exspecta:** expecta, J*ω*.—**suffla:** sufla, J*ω*.—**26. miluus errat:** milvus oberret, J*ª*.; milvus oberrat, H.—**31. farrata olla:** farratam ollam, J*ª*., H.—**35. hi mores:** in mores, J*ª*.—**38. exstat:** extat, J*ω*.—**48. venit amarum:** H.; venit, amarum, J*ω*.; venit amorum, J*ª*.—*sed mox paenituit. Vid. Prolegg.*, 193, 1.

## SATURA V.

**3. maesto:** moesto, J*ª*., H.—**8. Prognes:** Procnes, II.—**9, cenanda:** cocnanda, J*ω*., H.—**13. scloppo:** stloppo, J*ª*., H.—**17. dicis:** dicas, J*ª*., H.—**19. bullatis:** pullatis, J*ª*.; ampullatis *proposuit* J.—**24. dinoscere:** dignoscere, J*ª*.—**35. deducit:** J*ª*., H.; diducit, J*ω*.—**38. apposita:** J*ª*., H.; adpos., J*ω*.—**58. cheragra:** chiragra, J*ª*.—**66. 'cras hoc fiet.'** Idem cras fiet: cras hoc fiet idem —Cras fiet? H. **68. consumpsimus:** consumsimus, J*ª*.—**71. cantum:** canthum, J*ª*., H.—**76. tressis:** J*ª*., H.; tresis, J*ω*.—**82. pillea:** pilea, J*ª*., H.—**102. navem:** navim, J*ª*.—**105. speciem dinoscere:** specimen dignoscere, J*ª*.—**110. astringas:** adstringas, J*ª*.—**112. glutto:** gluto, J*ª*.—**117. sub:** J*ª*., H.; in, J*ω*.—**119. exsere:** J*ª*., H.; excre, J*ω*.—**122. cetera:** caetera, J*ª*. **123. tris:** tres, H.—**satyrum:** satyri, J*ª*.—**127. 'cessas nugator:'** J*ª*.; cessas nugator, J*ω*., H. *Vid. Comment.*—**131. erilis:** herilis, J*ª*., H.—**132. heia:** eia, J*ª*.—**135. hebenum:** ebenum, J*ª*., H. —**136. ex:** e, J*ª*.—**camelo:** J*ª*., H.; camello, J*ω*.—**138. varo:** J*ª*.; baro, J*ω*., H.—**142. ni:** nisi, J*ª*., H.—**145. exstinxerit:** J*ª*., H.; extinxerit, J*ω*.—**146. transilias:** transsilias, J*ª*.—**147. cena:** coena, J*ª*., H.—**148. exalet:** exhalet, J*ª*., H.—**149. nummi:** J*ª*.; nummos, J*ω*., H.—**150. pergant avidos sudare:** J*ª*.; peragant avido sudore, J*ω*., H.—**155. huncine:** hunccine, J*ª*., H.—**159. et tamen:** ac tamen, J*ª*.; ast tamen, H.—**163. adrodens:** abrodens, J*ª*.—**165. obscenum:** obscoenum, J*ª*.—**172. nec nunc:** ne nunc, J*ª*.—**arcessat:** accersar, H.; arcessor *al.*—**174. exieras:** exieris *al.*—**nec nunc:** ne nunc, J*ª*.—**190. Pulfennius:** Fulfennius, J*ª*.

## SATURA VI.

**5. iocis:** Heinr. *ex coni.;* iocos, J., H., Codd.—**6. egregius:** egregios *al.*—**senes:** senex, H.—**16. cenare:** coenare, Jᵃ., H.— **17. lagoena:** lagena, Jᵃ., H.—**20. tingat:** Jᵃ., H., Bramb.; tinguat, Jᵂ.—**holus:** olus, Jᵃ., H.—**empta:** emta, Jᵃ., H.—**24. tenuis salivas:** tenuem salivam, Jᵃ.—**30. dii:** Brambach; dei, J., H.—**31. caespite:** Brambach; cespite, J., H.—**33. cenam:** coenam, Jᵃ., H.—**34. negleget:** negliget, Jᵃ., H.—**37. tune bona incolumis minuas:** Jᵃ.; *haec verba et v.* 41 *verba* haec—metuas *transposuit Sinnerus quem secuti sunt* Jᵂ. *et* H.—**40. fenisecae:** faenisecae, Jᵃ.; foenisecae, H.—**50. conives:** connives, Jᵃ., H.—**51. inquis:** inquis. Jᵃ.—**64. dest:** deest, Jᵃ., H.—**66. Tadius:** Stadius Jᵃ. —**repone:** Jᵃ., H.; oppone, Jᵂ.—**67. faenoris:** Brambach; fenoris, Jᵂ.; foenoris, Jᵃ., H.—**sumptus:** sumtus, Jᵃ.—**ungue:** unge, Jᵃ.— **69. coquetur:** coquatur, Jᵃ., H.—**77. plausisse:** pavisse, Jᵃ.—**79. depunge:** depinge, Jᵃ., H.

# INDEX.

K

218                                   INDEX.

Flaccus, 1, 116.
flagellas puteal, 4, 49.
flexus metae, 3, 68.
Floralia, 5, 178.
foci cultrix, 3, 26.
foco admovit, 6, 1.
focus, 1, 72.
foedere certo, 5, 45.
folle, 5, 11.
fonte caballino, Prol., 1.
forcipe, 4, 40.
fores udas, 5, 166.
fortunare, 2, 45.
fossor, 5, 122.
fractus, 1, 18.
frangere Saturnum, 5, 50.
        rem patriam, 5, 165.
fratres aenos, 2, 56.
fretus, 4, 3.
frigere, 3, 109.
frigescant, 1, 109.
frigidus cinis, 6, 45.
frontem perisse, 5, 104.
fronte politus, 5, 116.
fruge Cleanthea, 5, 64.
fulta, 1, 78.
fulto, 5, 146.
fumo dare pondus, 5, 20.
fumosa Palilia, 1, 72.
fumosum sinciput, 6, 70.
fundo imo, 2, 51.
funem reduco, 5, 118.
funeris cena, 6, 33.
funus praeclarum, 2, 10.
fur, 1, 85.
Future as imperative, 1, 91.
        gnomic, 2, 5.
        participle, 1, 100.

G.

Gabinus cinctus, 5, 31 (note).
Galli, 5, 186.
garrit, 5, 96.
gaudere = ἀγαπᾶν, 6, 63.
        paratus, 1, 132.
gausape, 4, 37 ; 6, 46.
gemina lance, 4, 10.
geminet guttas, 3, 14.
Geminos (in G.) dividere, 5, 49.
        producis, 6, 18.

generoso honesto, 2, 74.
Genitive of material, 2, 52.
        free use of, 1, 14.
genius, 1, 113 ; 2, 3 ; 4, 27 ; 5, 151;
        6, 19. 48.
genuinum, 1, 115.
glutto, 5, 112.
Glyconi, 5, 9.
graece nugari, 1, 70.
Graiorum, 1, 127.
Graios, 6, 38.
grana, 5, 55.
granaria, 5, 110 ; 6, 25.
grande loqui, 1, 14 ; 5, 7.
grandes Galli, 5, 186.
        patinae, 2, 42.
grandi polenta, 3, 55.
grandia, 3, 45.
gravis alitus, 3, 89.
        Saturnus, 5, 50.
gurgite, 2, 15.
gurgulio, 4, 38.
guttas excutere, 2, 54.
gutture exalare, 3, 99.
        niti, 5, 6.

H.

habita tecum, 4, 52.
haeres, 2, 19.
hamo duplici, 5, 154.
hebenum, 5, 135.
hederae, Prol., 6.
Helicone, 5, 7.
Heliconidas, Prol., 4.
Hellebore, 3, 63 ; 4, 16 ; 5, 100.
heminas, 1, 130.
Hendiadys, 2, 52 ; 5, 131.
herba, 6, 26.
Hercule dextro, 2, 12.
heres proximus, 2, 12.
Ἑρμῆς κερδῷος, 6, 51.
heroas sensus, 1, 69.
Herodis dies, 5, 180.
hesterni Quirites, 3, 106.
hesternum cras, 5, 68.
        oscitat, 3, 59.
hianda, 5, 3.
hiantem ducere, 5, 176.
Hiatus, 3, 66.
hibernat, 6, 7.

220 INDEX.

K 2

turgescere somno, 5, 56.
turgescit bilis, 3, 8.
turgidus, 3, 98.
tus, 5, 135.
Tusco stemmate, 3, 22.
Tuscum fictile, 2, 60.
tutor, 3, 96.

## U.

uda labella, 2, 32.
udas fores, 5, 165.
udo, in udo esse, 1, 105.
ulcus putre, 3, 113.
ulterior cinere, 6, 41.
ultra, 3, 15.
umbo candidus, 5, 33.
umbra quinta, 3, 4.
Umbris pinguibus, 3, 74.
uncta fenestra, 5, 180.
   patella, 4, 17.
   pulmentaria, 3, 102.
uncto, sine uncto cenare, 6, 16.
unctus, 4, 33.
uncus, 5, 154 (note).
unde, 1, 73.
undique, 3, 59.
ungue caules, 6, 68.
unguine crasso, 6, 40.
unguis severos, 1, 65.
unum opus, 5, 43.
ὑπᾴδειν, 3, 20.
ὑποσκελίζειν, 1, 35.
ὑπόχαλκος, 5, 106.
urentis oculos, 2, 34.
urnas Vestalis, 2, 60.
urtica, 6, 70.
usque adeo, 1, 26.
usum vitae, 5, 94.
usus rerum, 5, 52.
ut omitted, 1, 56.
uxor proxima, 3, 43.

## V.

vafer, 1, 116. 132 ; 6, 20.
vago inguine, 6, 72.
vallis = sinus, 6, 8.
vanescere, 3, 13.
vapida lagoena, 6, 17.
   pice, 5, 148.
vapido pectore, 5, 117.

vaporata aure, 1, 126.
vappa, 5, 77.
varicosos centuriones, 5, 189.
varo (baro), 5, 138.
varo genio, 6, 18.
   pede, 4, 12.
vatibus, 5, 1.
vatum, Prol., 7.
ve-, 1, 97.
ve or vel redundant (?), 3, 29.
vegrandi, 1, 97.
Veientanum rubellum, 5, 147.
vel duo, vel nemo, 1, 3.
Velina, 5, 73.
velle suum, 5, 53.
   with perf. inf., 1, 41. 91.
vellere barbam, 1, 133 ; 2, 28.
vellus Calabrum, 2, 65.
velox, 4, 4.
vena singultiet, 6, 72.
   testiculi, 1, 103.
venas conpositas, 3, 91.
   stringere, 2, 66.
   tangere, 3, 107.
vendo = vendito, 1, 122.
veneno ferventi, 3, 37.
Veneri donatae pupae, 2, 70.
venire with the dative, 6, 39.
venosus, 1, 76.
venter, Prol., 11 ; 3, 98.
ventis rumpere, 3, 27.
ventos premere, 5, 11.
veratro, 1, 51.
verba dare, 3, 19 ; 4, 45.
   togae, 5, 14.
verecunda mensa, 5, 44.
veri speciem, 5, 105.
vernae discincto, 4, 22.
verrucosa, 1, 77.
versum cludere, 1, 93.
   tendere, 1, 65.
verte aliquid, 5, 137.
verterit, 5, 78.
vertigo, 5, 76.
verumne, 3, 7.
Vestalis urnas, 2, 60.
vetare superos, 2, 43.
vetavit, 5, 90.
veteres avias, 5, 92.
vetitos actus, 5, 99.

THE END.

# HARPER'S
# GREEK AND LATIN TEXTS.
## CAREFULLY REPRINTED FROM THE BEST EDITIONS.

ELEGANTLY PRINTED, 18MO, FLEXIBLE CLOTH BINDING, 75 CENTS A VOL.

---

This Series is intended to supply cheap and accurate pocket editions of the Classics, which shall be superior in mechanical execution to the small German editions now current in this country, and more convenient in form. The Texts of the "*Bibliotheca Classica*" and *Grammar-School Classics*, so far as they have been published, will be adopted. These editions have taken their place among scholars as valuable contributions to classical literature, and are admitted to be good examples of the judicious and practical nature of English scholarship; and as the editors have formed their texts from a careful examination of the best editions extant, it is believed that no texts better adapted for general use can be found. The volumes are handsomely printed in a good plain type, and on a firm fine paper, capable of receiving writing ink for notes, and are supplied at the moderate price of Seventy-five Cents a volume.

---

CÆSAR. C. Julii Cæsaris Commentarii de Bello Gallico. Recognovit GEO. LONG, M.A.

VERGILIUS. Publi Vergili Maronis Opera. Ex Recensione J. CONINGTON, M.A., Ling. et Lit. Lat. apud Oxon. Prof.

HORATIUS. Quinti Horatii Flacci Opera Omnia. Ex Recensione A. J. MACLEANE.

CICERO DE SENECTUTE ET DE AMICITIA. M. Tullii Ciceronis Cato Major sive de Senectute, Lælius sive de Amicitia, et Epistolæ Selectæ. Recensuit G. LONG, M.A.

SALLUST. C. Sallusti Crispi Catilina et Jugurtha. Recognovit GEO. LONG, M.A.

LUCRETIUS. T. Lucreti Cari de Rerum Natura Libri Sex. Recognovit HUGO A. I. MUNRO, M.A.

ÆSCHYLUS. Ex Novissima Recensione FREDERICI A. PALEY. Accessit Verborum quæ præcipue notanda sunt et Nominum Index.

SOPHOCLES. Ex Novissima Recensione GULIELMI DINDORFII. Accessit Verborum et Nominum Index.

EURIPIDES. Ex Recensione FREDERICI A. PALEY. Accessit Verborum et Nominum Index. 3 vols.

HERODOTUS. Recensuit JOSEPHUS WILLIAMS BLAKESLEY, S. T. B. Coll. ss. Trin. apud Cantabr. quondam Socius. 2 vols.

THUCYDIDES. Recensuit JOANNES GULIELMUS DONALDSON, S.T.P. Coll. ss. Trin. apud Cantabr. quondam Socius. 2 vols.

XENOPHON. Xenophontis Anabasis. Recensuit J. F. MACMICHAEL, A.B.

# RECOMMENDATIONS FROM DISTINGUISHED CLASSICAL SCHOLARS.

*From* C. C. FELTON, LL.D., *late President of Harvard College.*

I have had great pleasure in reading them (your edition of the Texts of Horace, Æschylus, and Euripides), from the beauty of the typography, the excellence of the paper, the convenience of the form, and the remarkable correctness of the printing. I never make a journey without one or more of these volumes in my pocket. I hope you will continue the series, so as to include every important work in Greek and Roman literature. These editions would be excellent to use in the recitation-room with college classes.

*From* Prof. PROUDFIT, *Rutgers College, New Brunswick, N. J.*

There is a tradition that Porson used to carry a Library of the Classics in his pockets. Your "Greek and Latin Texts" seem almost to make the thing possible. So light and lithe are they, so pleasant to the eye and portable to the pocket, that one may say, with Cicero, "*Delectant domi, non impediunt foris, nobiscum peregrinantur, rusticantur.*"

*From* Prof. HENRY DRISLER, *Columbia College, N. Y., Editor of "Liddell and Scott's Greek Lexicon."*

You have just hit the mark in undertaking to supply a series of class-room text-books from editions of established character, printed on handsome white paper, with clear type and black ink, in a form convenient to handle, and attractive to the eye.

*From* Prof. JAMES HADLEY, *Yale College, New Haven.*

The volumes thus far embraced in your "Greek and Latin Texts" have received the editorial care of able and distinguished scholars, and, so far as I have examined them, they appear to be printed with remarkable correctness. Their typographical elegance and clearness, as well as the compactness and lightness which fit them for the pocket, are qualities obvious to every eye. I regard the publication of such a series as an important service rendered to classical study and instruction, and as promising especial advantage to the colleges of our country.

*From* Rev. J. J. OWEN, D.D., *College of the City of New York.*

In publishing the "Greek and Latin Texts" in so beautiful and portable a form, you have, in my judgment, rendered a very great service to the cause of classical learning. The publication can not but be highly successful.

*From* Rev. HOWARD CROSBY, D.D., *late Professor of Greek at Rutgers College, N. J.*

Your series of Classical Texts have attained a most merited reputation as the very best classical issues emanating from an American source. Their perfection of type and accessories, and their careful, scholarly preparation, with their remarkable cheapness, will (and ought to) make them universally used in our schools and colleges.

*From* Prof. A. C. KENDRICK, *Rochester University.*

These editions are a credit to the American press. Text, type, and paper are alike unexceptionable. In reading these authors (Æschylus, Euripides, and Herodotus) I shall constantly recommend your editions to my classes.

*From* Prof. EDWARD GRAHAM DAWES, *Trinity College, Hartford.*

The teachers of America can not fail to be grateful to you for this admirable edition of the Classics. The accuracy of the text, the elegance of the typography, the freedom from commentary, and the price, all alike tend to commend these little volumes to every classical instructor. I shall introduce them in all my classes.

*From* Prof. G. MUSGRAVE GIGER, *College of New Jersey, Princeton.*

We have carefully examined the volume of "Harper's Greek and Latin Texts" containing the Works of Horace. In typographical accuracy and appearance it compares favorably with the charming edition of Didot, and never, perhaps, has Horace been more carefully and efficiently edited. * * * We feel confident that, if its merits were known, it could not fail to secure a most extended circulation.

*From* Prof. HENRY M. BAIRD, *University of the City of New York.*

From the volumes which I have examined I am led to form a very favorable opinion of this edition of the ancient Classics. We need just such a uniform series, consisting of small, portable volumes, containing a text based upon the most recent investigations of the great scholars of our day. I am glad to find the typography of your edition so much more elegant than the similar publications of either Tauchnitz or Teubner.

*From* TAYLER LEWIS, LL.D., *Union College, Schenectady, N. Y.*

These editions of the Classics you are publishing are just the thing for college use. I shall employ them wholly.

*From* Prof. W. S. TYLER, *Amherst College.*

The edition (Æschylus, Euripides, and Herodotus) seems to be made up of the most approved texts, carefully edited, beautifully printed, got up in a convenient form, and sold at a very reasonable price. The publishers deserve the thanks of the public, and especially of classical scholars, and I doubt not they will meet with the appreciation and reward which is their due.

*From* Prof. SAMUEL A. DUNCAN, *Dartmouth College, N. H.*

\* \* \* Your elegant edition of the Greek and Latin Texts. For convenience of form, beauty of appearance, and typographical execution, this edition of the Classics must stand unrivaled ; and deserving of equal commendation is the judgment which reproduces in such an accessible form the critical labors of such eminent scholars as the editors of the present series. You are certainly supplying a great desideratum, viz., a series of Greek and Latin authors attractive to the eye, of reliable scholarship, easily portable, and yet of a cost that places them within the means of all.

*From* Rev. WILLIAM C. CATTELL, *Professor of Latin and Greek, Lafayette College, Easton, Pa.*

It is the most elegant and accurate, as well as the cheapest edition of the Classics with which I am acquainted.

*From* Prof. A. S. PACKARD, *Bowdoin College, Maine.*

I admire the clearness of the type and the convenience of the edition for the use of the recitation-room. The names of the editors, whose text you have followed, give authority to the present edition.

*From* Prof. GOODWIN, *Harvard College.*

I congratulate you upon your perfect success in your undertaking, in which all lovers of the Classics must take a lively interest.

*From* Prof. JAMES R. BOISE, *University of Michigan.*

They are handsomely and, so far as I have had opportunity to examine them, accurately printed. They can not fail to be useful and convenient to American students.

*From* Dr. JAMES DE KOVEN, *Rector of Racine College, Wis.*

They will be of great assistance to all teachers of the Classics.

---

## HARPER'S SERIES OF GREEK AND LATIN TEXTS HAVE BEEN USED, EITHER WHOLLY OR IN PART, BY THE FOLLOWING PROFESSORS:

Prof. ANTHON, Columbia College, N. Y.; Prof. YOUNG, Ohio University; Prof. LIPSCOMB, Franklin College, Tenn. ; Prof. COOPER, Centre College, Ky. ; Prof. WILEY, Asbury University, Ind. ; Prof. HOYT, Asbury University, Ind. ; Prof. STURGUS, Hanover College, Ind.; Prof. HUNT, Wesleyan University, Ala.; Prof. SHORT, Columbia College, N.Y.; Prof. CARY, Antioch College, O. ; Prof. THOMAS, Georgetown College, O. ; Prof. SPAULDING, Iowa Wesleyan University ; Prof. ELLIS, Oberlin College, O. ; Prof. BUCKHAM, University of Vermont ; Prof. JOYNES, William and Mary College, Va. ; Prof. WADDELL, University of Georgia; Prof. PORTER, Beloit College, Wis. ; Prof. JONES, Lawrence University, Wis. ; Prof. BISHOP, Miami University, O. ; Prof. MATTHEWS, Centre College, Ky. ; Prof. LILLIE, Iowa State University ; Prof. NORTH, Hamilton College, Ky. ; Prof. WHEELER, Hobart College, N. Y. ; Prof. BALLANTINE, Indiana State University ; Prof. DENEEN, McKendree College, Ill. ; Prof. WYMAN, University of Alabama ; Prof. EMERSON, Beloit College ; Prof. HOWES, Shurtleff College, Ill. ; Prof. HUBBARD, University of North Carolina ; Prof. WILLIAMS, Ohio Wesleyan University ; Prof. BUTLER, Wisconsin University ; Prof. SUTTON, Washington College, Md. ; Prof. ELLIOTT, Miami University, O.

---

☞ HARPER & BROTHERS *will send any volume of their* GREEK AND LATIN TEXTS *by mail, postage paid, to any part of the United States, on receipt of* 75 *cents.*

# HARPER'S
# NEW CLASSICAL LIBRARY.

The want of a Series of LITERAL TRANSLATIONS of the Greek and Latin authors who are usually studied in the American course of Academic, Classical, and Collegiate education, has been long felt by the most intelligent and assiduous classical teachers. That they are capable of being abused by the indolent and unfaithful pupil is no plea against their utility when employed in their legitimate place. A translation of an ancient writer into English, as perfectly literal as is permitted by the idioms of the respective languages, affords an invaluable aid to the instructor in the accomplishment of his arduous task. If executed with fidelity and skill, it saves much time and labor in the consultation of dictionaries, and embodies the best results of philological acumen and research in the shortest possible space. Pages of learned commentary are thus concentrated in the rendering of a single word.

The works which have been issued are reprints from "BOHN'S CLASSICAL LIBRARY," brought out uniform with the English edition, and comprise faithful translations of the principal Greek and Latin Classics.

Each work is given without abridgment, and includes short suggestive notes, adapted to the comprehension as well as the actual wants of the student. Copious and accurate indices are appended to every translation. No verson is adopted without ample and thorough revision, correcting its errors by the lights of modern research, and placing it on a level with the present improved state of philological learning.

This NEW CLASSICAL LIBRARY has received a cordial welcome from the whole corps of American classical teachers. The important uses of such works in their daily vocations are too obvious to require discussion. Nor is the interest of the series confined to teachers alone. Every reading man, though destitute of a knowledge of the ancient languages, feels a laudable curiosity to form an acquaintance with the incomparable models of literary art which they have preserved. In the literal translations with which he is furnished by the present series he will find the information that he seeks, enabling him to comprehend current classical allusions with facility, to become familiar with the true spirit of the ancients, and to share in conversation and studies which presuppose a knowledge of Greek and Roman antiquity.

The following volumes are now ready. 12mo, Cloth, $1 50 per volume.

| | |
|---|---|
| CÆSAR. | JUVENAL. |
| VIRGIL. | XENOPHON. |
| SALLUST. | HOMER'S ILIAD. |
| HORACE. | HOMER'S ODYSSEY. |
| CICERO'S ORATIONS. | HERODOTUS. |
| CICERO'S OFFICES, &c. | DEMOSTHENES. 2 VOLS. |
| CICERO ON ORATORY | THUCYDIDES. |
| AND ORATORS. | ÆSCHYLUS. |
| TACITUS. 2 VOLS. | SOPHOCLES. |
| TERENCE. | EURIPIDES. 2 VOLS. |

LIVY. 2 VOLS.

☞ HARPER & BROTHERS *will send any volume of the* NEW CLASSICAL LIBRARY *by mail, postage paid, to any part of the United States, on receipt of* $1 50.

# ANTHON'S SERIES

OF

# SCHOOL AND COLLEGE CLASSICS.

The unrivaled success which has attended the scholastic labors of Professor Anthon best attests the distinguished merit with which the following series has been regarded by the learned world. The *London Athenæum* says : "*Dr. Anthon has done more for sound classical school literature than any half dozen Englishmen ; his books are admirably edited.* His merits, as an editor of the school classics, are so well understood and appreciated in this country, as well as in his own, that commendation would be superfluous."

We consider his series of "School Classics" to stand unrivaled in their department of education, whether we regard the extent of scholarship which they display, or the easy gradation by which the student is led from the first principles of a complex language to its final and accurate combinations. A union of the highest classical knowledge, with the power of adapting it to the student, is of rare occurrence : these attributes characterize this excellent series.—*Examiner*, London.

The volumes of this series are neatly and strongly bound in Sheep.

*Classical Dictionary.* 8vo, $6 00.

*Latin-English and English-Latin Dictionary.* 8vo, $3 50.

*Ancient Geography.* 8vo, $3 00.

*Manual of Greek Literature.* 12mo, $1 50.

*Manual of Greek Antiquities.* 12mo, $1 50.

*Manual of Roman Antiquities.* 12mo, $1 50.

*Latin Lessons.* 12mo, $1 25.

*Latin Prose Composition.* 12mo, $1 25.—*Key.* 12mo, 75 cts.

*Zumpt's Latin Grammar.* 12mo, $1 50. — *Abridged.* 12mo, $1 00.

*Latin Versification.* 12mo, $1 25.—*Key.* 12mo, 75 cts.

*Latin Prosody.* 12mo, $1 25.

*Cæsar.* Map, Portrait, &c. 12mo, $1 50.

*Virgil's Æneid.* 12mo, $1 75.

*Virgil's Eclogues and Georgics.* 12mo, $1 75.

*Sallust.* 12mo, $1 50.

*Horace.* 12mo, $1 75.

*Cicero's Orations.* 12mo, $1 50.

*Cicero's Tusculan Disputations.* 12mo, $1 50.

*Cicero de Senectute, Amicitia, &c.* 12mo, $1 50.

*Cicero de Officiis.* 12mo, $1 50.

*Tacitus.* 12mo, $1 50.

*Cornelius Nepos.* 12mo, $1 50.

*Juvenal and Persius.* 12mo, $1 50.

*First Greek Lessons.* 12mo, $1 25.

*Greek Prose Composition.* 12mo, $1 25.

*Greek Grammar.* 12mo, $1 25.

*New Greek Grammar.* 12mo, $1 50.

*Greek Prosody.* 12mo, $1 25.

*Jacobs's Greek Reader.* 12mo, $1 50.

*Xenophon's Anabasis.* 12mo, $1 50.

*Xenophon's Memorabilia of Socrates.* 12mo, $1 50.

*Homer's Iliad.* 12mo, $1 75.

☞ HARPER & BROTHERS *will send any of the above works by mail, postage prepaid, to any part of the United States, on receipt of the price.*

# THE STUDENT'S SERIES,

PUBLISHED BY HARPER & BROTHERS, NEW YORK.

*WITH MAPS AND WOODCUTS.*

THE STUDENT'S HISTORY OF GREECE, from the Earliest Times to the Roman Conquest. With Supplementary Chapters on the History of Literature and Art. By WM. SMITH, LL.D. 12mo, 724 pages, Cloth, $2 00.

&#9758; A SMALLER HISTORY OF GREECE, for Younger Students and Common Schools. 16mo, 272 pages, Cloth, $1 00.

THE STUDENT'S HISTORY OF ROME, from the Earliest Times to the Establishment of the Empire. With Chapters on the History of Literature and Art. By H. G. LIDDELL, D.D., Dean of Christ Church, Oxford. 12mo, 778 pages, Cloth, $2 00.

&#9758; A SMALLER HISTORY OF ROME, from the Earliest Times to the Establishment of the Empire. By WM. SMITH, LL.D. With a Continuation to A.D. 476, by EUGENE LAWRENCE, A.M. 16mo, Cloth, $1 00.

THE STUDENT'S GIBBON. The History of the Decline and Fall of the Roman Empire. By EDWARD GIBBON. Abridged. Incorporating the Researches of Recent Commentators. By WM. SMITH, LL.D. 12mo, 706 pages, Cloth, $2 00.

THE STUDENT'S STRICKLAND. Lives of the Queens of England, from the Roman Conquest. By AGNES STRICKLAND, Author of "Lives of the Queens of Scotland." Abridged by the Author. Revised and Edited by CAROLINE G. PARKER. 12mo, 675 pages, Cloth, $2 00.

THE STUDENT'S HUME. A History of England, from the Earliest Times to the Revolution in 1688. By DAVID HUME. Abridged. Incorporating the Corrections and Researches of Recent Historians, and continuing down to the Year 1858. 12mo, 806 pages, Cloth, $2 00.

&#9758; A SMALLER HISTORY OF ENGLAND, from the Earliest Times to the Year 1862. Edited by WM. SMITH, LL.D. 16mo, Cloth, $1 00.

THE STUDENT'S HISTORY OF FRANCE, from the Earliest Times to the Establishment of the Second Empire in 1852. 12mo, 742 pages, Cloth, $2 00.

THE STUDENT'S ANCIENT HISTORY OF THE EAST, from the Earliest Times to the Conquest of Alexander the Great. Including Egypt, Assyria, Babylonia, Media, Persia, Asia Minor, and Phœnicia. By PHILIP SMITH, B.A., Author of the "History of the World." Edited by WM. SMITH, D.C.L., LL.D. 12mo, 649 pages, Cloth, $2 00.

THE STUDENT'S HALLAM. View of the State of Europe during the Middle Ages. By HENRY HALLAM, LL.D., F.R.A.S. Incorporating in the Text the Author's Latest Researches, with Additions from Recent Writers, and adapted to the Use of Students. Edited by WM. SMITH, D.C.L., LL.D. 12mo, 718 pages, Cloth, $2 00.

THE STUDENT'S HALLAM'S CONSTITUTIONAL HISTORY OF ENGLAND. The Constitutional History of England, from the Accession of Henry VII. to the Death of George II. By HENRY HALLAM, LL.D., F.R.A.S. Incorporating the Author's Latest Additions and Corrections, and adapted to the Use of Students. By WM. SMITH, D.C.L., LL.D. 12mo, 747 pages, Cloth, $2 00.

THE STUDENT'S OLD TESTAMENT HISTORY, from the Creation to the Return of the Jews from Captivity. Edited by WM. SMITH, LL.D. 12mo, 715 pages, Cloth, $2 00.

THE STUDENT'S NEW TESTAMENT HISTORY. With an Introduction, connecting the History of the Old and New Testaments. Edited by WM. SMITH, LL.D. 12mo, 780 pages, Cloth, $2 00.

&#9758; A SMALLER SCRIPTURE HISTORY. In Three Parts: Old Testament History; Connection of Old and New Testaments; New Testament History to A.D. 70. Edited by WM. SMITH, LL.D. 16mo, 375 pages, Cloth, $1 00.

THE STUDENT'S LYELL'S GEOLOGY. The Elements of Geology. By Sir CHARLES LYELL, Bart., F.R.S. 12mo, 640 pages, Cloth, $2 00.

*Sent by mail, postage free, on receipt of the price.*